THE MIGHTY CAPTAIN MARVEL

BAND OF SISTERS

MARGARET STOHL
WRITER

ISSUES #5-8

MICHELE BANDINI
ARTIST

ERICK ARCINIEGA
WITH **MICHAEL GARLAND** (#5)
COLOR ARTISTS

ELIZABETH TORQUE
COVER ART

ISSUE #9

RO STEIN & TED BRANDT
ARTISTS

ERICK ARCINIEGA
COLOR ARTIST

MEGHAN HETRICK
COVER ART

VC'S JOE CARAMAGNA
LETTERER

SANA AMANAT WITH CHARLES BEACHAM & MARK BASSO
EDITORS

COLLECTION EDITOR **JENNIFER GRÜNWALD** ASSISTANT EDITOR **CAITLIN O'CONNELL**
ASSOCIATE MANAGING EDITOR **KATERI WOODY** EDITOR, SPECIAL PROJECTS **MARK D. BEAZLEY**
VP PRODUCTION & SPECIAL PROJECTS **JEFF YOUNGQUIST** SVP PRINT, SALES & MARKETING **DAVID GABRIEL**
SPECIAL THANKS TO **ANTHONY GAMBINO**

EDITOR IN CHIEF **AXEL ALONSO** CHIEF CREATIVE OFFICER **JOE QUESADA**
PRESIDENT **DAN BUCKLEY** EXECUTIVE PRODUCER **ALAN FINE**

THE MIGHTY CAPTAIN MARVEL VOL. 2: BAND OF SISTERS. Contains material originally published in magazine form as THE MIGHTY CAPTAIN MARVEL #5-9. First printing 2017. ISBN# 978-1-302-90606-1. Published by MARVEL WORLDWIDE, INC., a subsidiary of MARVEL ENTERTAINMENT, LLC. OFFICE OF PUBLICATION: 135 West 50th Street, New York, NY 10020. Copyright © 2017 MARVEL No similarity between any of the names, characters, persons, and/or institutions in this magazine with those of any living or dead person or institution is intended, and any such similarity which may exist is purely coincidental. **Printed in Canada.** DAN BUCKLEY, President, Marvel Entertainment; JOE QUESADA, Chief Creative Officer; TOM BREVOORT, SVP of Publishing; DAVID BOGART, SVP of Business Affairs & Operations, Publishing & Partnership; C.B. CEBULSKI, VP of Brand Management & Development, Asia; DAVID GABRIEL, SVP of Sales & Marketing, Publishing; JEFF YOUNGQUIST, VP of Production & Special Projects; DAN CARR, Executive Director of Publishing Technology; ALEX MORALES, Director of Publishing Operations; SUSAN CRESPI, Production Manager; STAN LEE, Chairman Emeritus. For information regarding advertising in Marvel Comics or on Marvel.com, please contact Jonathan Parkhideh, VP of Digital Media & Marketing Solutions, at jparkhideh@marvel.com. For Marvel subscription inquiries, please call 888-511-5480. **Manufactured between** 11/3/2017 and 12/4/2017 by SOLISCO PRINTERS, SCOTT, QC, CANADA.

10 9 8 7 6 5 4 3 2 1

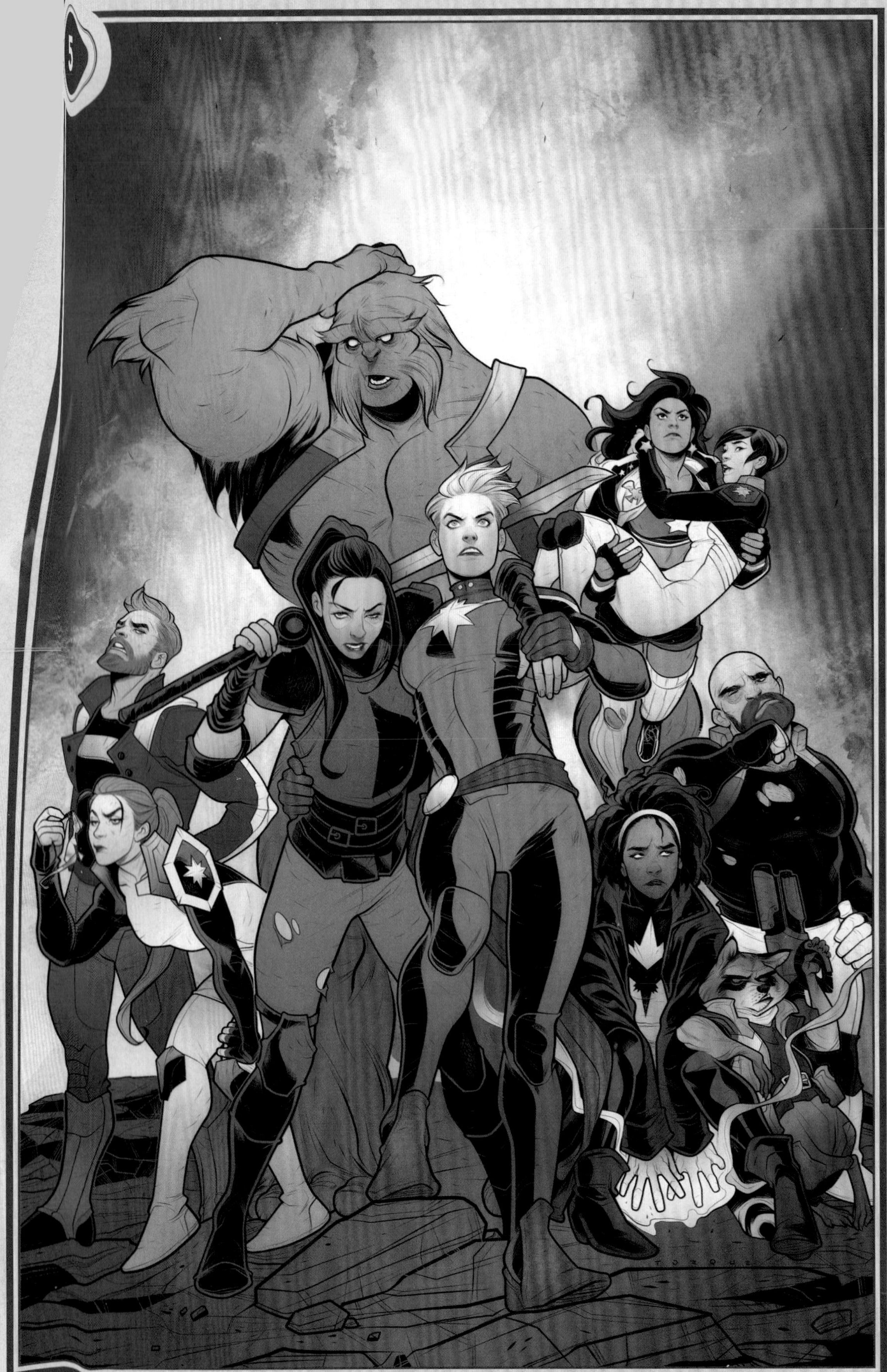
5

NO CHALLENGE IS TOO GREAT FOR THE FORMER AIR FORCE PILOT TURNED SUPER HERO. CAROL DANVERS HAS COME A LONG WAY SINCE AN INCIDENT WITH ALIEN TECHNOLOGY LEFT HER WITH AMAZING POWERS. PART KREE, PART HUMAN, CAROL IS NOW THE MOST POWERFUL AND POPULAR SUPER HERO ON EARTH, AND FROM THE ALPHA FLIGHT SPACE STATION MILES ABOVE THE PLANET, SHE AND HER CREW DEFEND THE WORLD FROM INTERGALACTIC THREATS.

THE MIGHTY CAPTAIN MARVEL

BAND OF SISTERS

RECENTLY, CAROL STOPPED THE PLOT OF DR. EVE, A NEFARIOUS GENETICIST WHO ABDUCTED KREE CHILDREN TO USE THEIR DNA TO TURN CAPTAIN MARVEL INTO A LIVING WEAPON. BUT THE SUCCESS CAME AT A COST — BEAN, CAROL'S ADOPTED HALA CHILD SACRIFICED HERSELF, BECOMING PURE HLA ENERGY.

BACK ON EARTH A COSMIC CUBE TRANSFORMED CAPTAIN AMERICA INTO A HYDRA SLEEPER AGENT. CAROL IS UNAWARE ON HER POST AT ALPHA FLIGHT, ATTEMPTING TO BUILD A SHIELD THAT WOULD PROTECT EARTH FROM THE INCOMING CHITAURI ATTACK. WILL EARTH'S FIRST LINE OF DEFENSE BE READY IN TIME?

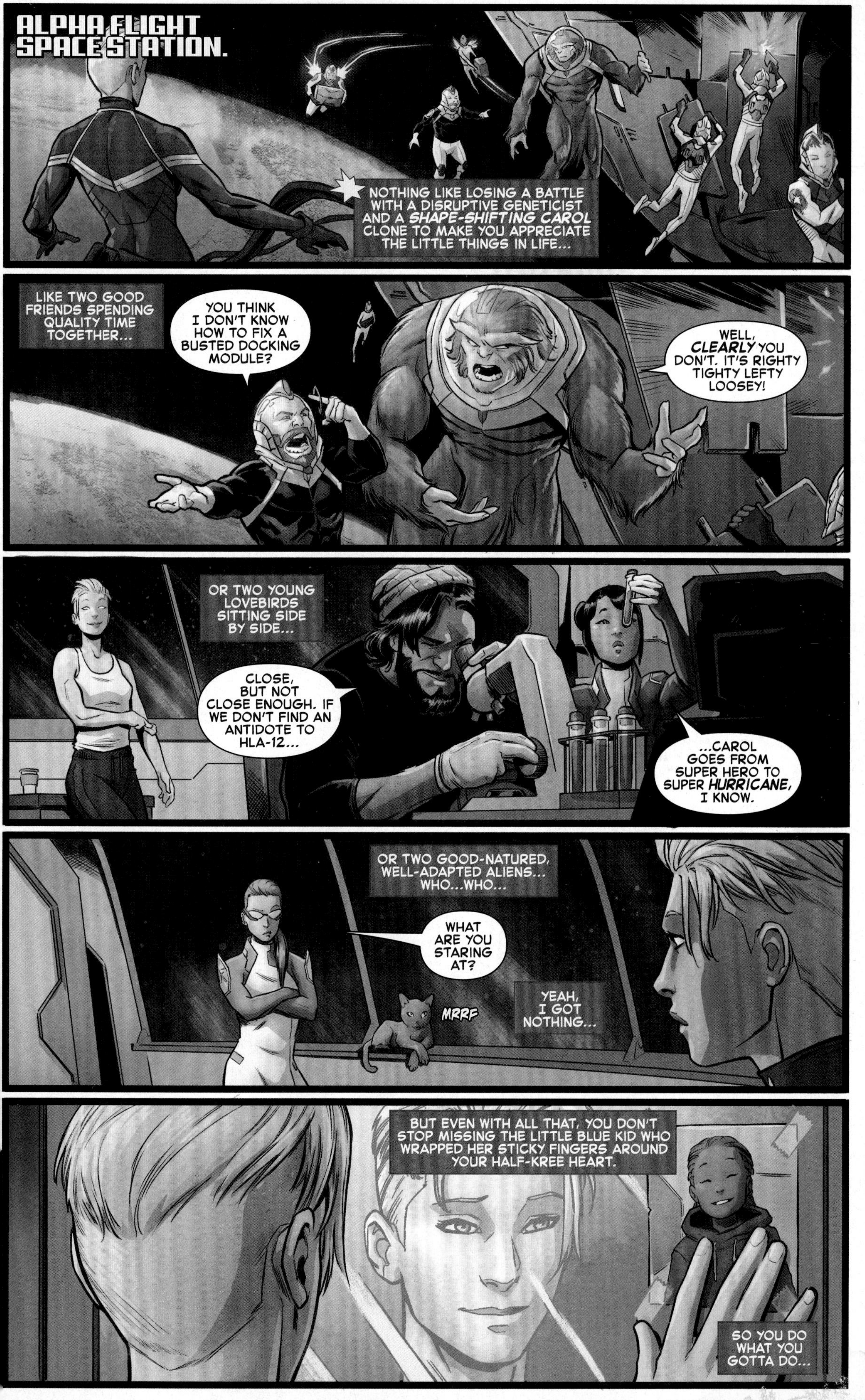
ALPHA FLIGHT SPACE STATION.
NOTHING LIKE LOSING A BATTLE WITH A DISRUPTIVE GENETICIST AND A SHAPE-SHIFTING CAROL CLONE TO MAKE YOU APPRECIATE THE LITTLE THINGS IN LIFE...
LIKE TWO GOOD FRIENDS SPENDING QUALITY TIME TOGETHER...
YOU THINK I DON'T KNOW HOW TO FIX A BUSTED DOCKING MODULE?
WELL, CLEARLY YOU DON'T. IT'S RIGHTY TIGHTY LEFTY LOOSEY!
OR TWO YOUNG LOVEBIRDS SITTING SIDE BY SIDE...
CLOSE, BUT NOT CLOSE ENOUGH. IF WE DON'T FIND AN ANTIDOTE TO HLA-12...
...CAROL GOES FROM SUPER HERO TO SUPER HURRICANE, I KNOW.
OR TWO GOOD-NATURED, WELL-ADAPTED ALIENS... WHO...WHO...
WHAT ARE YOU STARING AT?
MRRF
YEAH, I GOT NOTHING...
BUT EVEN WITH ALL THAT, YOU DON'T STOP MISSING THE LITTLE BLUE KID WHO WRAPPED HER STICKY FINGERS AROUND YOUR HALF-KREE HEART.
SO YOU DO WHAT YOU GOTTA DO...

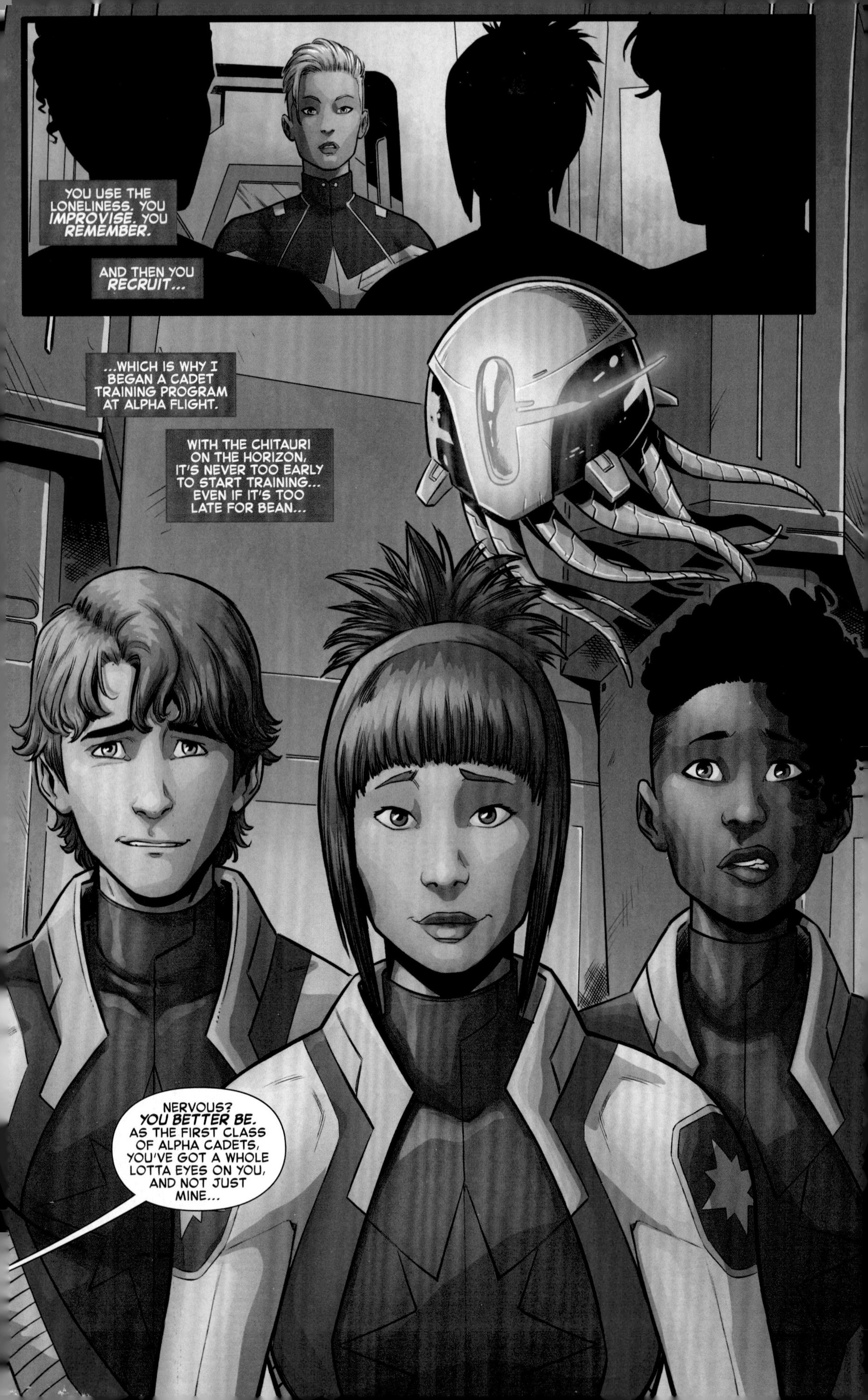

YOU USE THE LONELINESS. YOU IMPROVISE. YOU REMEMBER.
AND THEN YOU RECRUIT...
...WHICH IS WHY I BEGAN A CADET TRAINING PROGRAM AT ALPHA FLIGHT.
WITH THE CHITAURI ON THE HORIZON, IT'S NEVER TOO EARLY TO START TRAINING... EVEN IF IT'S TOO LATE FOR BEAN...
NERVOUS? YOU BETTER BE. AS THE FIRST CLASS OF ALPHA CADETS, YOU'VE GOT A WHOLE LOTTA EYES ON YOU, AND NOT JUST MINE...

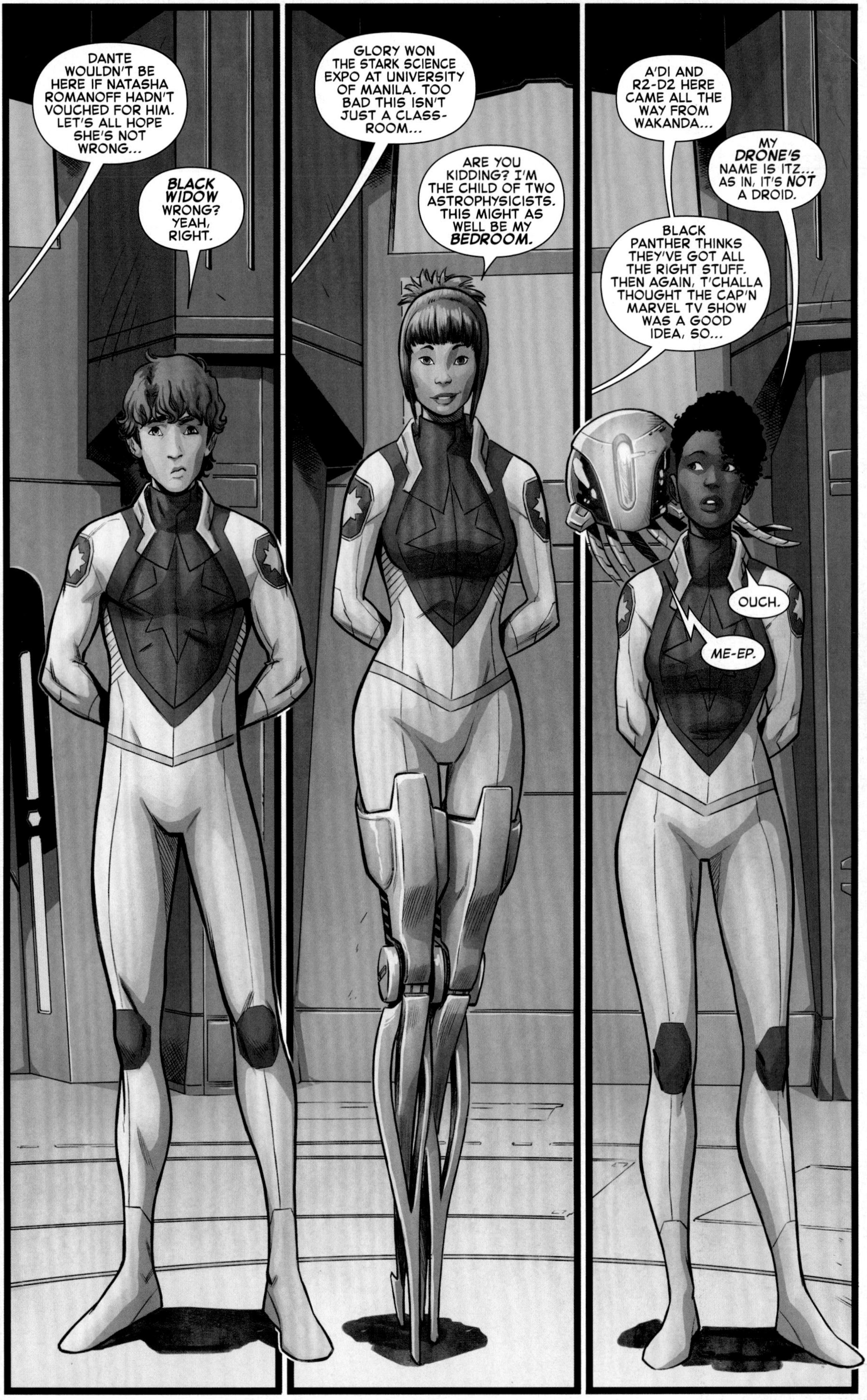
DANTE WOULDN'T BE HERE IF NATASHA ROMANOFF HADN'T VOUCHED FOR HIM. LET'S ALL HOPE SHE'S NOT WRONG...
BLACK WIDOW WRONG? YEAH, RIGHT.
GLORY WON THE STARK SCIENCE EXPO AT UNIVERSITY OF MANILA. TOO BAD THIS ISN'T JUST A CLASS-ROOM...
ARE YOU KIDDING? I'M THE CHILD OF TWO ASTROPHYSICISTS. THIS MIGHT AS WELL BE MY *BEDROOM.*
A'DI AND R2-D2 HERE CAME ALL THE WAY FROM WAKANDA...
MY *DRONE'S* NAME IS ITZ... AS IN, IT'S *NOT* A DROID.
BLACK PANTHER THINKS THEY'VE GOT ALL THE RIGHT STUFF. THEN AGAIN, T'CHALLA THOUGHT THE CAP'N MARVEL TV SHOW WAS A GOOD IDEA, SO...
OUCH.
ME-EP.

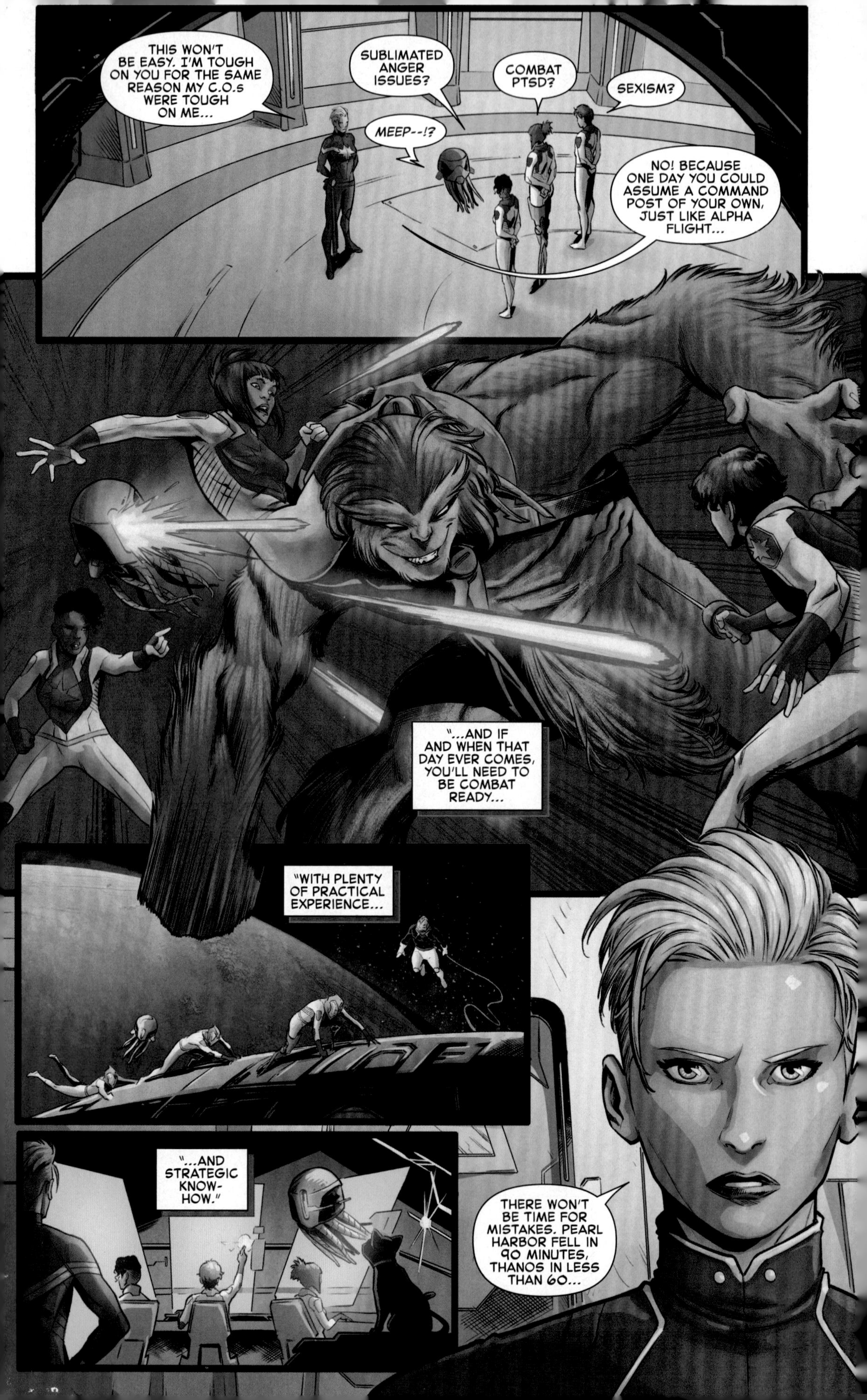
THIS WON'T BE EASY. I'M TOUGH ON YOU FOR THE SAME REASON MY C.O.s WERE TOUGH ON ME...
SUBLIMATED ANGER ISSUES?
COMBAT PTSD?
SEXISM?
MEEP--!?
NO! BECAUSE ONE DAY YOU COULD ASSUME A COMMAND POST OF YOUR OWN, JUST LIKE ALPHA FLIGHT...
"...AND IF AND WHEN THAT DAY EVER COMES, YOU'LL NEED TO BE COMBAT READY...
"WITH PLENTY OF PRACTICAL EXPERIENCE...
"...AND STRATEGIC KNOW-HOW."
THERE WON'T BE TIME FOR MISTAKES. PEARL HARBOR FELL IN 90 MINUTES, THANOS IN LESS THAN 60...

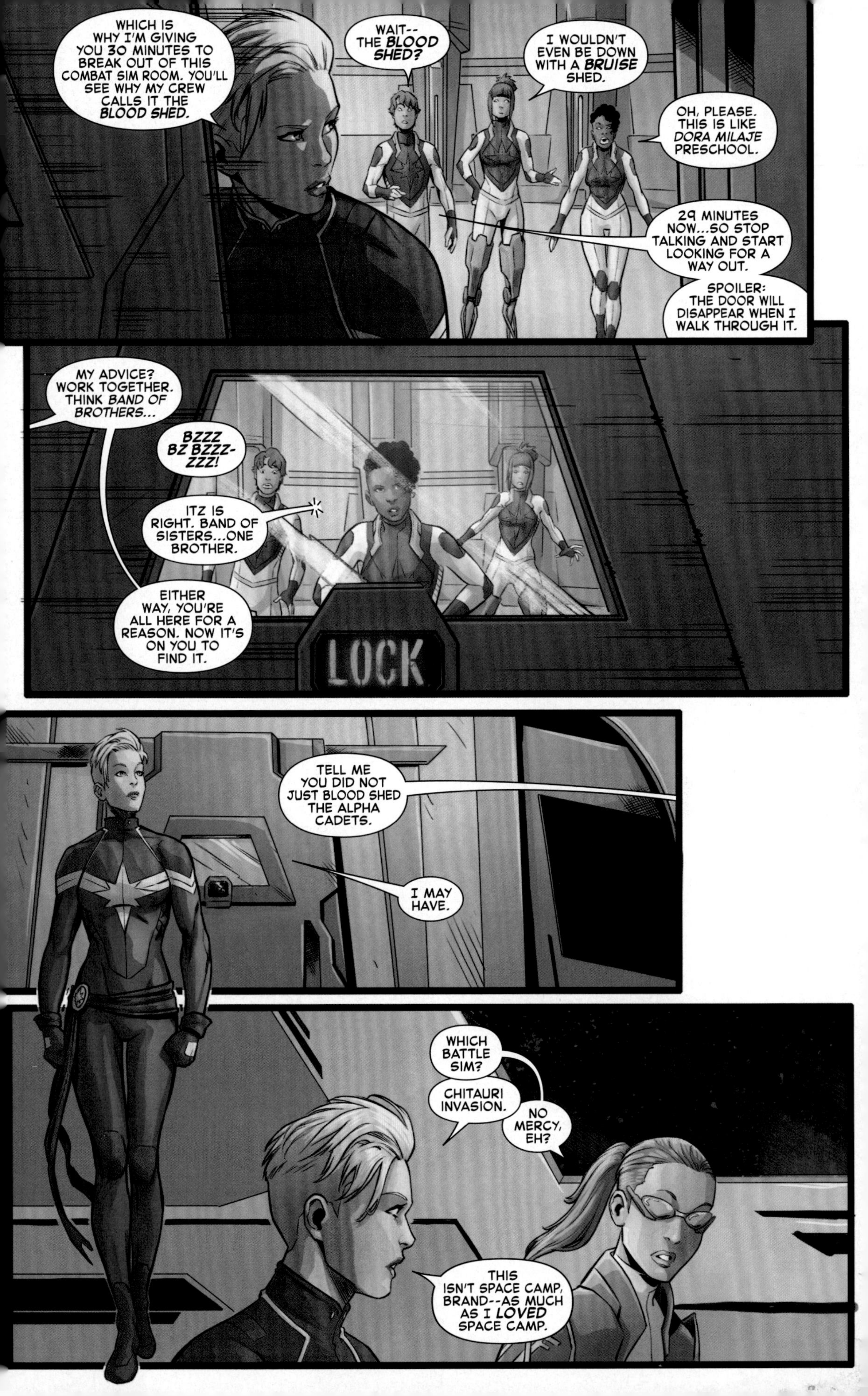

WHICH IS WHY I'M GIVING YOU 30 MINUTES TO BREAK OUT OF THIS COMBAT SIM ROOM. YOU'LL SEE WHY MY CREW CALLS IT THE *BLOOD SHED.*
WAIT-- THE *BLOOD SHED?*
I WOULDN'T EVEN BE DOWN WITH A *BRUISE* SHED.
OH, PLEASE. THIS IS LIKE *DORA MILAJE* PRESCHOOL.
29 MINUTES NOW...SO STOP TALKING AND START LOOKING FOR A WAY OUT.
SPOILER: THE DOOR WILL DISAPPEAR WHEN I WALK THROUGH IT.
MY ADVICE? WORK TOGETHER. THINK *BAND OF BROTHERS...*
BZZZ BZ BZZZ-ZZZ!
ITZ IS RIGHT. BAND OF SISTERS...ONE BROTHER.
EITHER WAY, YOU'RE ALL HERE FOR A REASON. NOW IT'S ON YOU TO FIND IT.
LOCK
TELL ME YOU DID NOT JUST BLOOD SHED THE ALPHA CADETS.
I MAY HAVE.
WHICH BATTLE SIM?
CHITAURI INVASION.
NO MERCY, EH?
THIS ISN'T SPACE CAMP, BRAND--AS MUCH AS I *LOVED* SPACE CAMP.

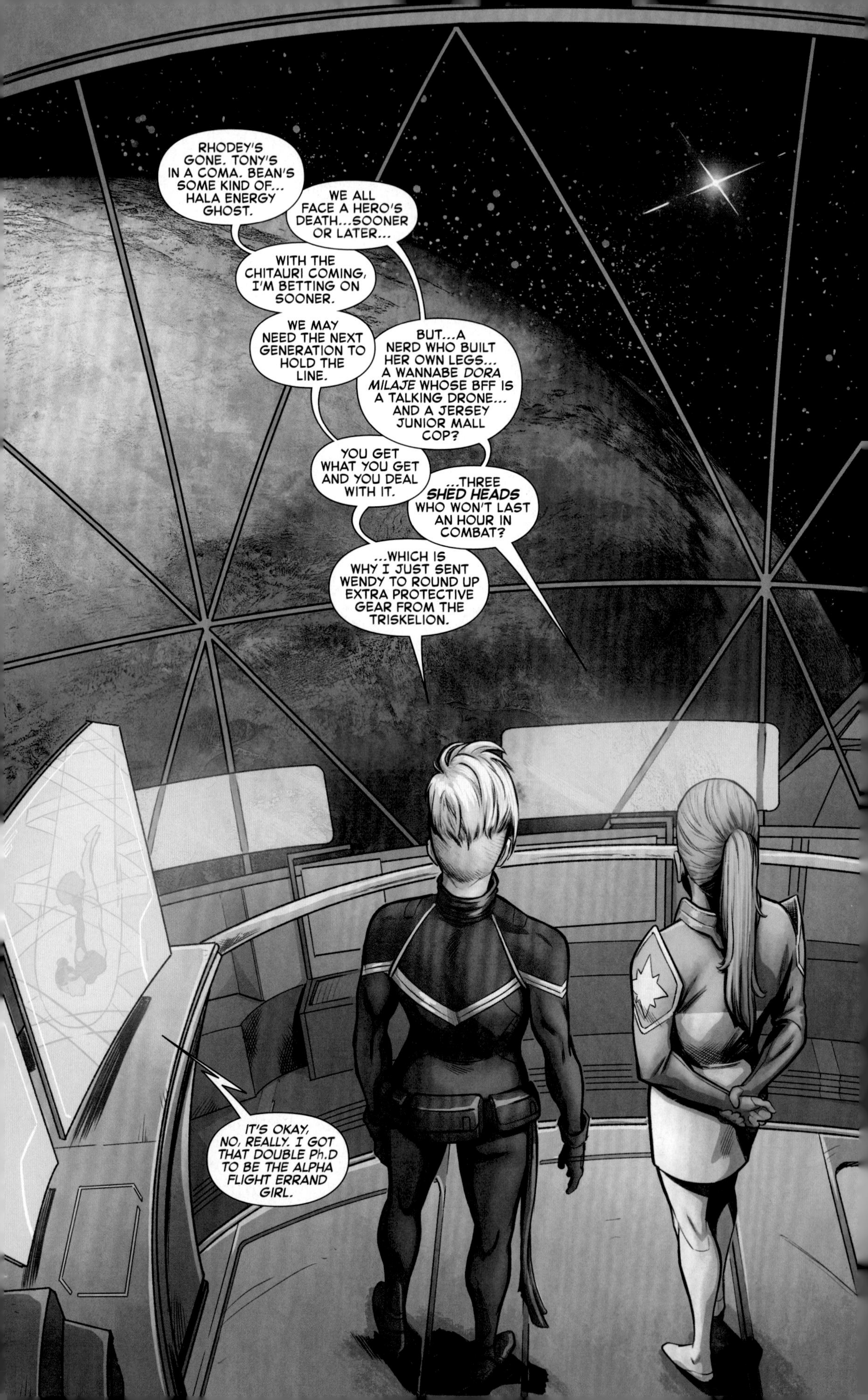
RHODEY'S GONE. TONY'S IN A COMA. BEAN'S SOME KIND OF... HALA ENERGY GHOST.
WE ALL FACE A HERO'S DEATH...SOONER OR LATER...
WITH THE CHITAURI COMING, I'M BETTING ON SOONER.
WE MAY NEED THE NEXT GENERATION TO HOLD THE LINE.
BUT...A NERD WHO BUILT HER OWN LEGS... A WANNABE *DORA MILAJE* WHOSE BFF IS A TALKING DRONE... AND A JERSEY JUNIOR MALL COP?
YOU GET WHAT YOU GET AND YOU DEAL WITH IT.
...THREE ***SHED HEADS*** WHO WON'T LAST AN HOUR IN COMBAT?
...WHICH IS WHY I JUST SENT WENDY TO ROUND UP EXTRA PROTECTIVE GEAR FROM THE TRISKELION.
IT'S OKAY, NO, REALLY. I GOT THAT DOUBLE Ph.D TO BE THE ALPHA FLIGHT ERRAND GIRL.

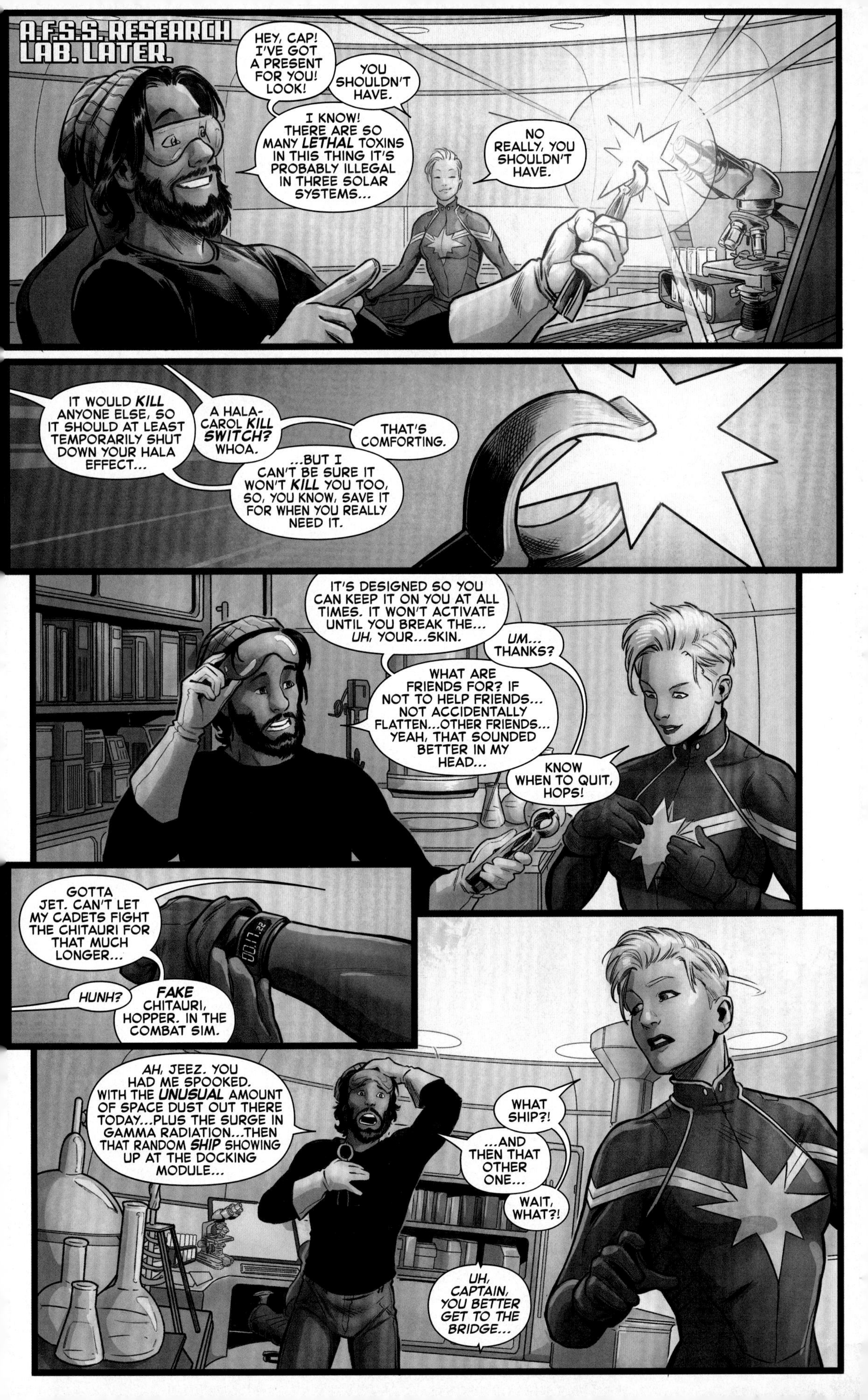
A.F.S.S. RESEARCH LAB. LATER.
HEY, CAP! I'VE GOT A PRESENT FOR YOU! LOOK!
YOU SHOULDN'T HAVE.
I KNOW! THERE ARE SO MANY LETHAL TOXINS IN THIS THING IT'S PROBABLY ILLEGAL IN THREE SOLAR SYSTEMS...
NO REALLY, YOU SHOULDN'T HAVE.
IT WOULD KILL ANYONE ELSE, SO IT SHOULD AT LEAST TEMPORARILY SHUT DOWN YOUR HALA EFFECT...
A HALA-CAROL KILL SWITCH? WHOA.
THAT'S COMFORTING.
...BUT I CAN'T BE SURE IT WON'T KILL YOU TOO, SO, YOU KNOW, SAVE IT FOR WHEN YOU REALLY NEED IT.
IT'S DESIGNED SO YOU CAN KEEP IT ON YOU AT ALL TIMES. IT WON'T ACTIVATE UNTIL YOU BREAK THE... UH, YOUR...SKIN.
UM... THANKS?
WHAT ARE FRIENDS FOR? IF NOT TO HELP FRIENDS... NOT ACCIDENTALLY FLATTEN...OTHER FRIENDS... YEAH, THAT SOUNDED BETTER IN MY HEAD...
KNOW WHEN TO QUIT, HOPS!
GOTTA JET. CAN'T LET MY CADETS FIGHT THE CHITAURI FOR THAT MUCH LONGER...
HUNH?
FAKE CHITAURI, HOPPER. IN THE COMBAT SIM.
AH, JEEZ. YOU HAD ME SPOOKED. WITH THE UNUSUAL AMOUNT OF SPACE DUST OUT THERE TODAY...PLUS THE SURGE IN GAMMA RADIATION...THEN THAT RANDOM SHIP SHOWING UP AT THE DOCKING MODULE...
WHAT SHIP?!
...AND THEN THAT OTHER ONE...
WAIT, WHAT?!
UH, CAPTAIN, YOU BETTER GET TO THE BRIDGE...

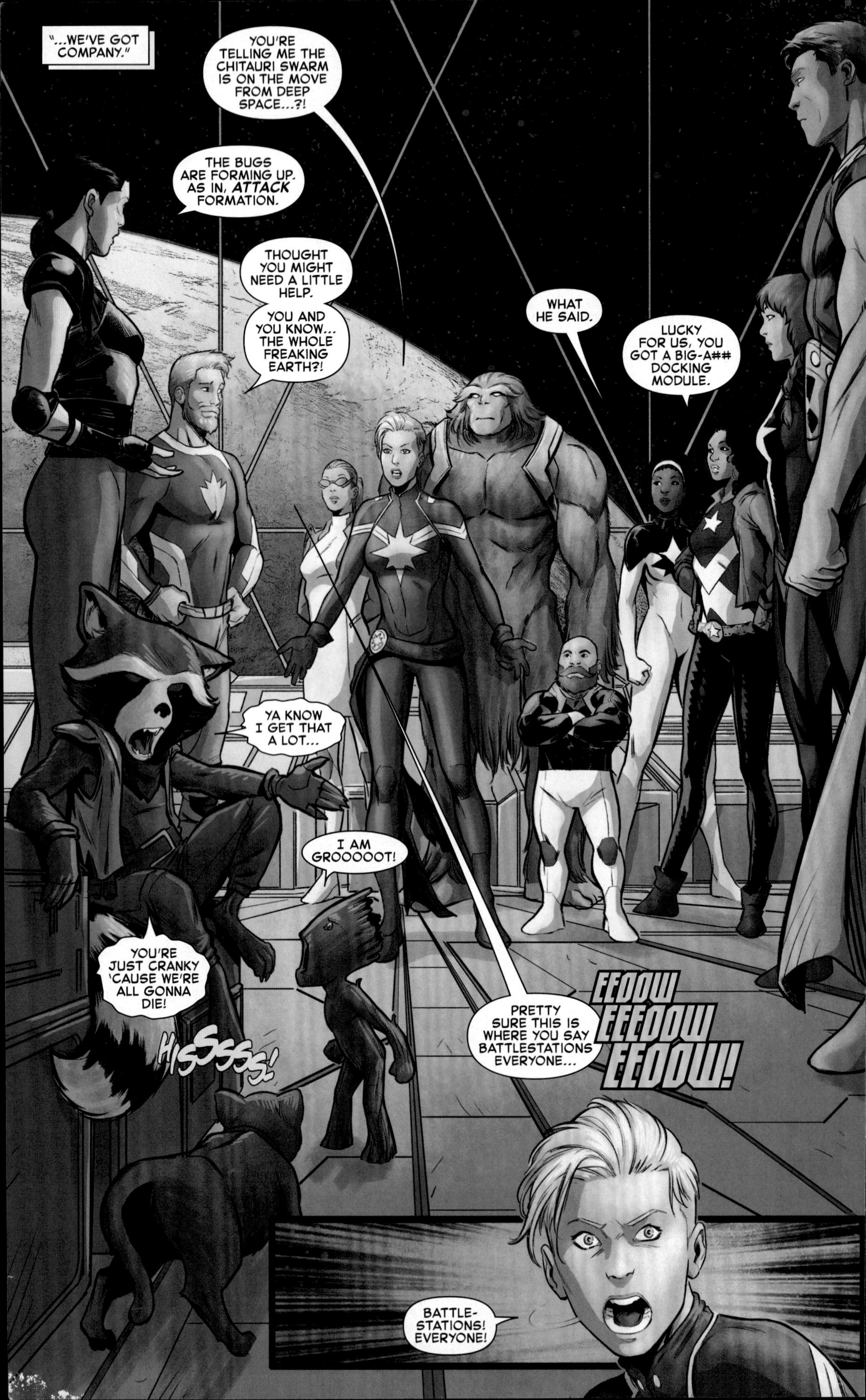
"...WE'VE GOT COMPANY."
YOU'RE TELLING ME THE CHITAURI SWARM IS ON THE MOVE FROM DEEP SPACE...?!
THE BUGS ARE FORMING UP. AS IN, ATTACK FORMATION.
THOUGHT YOU MIGHT NEED A LITTLE HELP.
YOU AND YOU KNOW... THE WHOLE FREAKING EARTH?!
WHAT HE SAID.
LUCKY FOR US, YOU GOT A BIG-A## DOCKING MODULE.
YA KNOW I GET THAT A LOT...
I AM GROOOOOT!
YOU'RE JUST CRANKY 'CAUSE WE'RE ALL GONNA DIE!
HISSSSS!
PRETTY SURE THIS IS WHERE YOU SAY BATTLESTATIONS EVERYONE...
EEOOW EEEOOW EEOOW!
BATTLE-STATIONS! EVERYONE!

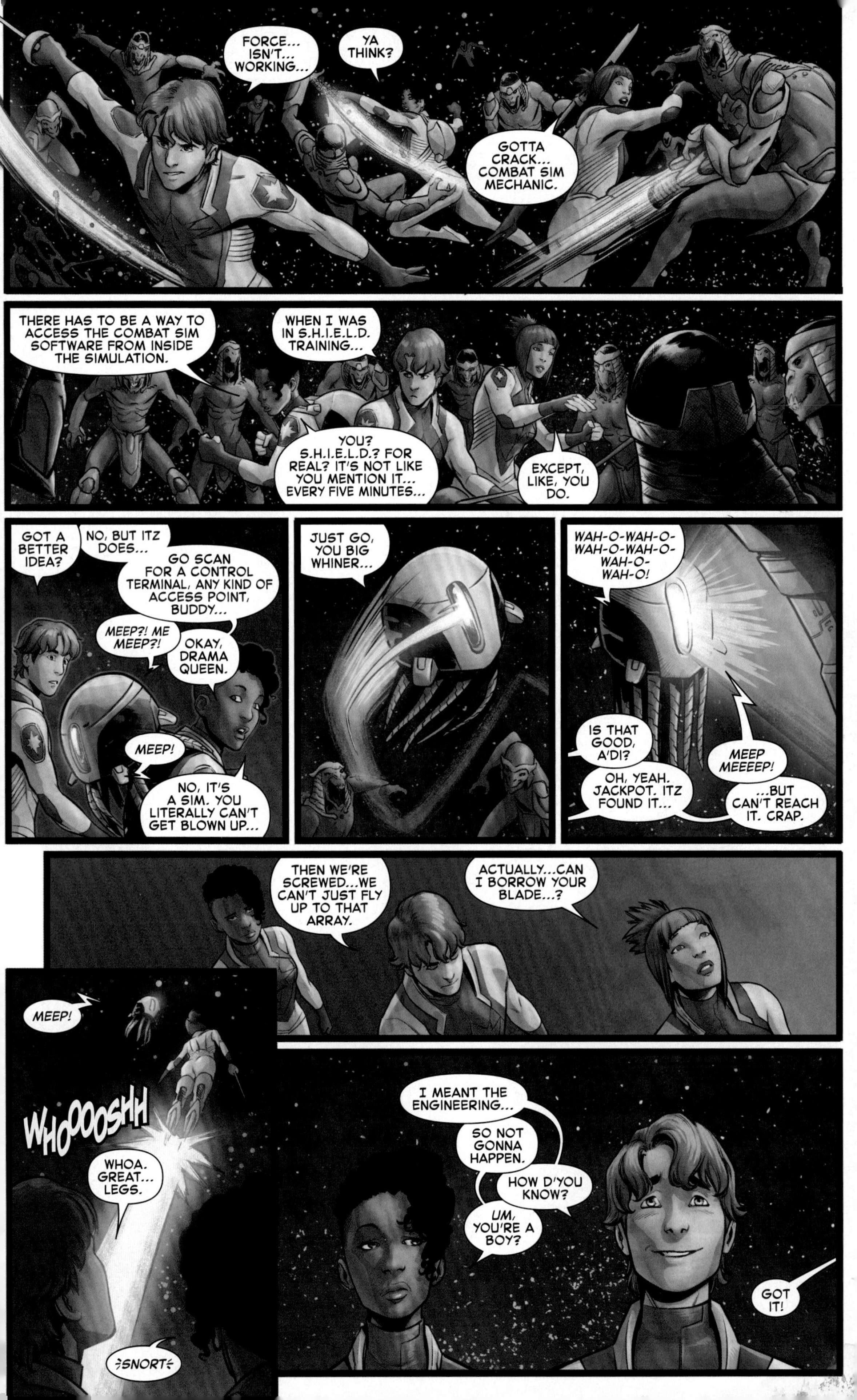

FORCE... ISN'T... WORKING...
YA THINK?
GOTTA CRACK... COMBAT SIM MECHANIC.
THERE HAS TO BE A WAY TO ACCESS THE COMBAT SIM SOFTWARE FROM INSIDE THE SIMULATION.
WHEN I WAS IN S.H.I.E.L.D. TRAINING...
YOU? S.H.I.E.L.D.? FOR REAL? IT'S NOT LIKE YOU MENTION IT... EVERY FIVE MINUTES...
EXCEPT, LIKE, YOU DO.
GOT A BETTER IDEA?
NO, BUT ITZ DOES...
GO SCAN FOR A CONTROL TERMINAL, ANY KIND OF ACCESS POINT, BUDDY...
MEEP?! ME MEEP?!
OKAY, DRAMA QUEEN.
MEEP!
NO, IT'S A SIM. YOU LITERALLY CAN'T GET BLOWN UP...
JUST GO, YOU BIG WHINER...
WAH-O-WAH-O-WAH-O-WAH-O-WAH-O-WAH-O!
IS THAT GOOD, A'DI?
OH, YEAH. JACKPOT. ITZ FOUND IT...
MEEP MEEEEP!
...BUT CAN'T REACH IT. CRAP.
THEN WE'RE SCREWED...WE CAN'T JUST FLY UP TO THAT ARRAY.
ACTUALLY...CAN I BORROW YOUR BLADE...?
MEEP!
WHOOOOSHH
WHOA. GREAT... LEGS.
SNORT
I MEANT THE ENGINEERING...
SO NOT GONNA HAPPEN.
HOW D'YOU KNOW?
UM, YOU'RE A BOY?
GOT IT!

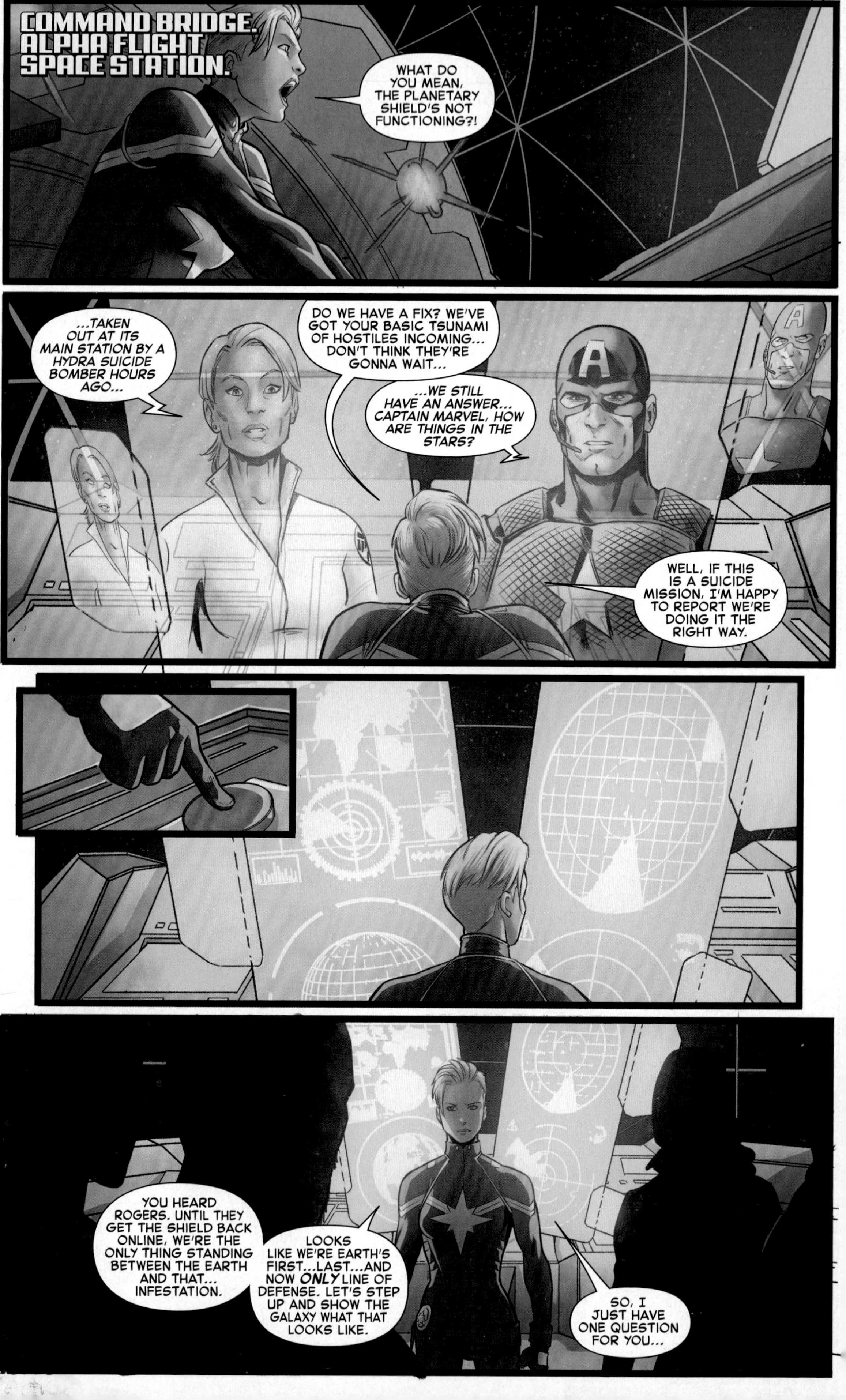
COMMAND BRIDGE. ALPHA FLIGHT SPACE STATION.
WHAT DO YOU MEAN, THE PLANETARY SHIELD'S NOT FUNCTIONING?!
...TAKEN OUT AT ITS MAIN STATION BY A HYDRA SUICIDE BOMBER HOURS AGO...
DO WE HAVE A FIX? WE'VE GOT YOUR BASIC TSUNAMI OF HOSTILES INCOMING... DON'T THINK THEY'RE GONNA WAIT...
...WE STILL HAVE AN ANSWER... CAPTAIN MARVEL, HOW ARE THINGS IN THE STARS?
WELL, IF THIS IS A SUICIDE MISSION, I'M HAPPY TO REPORT WE'RE DOING IT THE RIGHT WAY.
YOU HEARD ROGERS. UNTIL THEY GET THE SHIELD BACK ONLINE, WE'RE THE ONLY THING STANDING BETWEEN THE EARTH AND THAT... INFESTATION.
LOOKS LIKE WE'RE EARTH'S FIRST...LAST...AND NOW *ONLY* LINE OF DEFENSE. LET'S STEP UP AND SHOW THE GALAXY WHAT THAT LOOKS LIKE.
SO, I JUST HAVE ONE QUESTION FOR YOU...

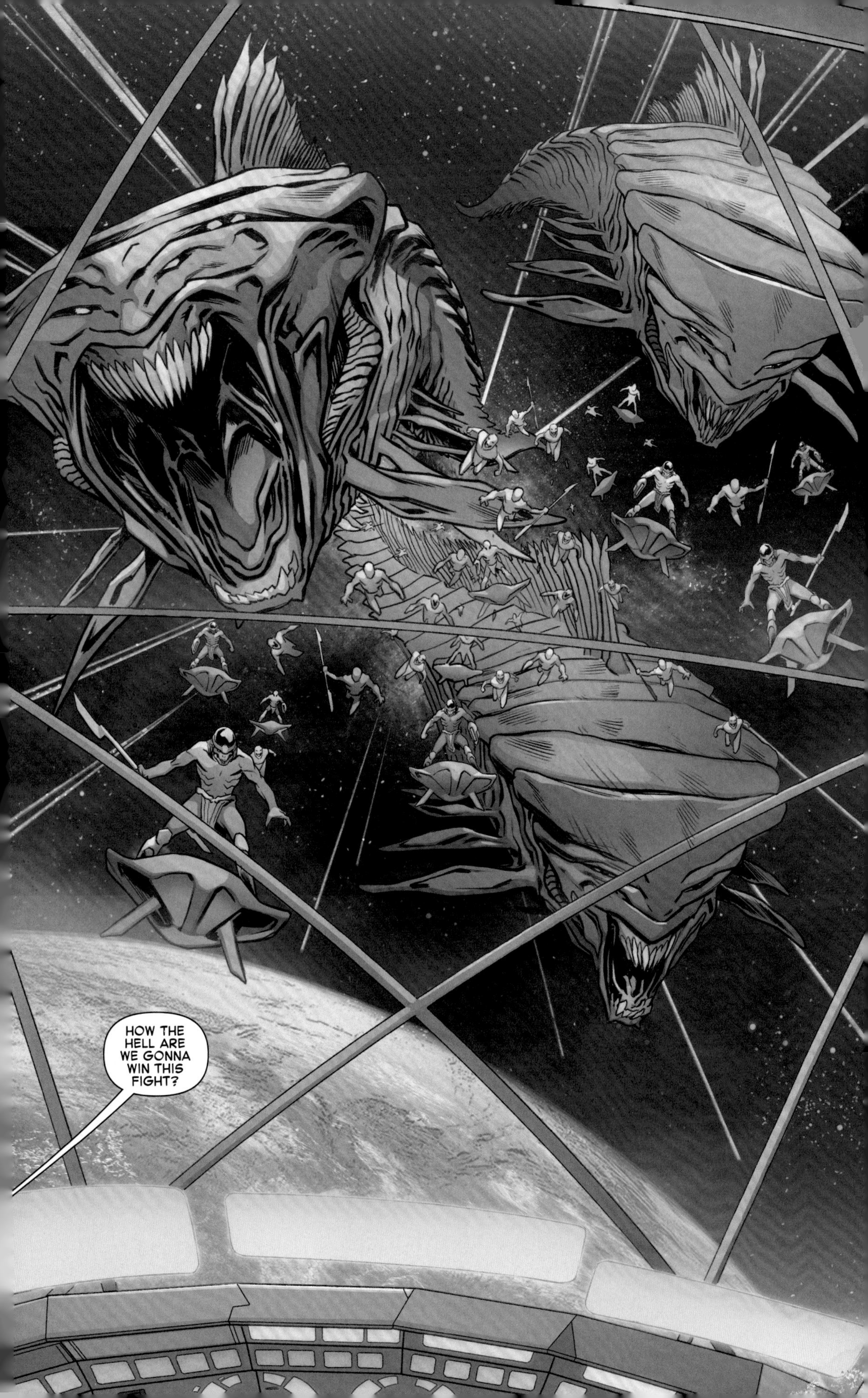
HOW THE HELL ARE WE GONNA WIN THIS FIGHT?

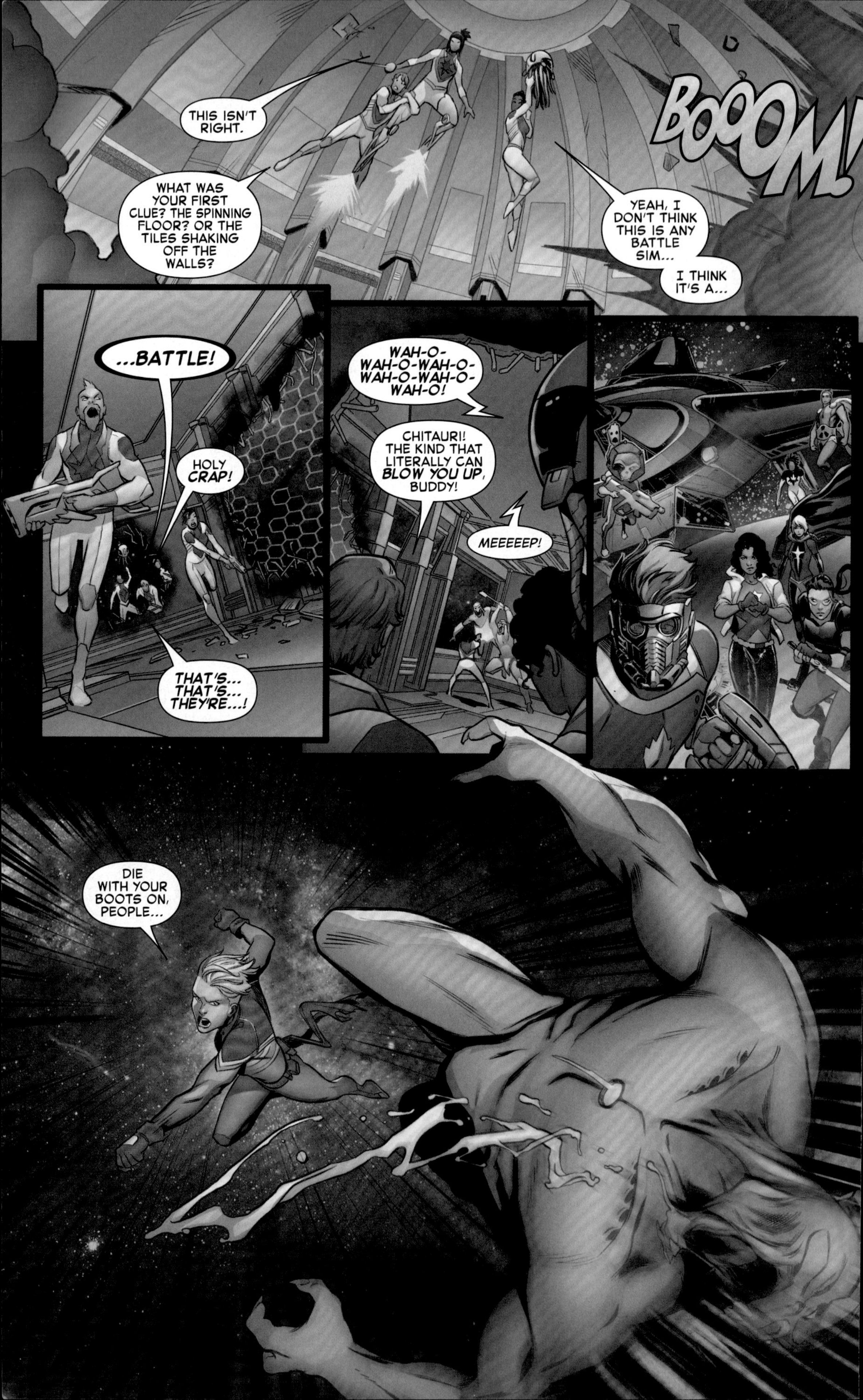
THIS ISN'T RIGHT.
WHAT WAS YOUR FIRST CLUE? THE SPINNING FLOOR? OR THE TILES SHAKING OFF THE WALLS?
BOOOM!
YEAH, I DON'T THINK THIS IS ANY BATTLE SIM...
I THINK IT'S A...
...BATTLE!
HOLY CRAP!
THAT'S... THAT'S... THEY'RE...!
WAH-O-WAH-O-WAH-O-WAH-O-WAH-O-WAH-O!
CHITAURI! THE KIND THAT LITERALLY CAN BLOW YOU UP, BUDDY!
MEEEEEP!
DIE WITH YOUR BOOTS ON, PEOPLE...

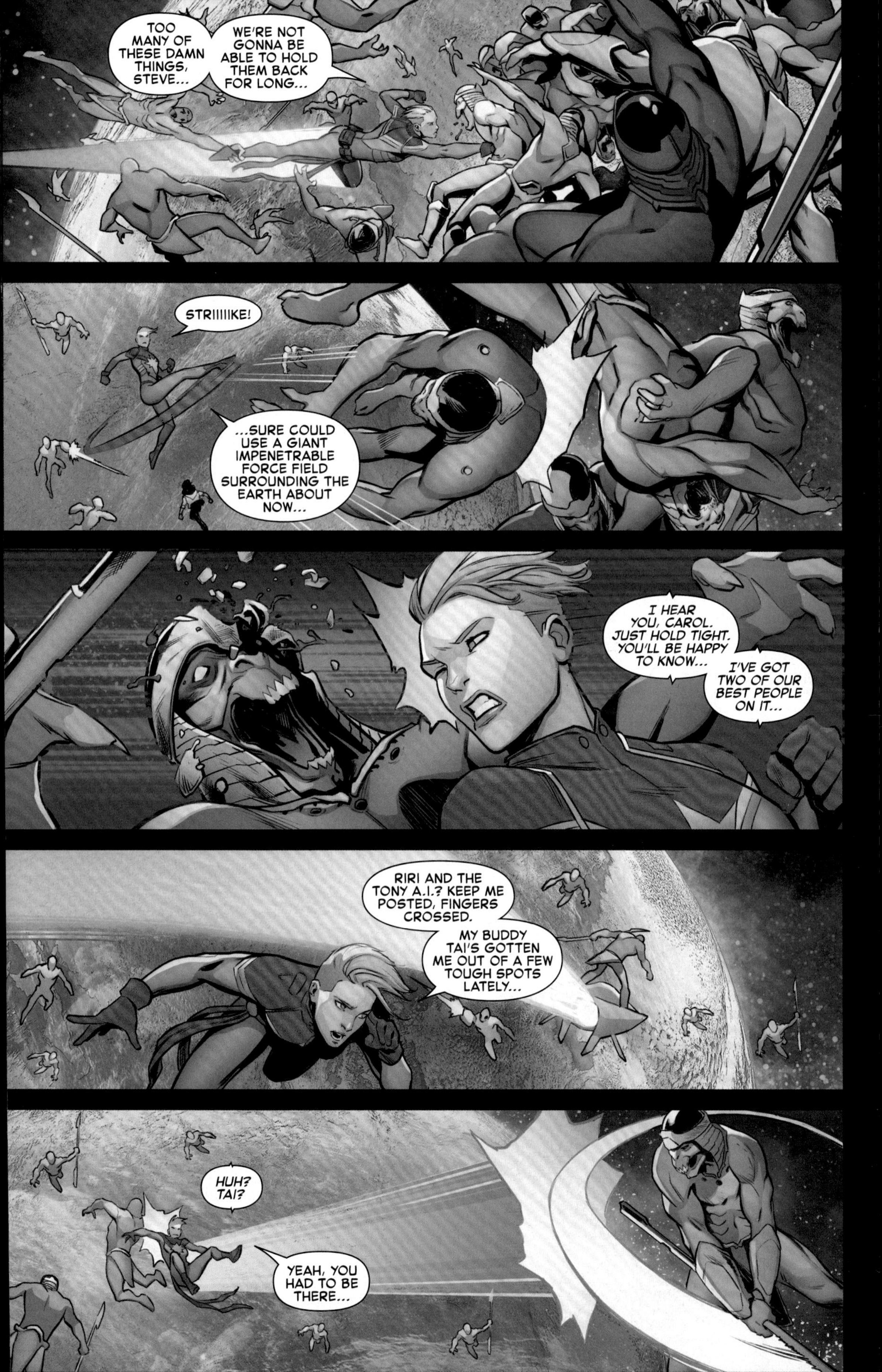
TOO MANY OF THESE DAMN THINGS, STEVE...
WE'RE NOT GONNA BE ABLE TO HOLD THEM BACK FOR LONG...
STRIIIIIKE!
...SURE COULD USE A GIANT IMPENETRABLE FORCE FIELD SURROUNDING THE EARTH ABOUT NOW...
I HEAR YOU, CAROL. JUST HOLD TIGHT. YOU'LL BE HAPPY TO KNOW...
I'VE GOT TWO OF OUR BEST PEOPLE ON IT...
RIRI AND THE TONY A.I.? KEEP ME POSTED, FINGERS CROSSED.
MY BUDDY TAI'S GOTTEN ME OUT OF A FEW TOUGH SPOTS LATELY...
HUH? TAI?
YEAH, YOU HAD TO BE THERE...

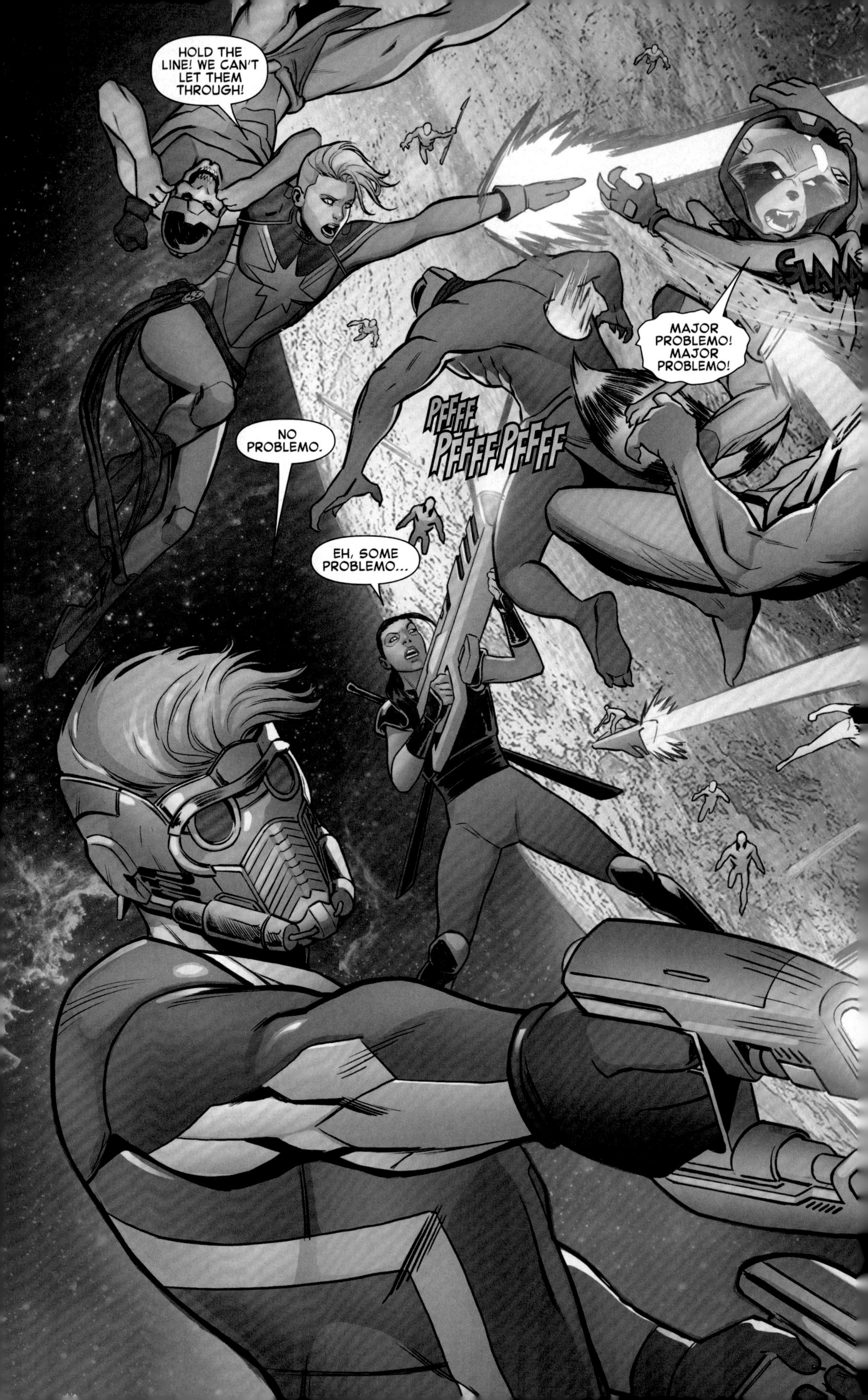
HOLD THE LINE! WE CAN'T LET THEM THROUGH!
MAJOR PROBLEMO! MAJOR PROBLEMO!
NO PROBLEMO.
PFFFF PFFFF PFFFF
EH, SOME PROBLEMO...

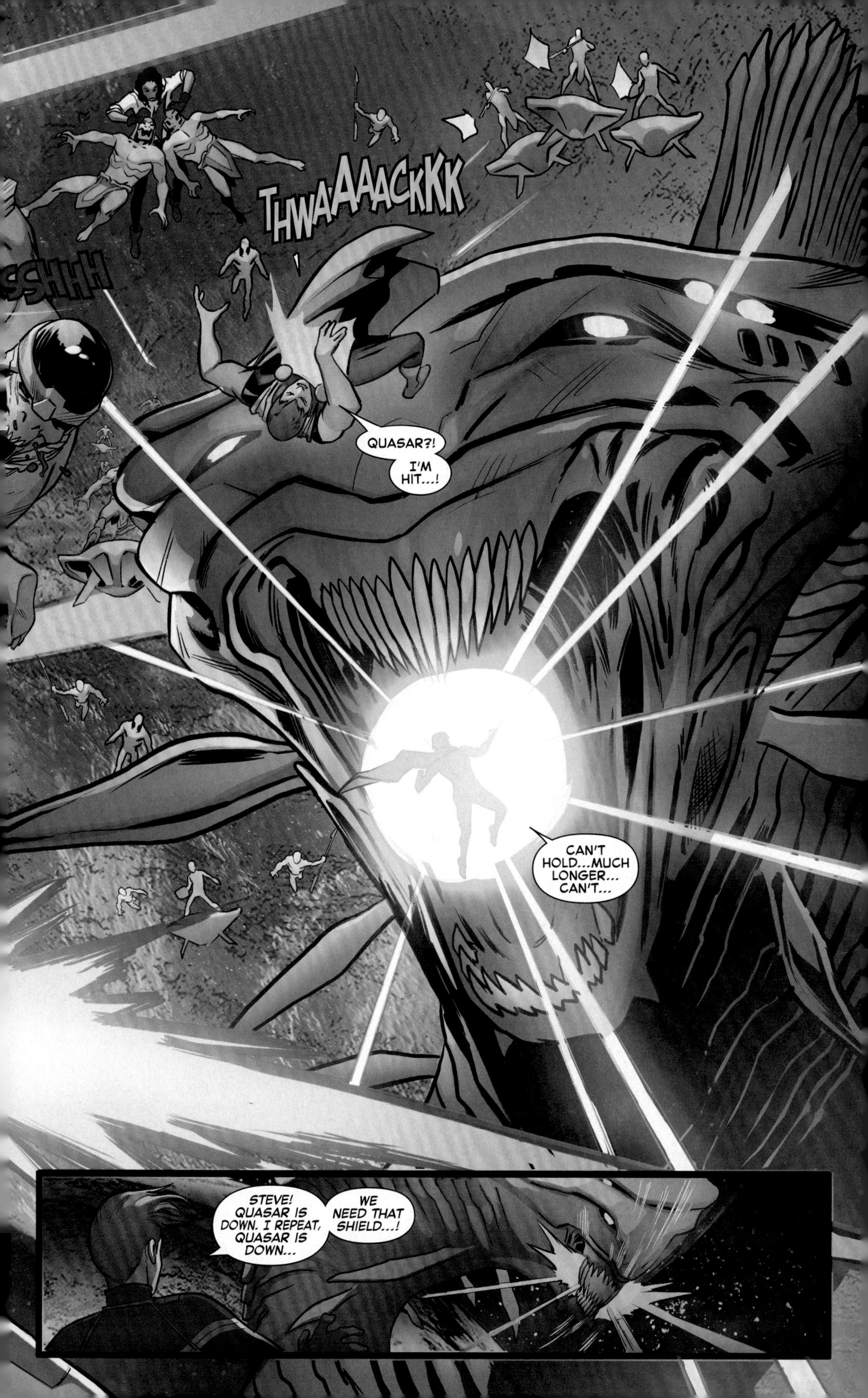
THWAAAACKKK
QUASAR?!
I'M HIT...!
CAN'T HOLD...MUCH LONGER... CAN'T...
STEVE! QUASAR IS DOWN. I REPEAT, QUASAR IS DOWN...
WE NEED THAT SHIELD...!

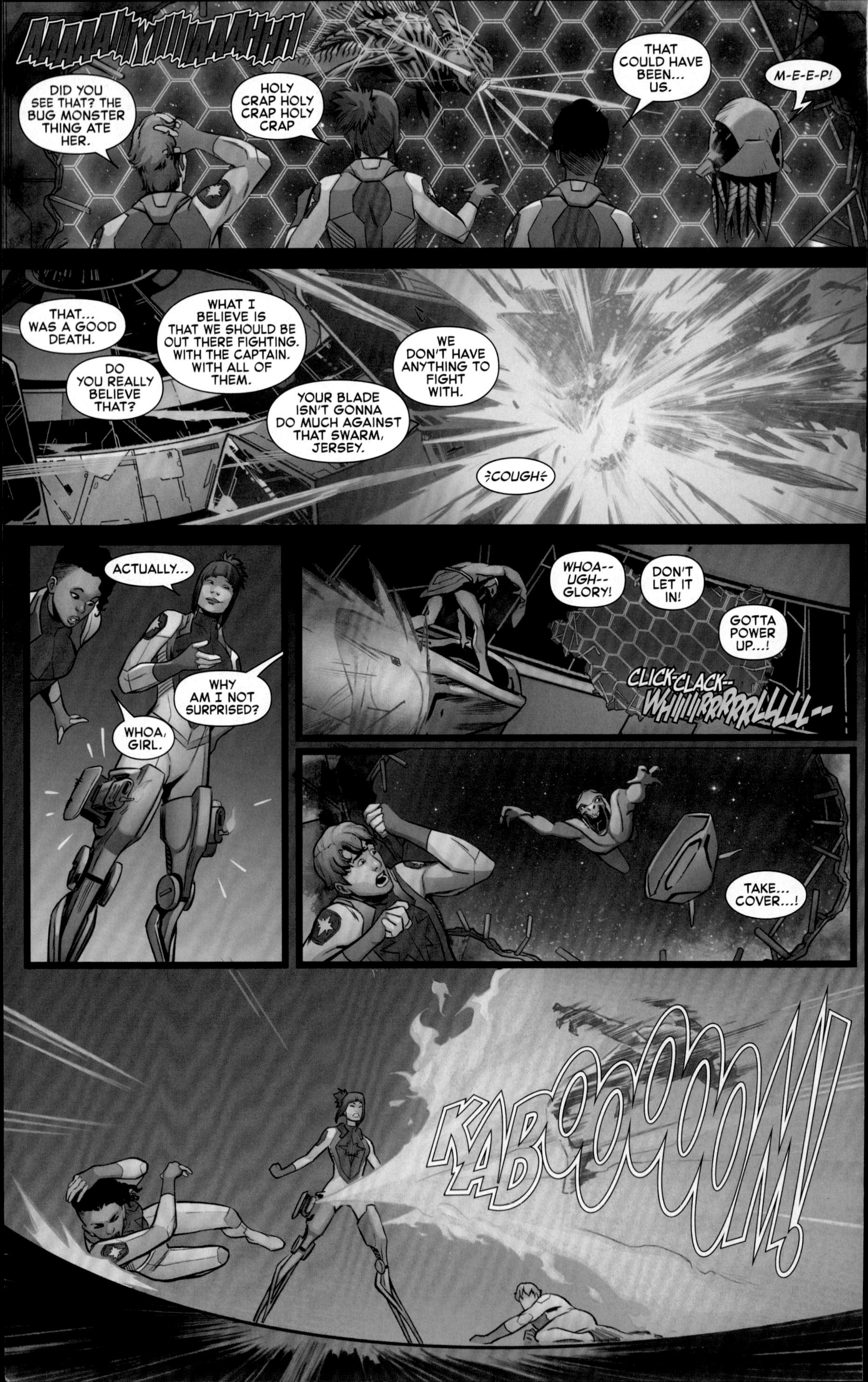
AAAAUIYIIIIAAAHHH
DID YOU SEE THAT? THE BUG MONSTER THING ATE HER.
HOLY CRAP HOLY CRAP HOLY CRAP
THAT COULD HAVE BEEN... US.
M-E-E-P!
THAT... WAS A GOOD DEATH.
DO YOU REALLY BELIEVE THAT?
WHAT I BELIEVE IS THAT WE SHOULD BE OUT THERE FIGHTING. WITH THE CAPTAIN. WITH ALL OF THEM.
YOUR BLADE ISN'T GONNA DO MUCH AGAINST THAT SWARM, JERSEY.
WE DON'T HAVE ANYTHING TO FIGHT WITH.
COUGH
ACTUALLY...
WHY AM I NOT SURPRISED?
WHOA, GIRL.
WHOA-- UGH-- GLORY!
DON'T LET IT IN!
GOTTA POWER UP...!
CLICK-CLACK-
WHIIIRRRRLLLLL--
TAKE... COVER...!
KABOOOOOOM!

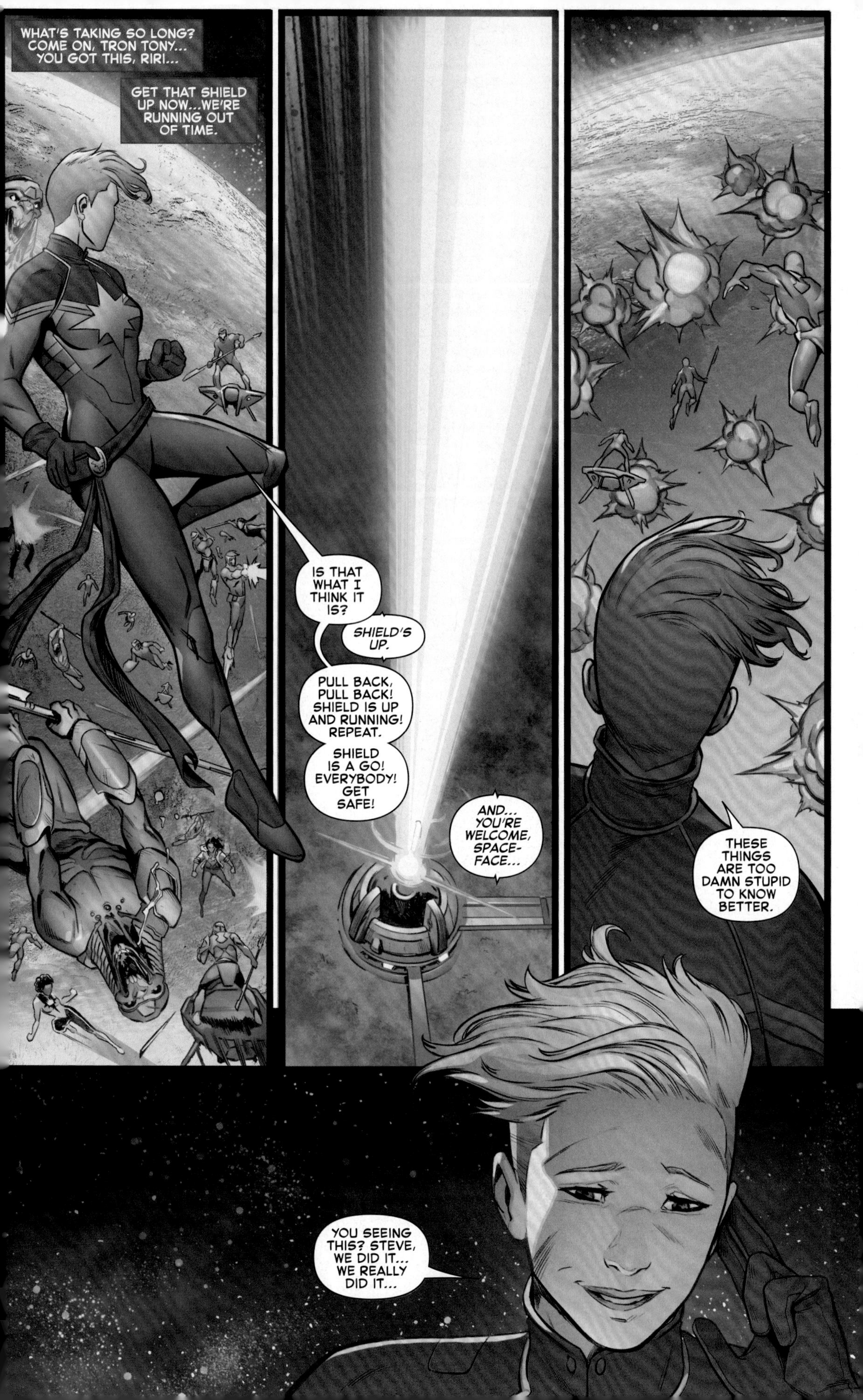
WHAT'S TAKING SO LONG? COME ON, TRON TONY... YOU GOT THIS, RIRI...
GET THAT SHIELD UP NOW...WE'RE RUNNING OUT OF TIME.
IS THAT WHAT I THINK IT IS?
SHIELD'S UP.
PULL BACK, PULL BACK! SHIELD IS UP AND RUNNING! REPEAT.
SHIELD IS A GO! EVERYBODY! GET SAFE!
AND... YOU'RE WELCOME, SPACE-FACE...
THESE THINGS ARE TOO DAMN STUPID TO KNOW BETTER.
YOU SEEING THIS? STEVE, WE DID IT... WE REALLY DID IT...

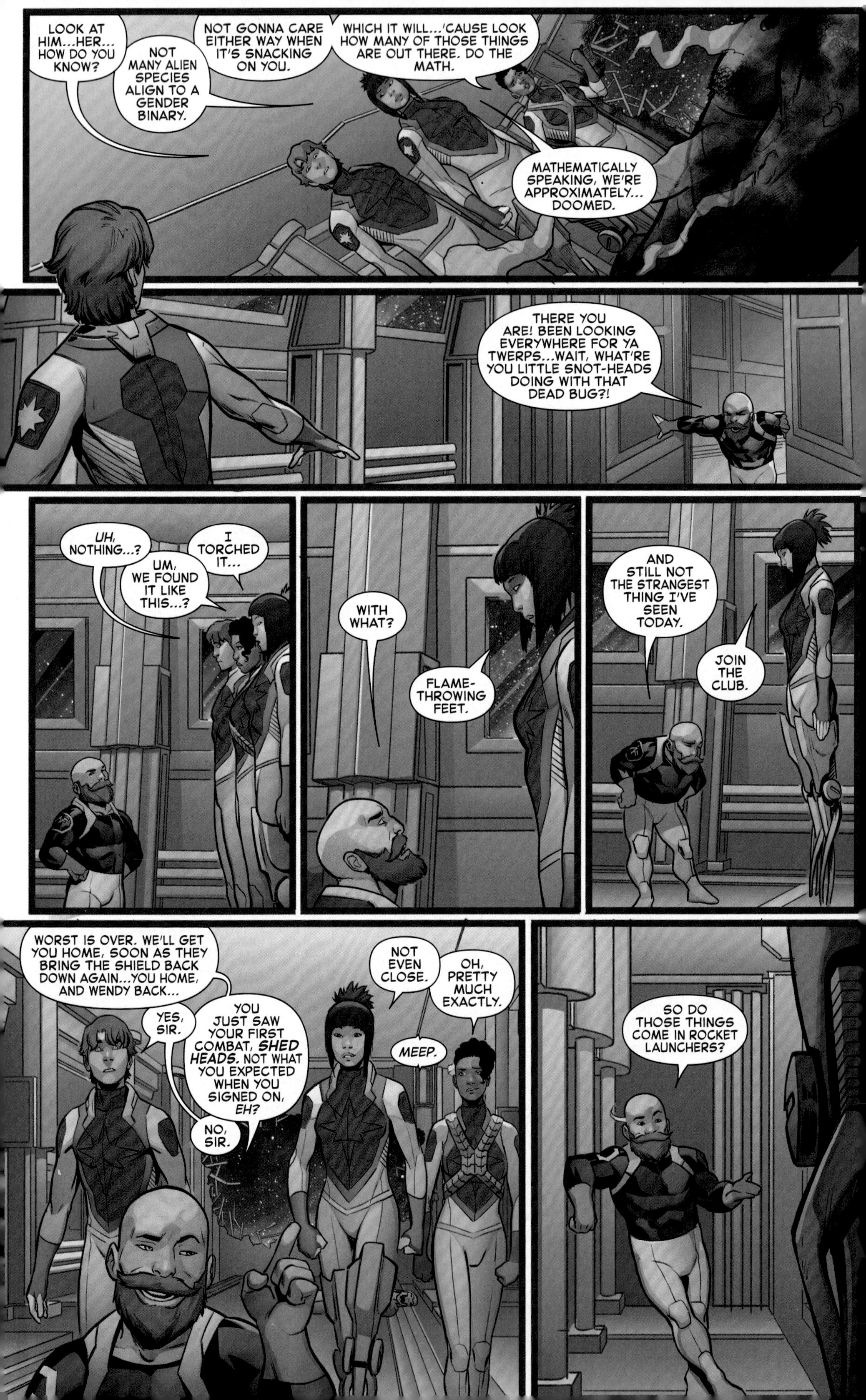
LOOK AT HIM...HER... HOW DO YOU KNOW?
NOT MANY ALIEN SPECIES ALIGN TO A GENDER BINARY.
NOT GONNA CARE EITHER WAY WHEN IT'S SNACKING ON YOU.
WHICH IT WILL...'CAUSE LOOK HOW MANY OF THOSE THINGS ARE OUT THERE. DO THE MATH.
MATHEMATICALLY SPEAKING, WE'RE APPROXIMATELY... DOOMED.
THERE YOU ARE! BEEN LOOKING EVERYWHERE FOR YA TWERPS...WAIT, WHAT'RE YOU LITTLE SNOT-HEADS DOING WITH THAT DEAD BUG?!
UH, NOTHING...?
UM, WE FOUND IT LIKE THIS...?
I TORCHED IT...
WITH WHAT?
FLAME-THROWING FEET.
AND STILL NOT THE STRANGEST THING I'VE SEEN TODAY.
JOIN THE CLUB.
WORST IS OVER. WE'LL GET YOU HOME, SOON AS THEY BRING THE SHIELD BACK DOWN AGAIN...YOU HOME, AND WENDY BACK...
YES, SIR.
YOU JUST SAW YOUR FIRST COMBAT, SHED HEADS. NOT WHAT YOU EXPECTED WHEN YOU SIGNED ON, EH?
NO, SIR.
NOT EVEN CLOSE.
OH, PRETTY MUCH EXACTLY.
MEEP.
SO DO THOSE THINGS COME IN ROCKET LAUNCHERS?

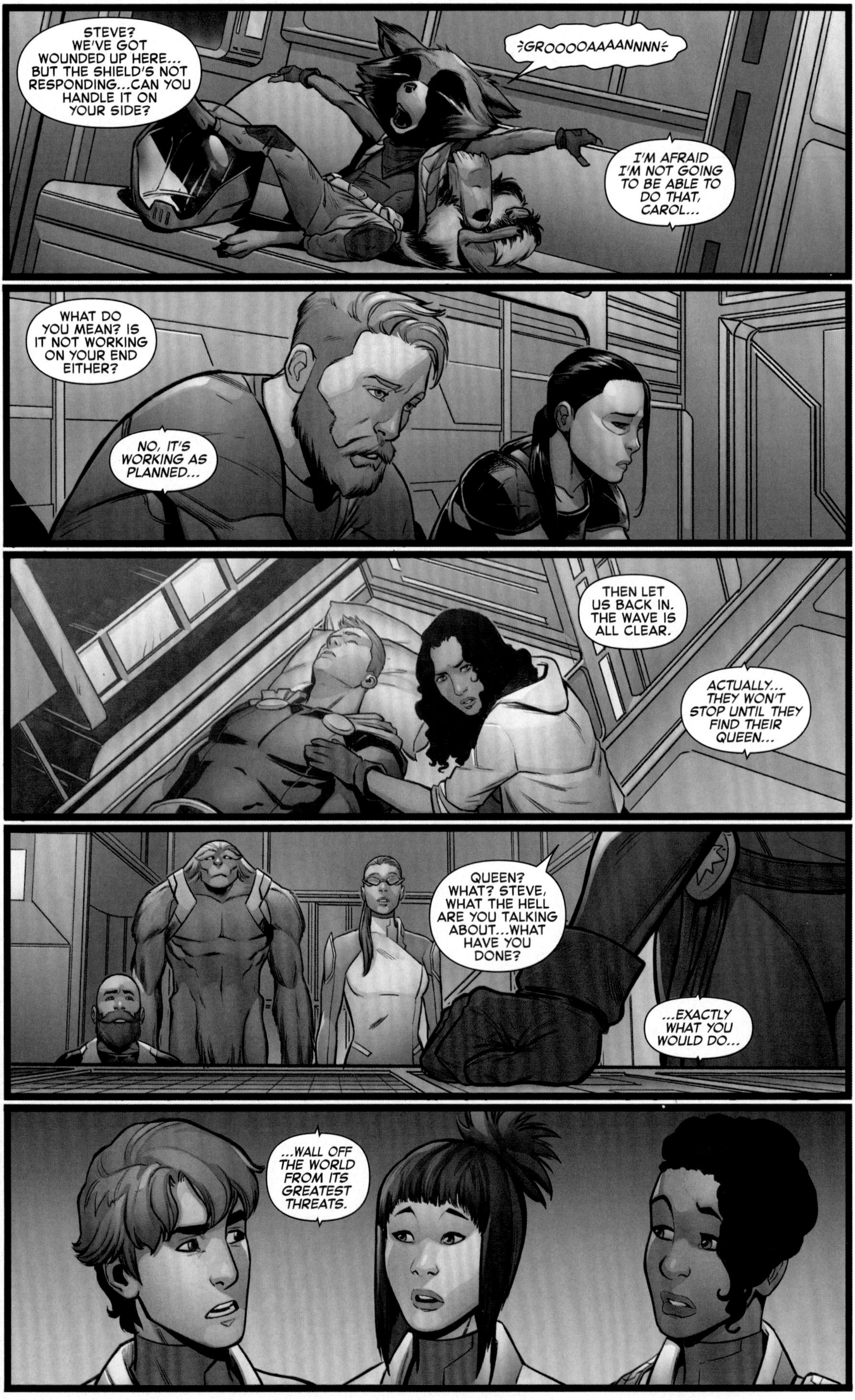
STEVE? WE'VE GOT WOUNDED UP HERE... BUT THE SHIELD'S NOT RESPONDING...CAN YOU HANDLE IT ON YOUR SIDE?
GROOOOAAAANNNN
I'M AFRAID I'M NOT GOING TO BE ABLE TO DO THAT, CAROL...
WHAT DO YOU MEAN? IS IT NOT WORKING ON YOUR END EITHER?
NO, IT'S WORKING AS PLANNED...
THEN LET US BACK IN. THE WAVE IS ALL CLEAR.
ACTUALLY... THEY WON'T STOP UNTIL THEY FIND THEIR QUEEN...
QUEEN? WHAT? STEVE, WHAT THE HELL ARE YOU TALKING ABOUT...WHAT HAVE YOU DONE?
...EXACTLY WHAT YOU WOULD DO...
...WALL OFF THE WORLD FROM ITS GREATEST THREATS.

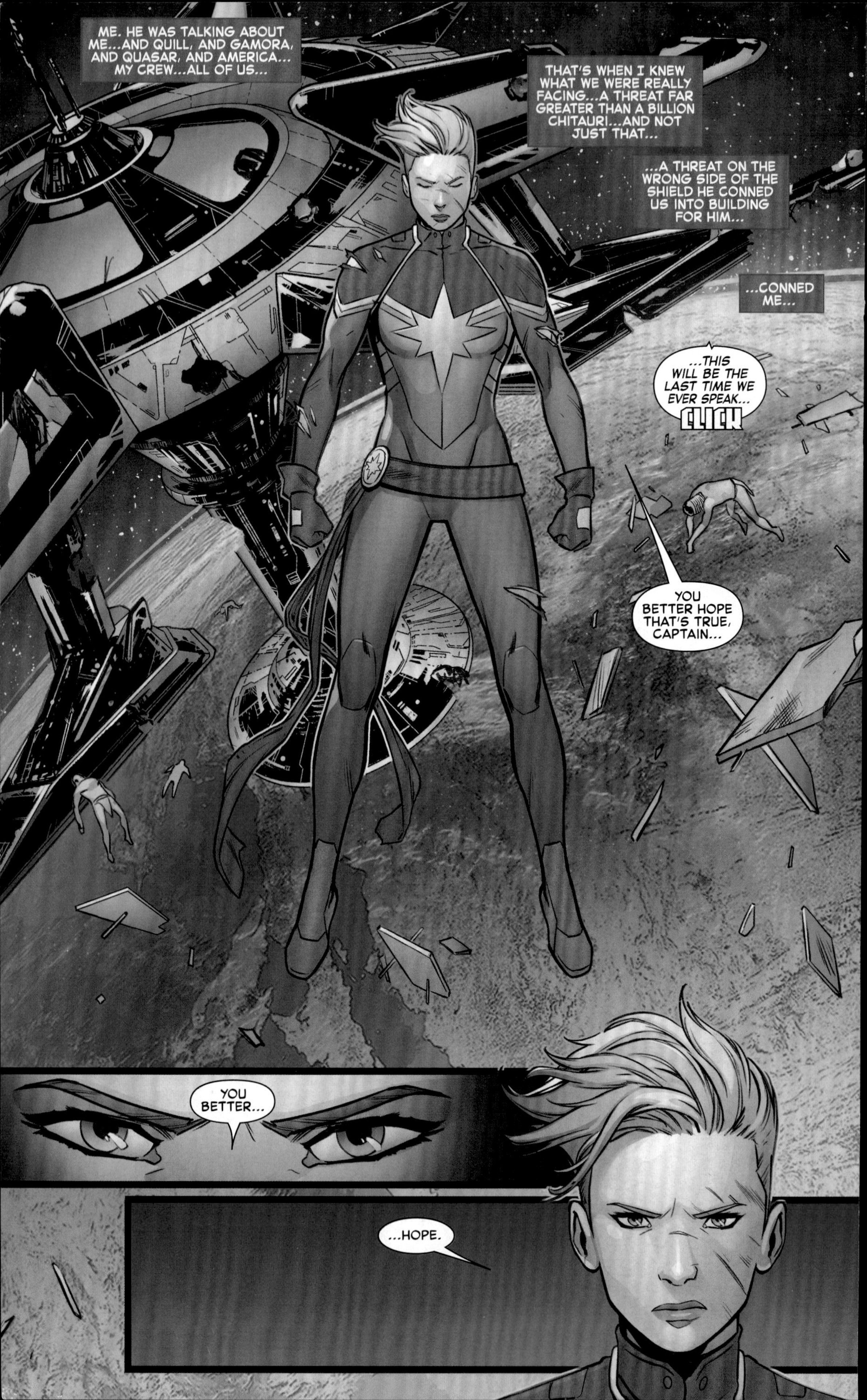
ME. HE WAS TALKING ABOUT ME...AND QUILL, AND GAMORA, AND QUASAR, AND AMERICA... MY CREW...ALL OF US...
THAT'S WHEN I KNEW WHAT WE WERE REALLY FACING...A THREAT FAR GREATER THAN A BILLION CHITAURI...AND NOT JUST THAT...
...A THREAT ON THE WRONG SIDE OF THE SHIELD HE CONNED US INTO BUILDING FOR HIM...
...CONNED ME...
...THIS WILL BE THE LAST TIME WE EVER SPEAK...
CLICK
YOU BETTER HOPE THAT'S TRUE, CAPTAIN...
YOU BETTER...
...HOPE.

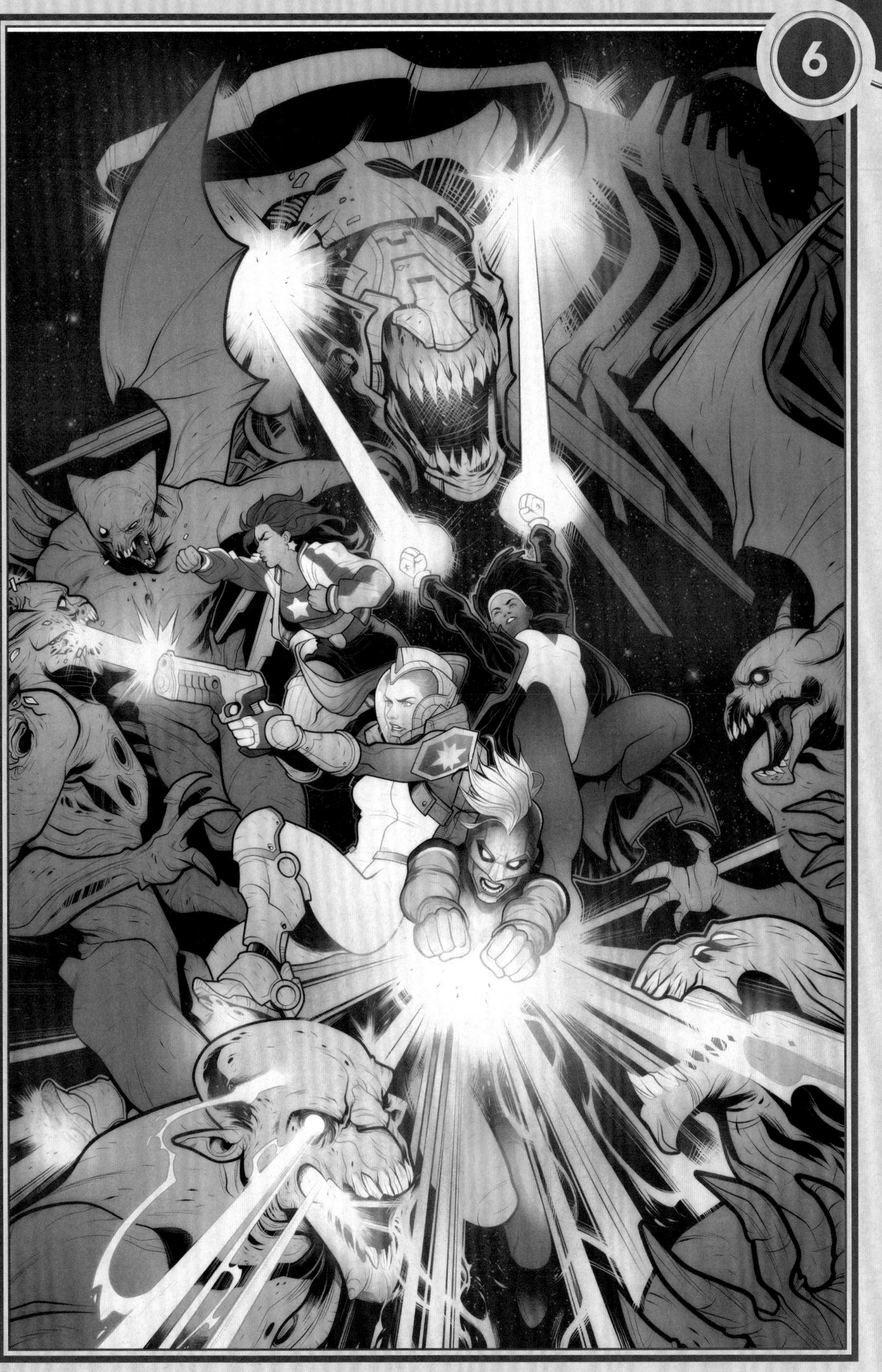
6

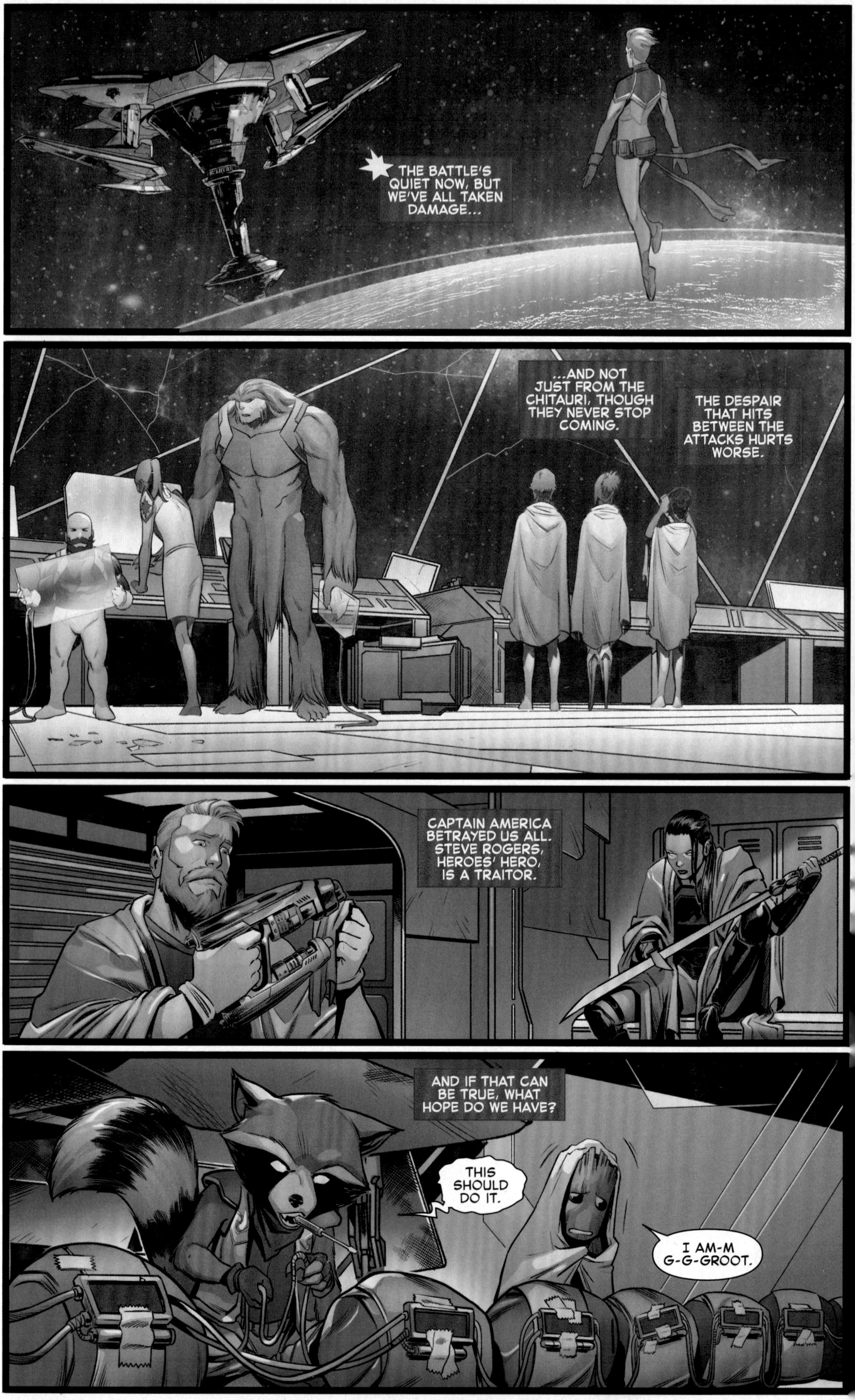
THE BATTLE'S QUIET NOW, BUT WE'VE ALL TAKEN DAMAGE...
...AND NOT JUST FROM THE CHITAURI, THOUGH THEY NEVER STOP COMING.
THE DESPAIR THAT HITS BETWEEN THE ATTACKS HURTS WORSE.
CAPTAIN AMERICA BETRAYED US ALL. STEVE ROGERS, HEROES' HERO, IS A TRAITOR.
AND IF THAT CAN BE TRUE, WHAT HOPE DO WE HAVE?
THIS SHOULD DO IT.
I AM-M G-G-GROOT.

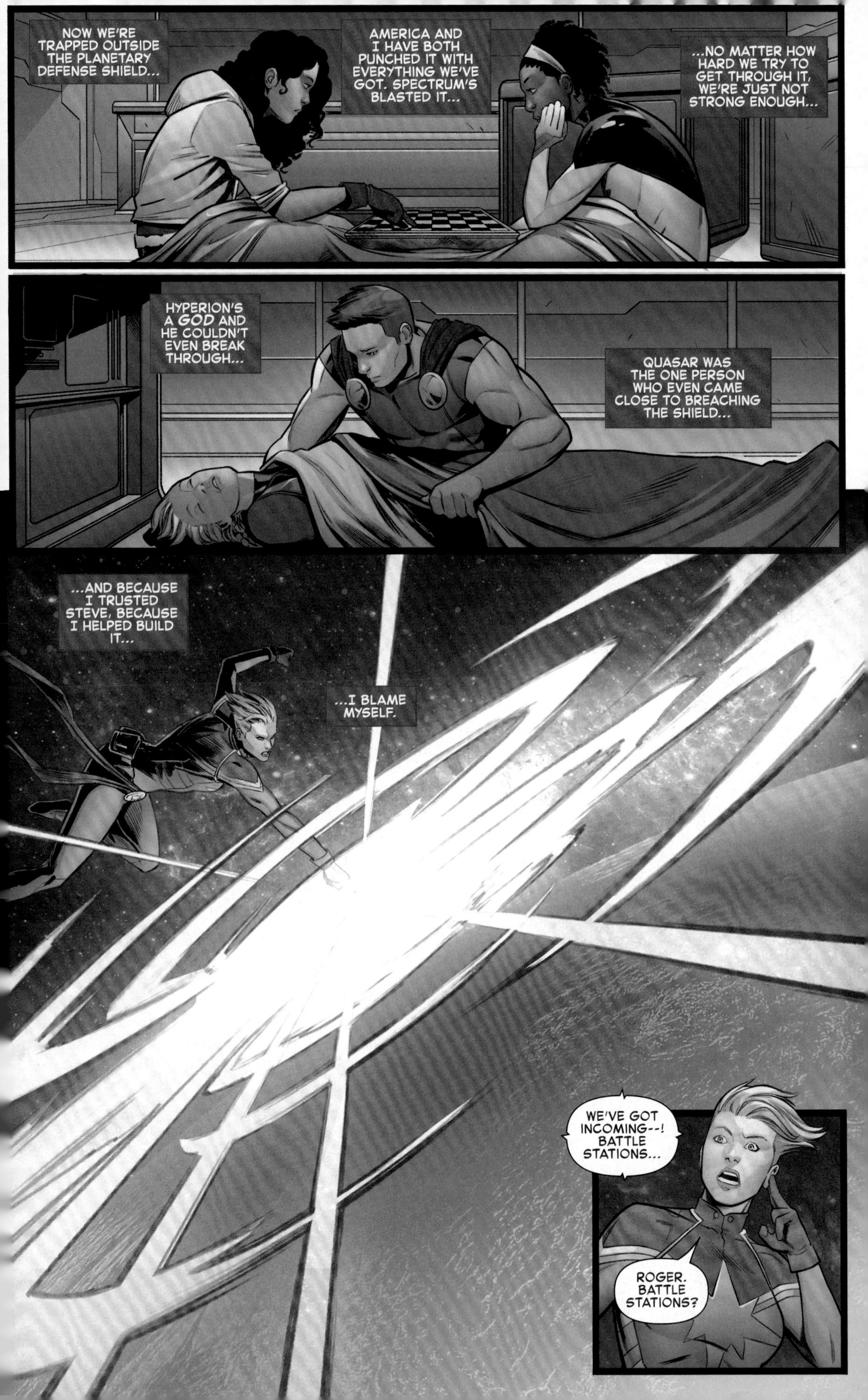
NOW WE'RE TRAPPED OUTSIDE THE PLANETARY DEFENSE SHIELD...
AMERICA AND I HAVE BOTH PUNCHED IT WITH EVERYTHING WE'VE GOT. SPECTRUM'S BLASTED IT...
...NO MATTER HOW HARD WE TRY TO GET THROUGH IT, WE'RE JUST NOT STRONG ENOUGH...
HYPERION'S A *GOD* AND HE COULDN'T EVEN BREAK THROUGH...
QUASAR WAS THE ONE PERSON WHO EVEN CAME CLOSE TO BREACHING THE SHIELD...
...AND BECAUSE I TRUSTED STEVE, BECAUSE I HELPED BUILD IT...
...I BLAME MYSELF.
WE'VE GOT INCOMING--! BATTLE STATIONS...
ROGER. BATTLE STATIONS?

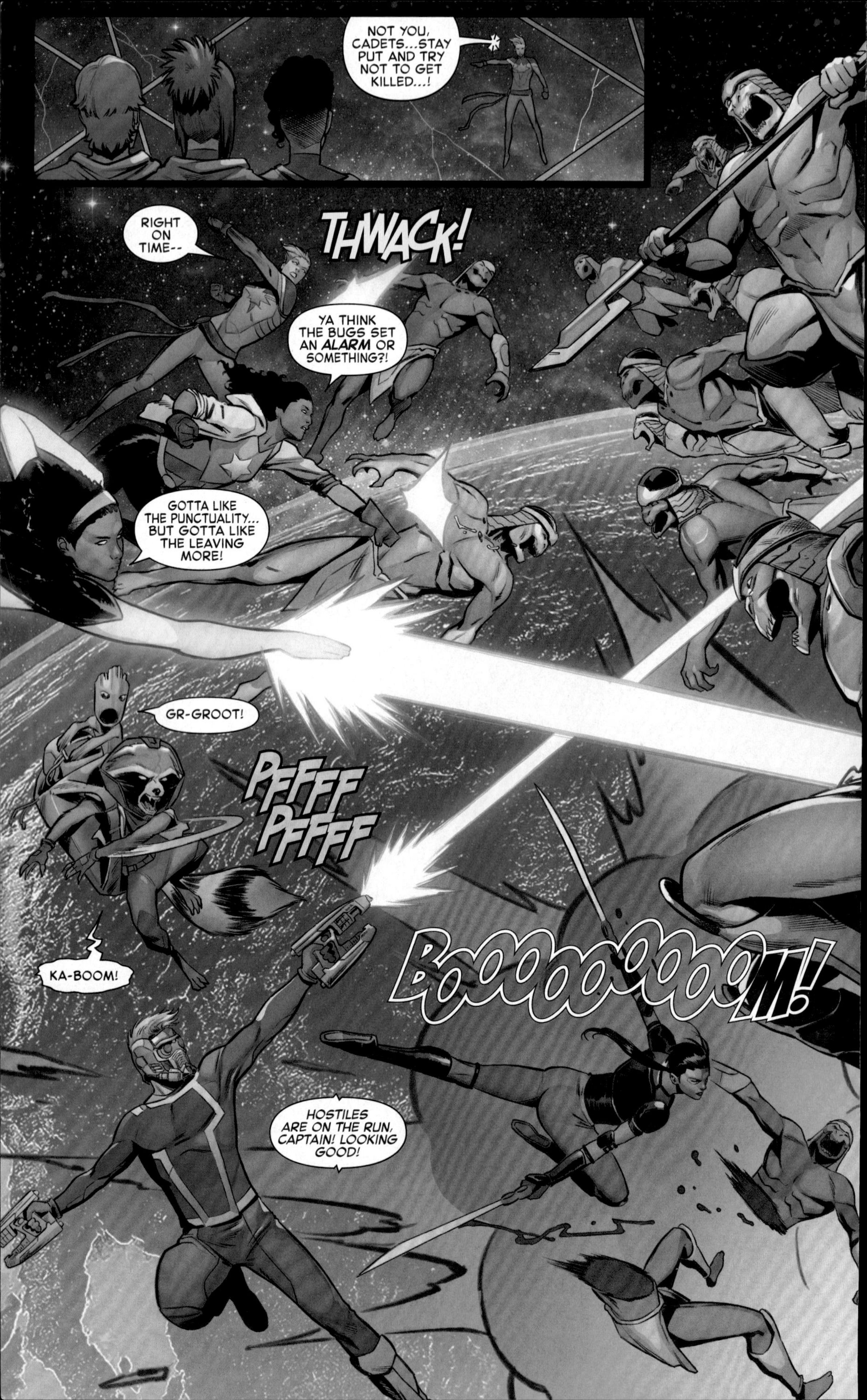

NOT YOU, CADETS...STAY PUT AND TRY NOT TO GET KILLED...!
RIGHT ON TIME--
THWACK!
YA THINK THE BUGS SET AN ALARM OR SOMETHING?!
GOTTA LIKE THE PUNCTUALITY... BUT GOTTA LIKE THE LEAVING MORE!
GR-GROOT!
PFFFF PFFFF
KA-BOOM!
BOOOOOOOOOM!
HOSTILES ARE ON THE RUN, CAPTAIN! LOOKING GOOD!

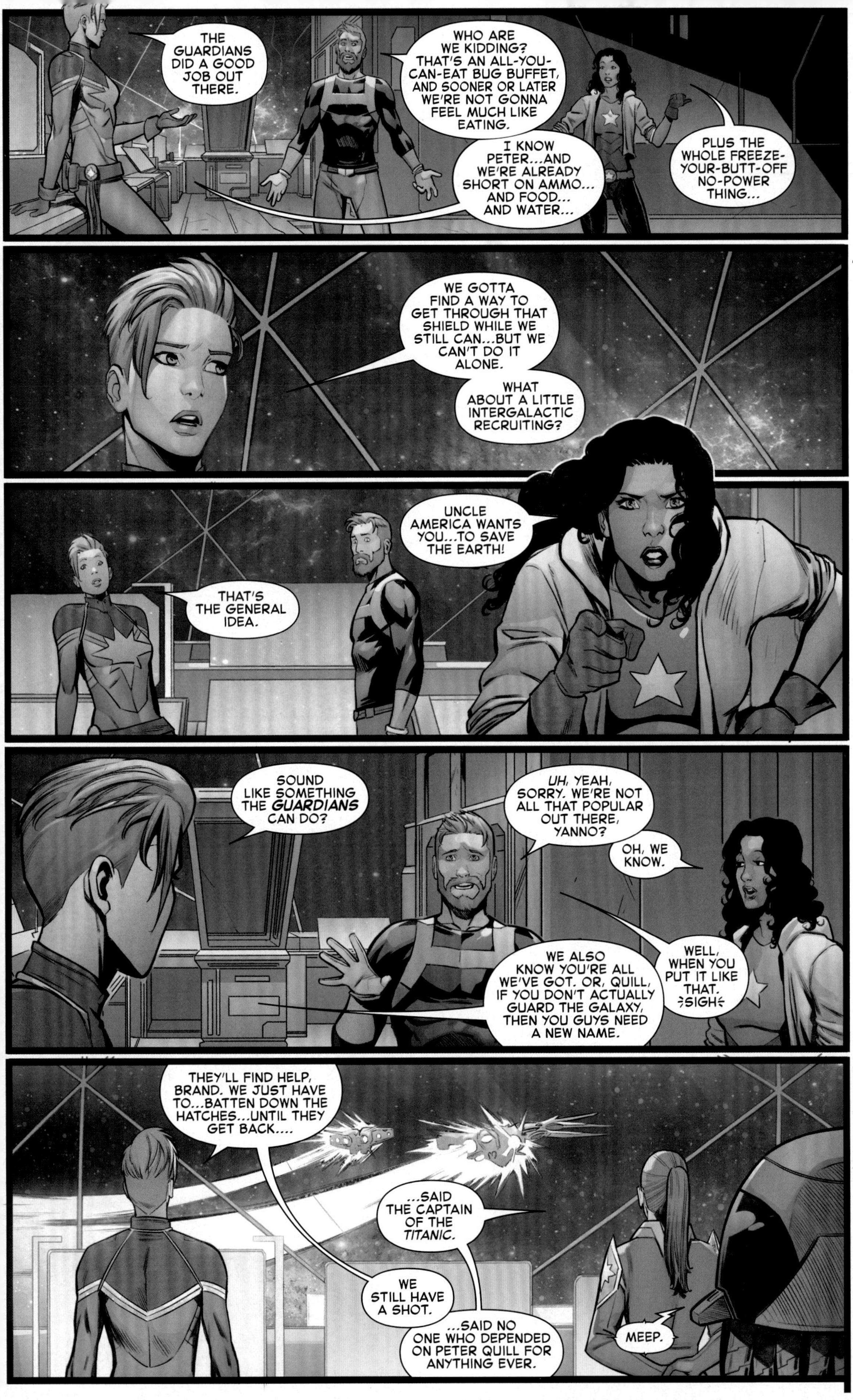
THE GUARDIANS DID A GOOD JOB OUT THERE.
WHO ARE WE KIDDING? THAT'S AN ALL-YOU-CAN-EAT BUG BUFFET, AND SOONER OR LATER WE'RE NOT GONNA FEEL MUCH LIKE EATING.
I KNOW PETER...AND WE'RE ALREADY SHORT ON AMMO... AND FOOD... AND WATER...
PLUS THE WHOLE FREEZE-YOUR-BUTT-OFF NO-POWER THING...
WE GOTTA FIND A WAY TO GET THROUGH THAT SHIELD WHILE WE STILL CAN...BUT WE CAN'T DO IT ALONE.
WHAT ABOUT A LITTLE INTERGALACTIC RECRUITING?
UNCLE AMERICA WANTS YOU...TO SAVE THE EARTH!
THAT'S THE GENERAL IDEA.
SOUND LIKE SOMETHING THE GUARDIANS CAN DO?
UH, YEAH, SORRY. WE'RE NOT ALL THAT POPULAR OUT THERE, YANNO?
OH, WE KNOW.
WE ALSO KNOW YOU'RE ALL WE'VE GOT. OR, QUILL, IF YOU DON'T ACTUALLY GUARD THE GALAXY, THEN YOU GUYS NEED A NEW NAME.
WELL, WHEN YOU PUT IT LIKE THAT. SIGH
THEY'LL FIND HELP, BRAND. WE JUST HAVE TO...BATTEN DOWN THE HATCHES...UNTIL THEY GET BACK....
...SAID THE CAPTAIN OF THE TITANIC.
WE STILL HAVE A SHOT.
...SAID NO ONE WHO DEPENDED ON PETER QUILL FOR ANYTHING EVER.
MEEP.

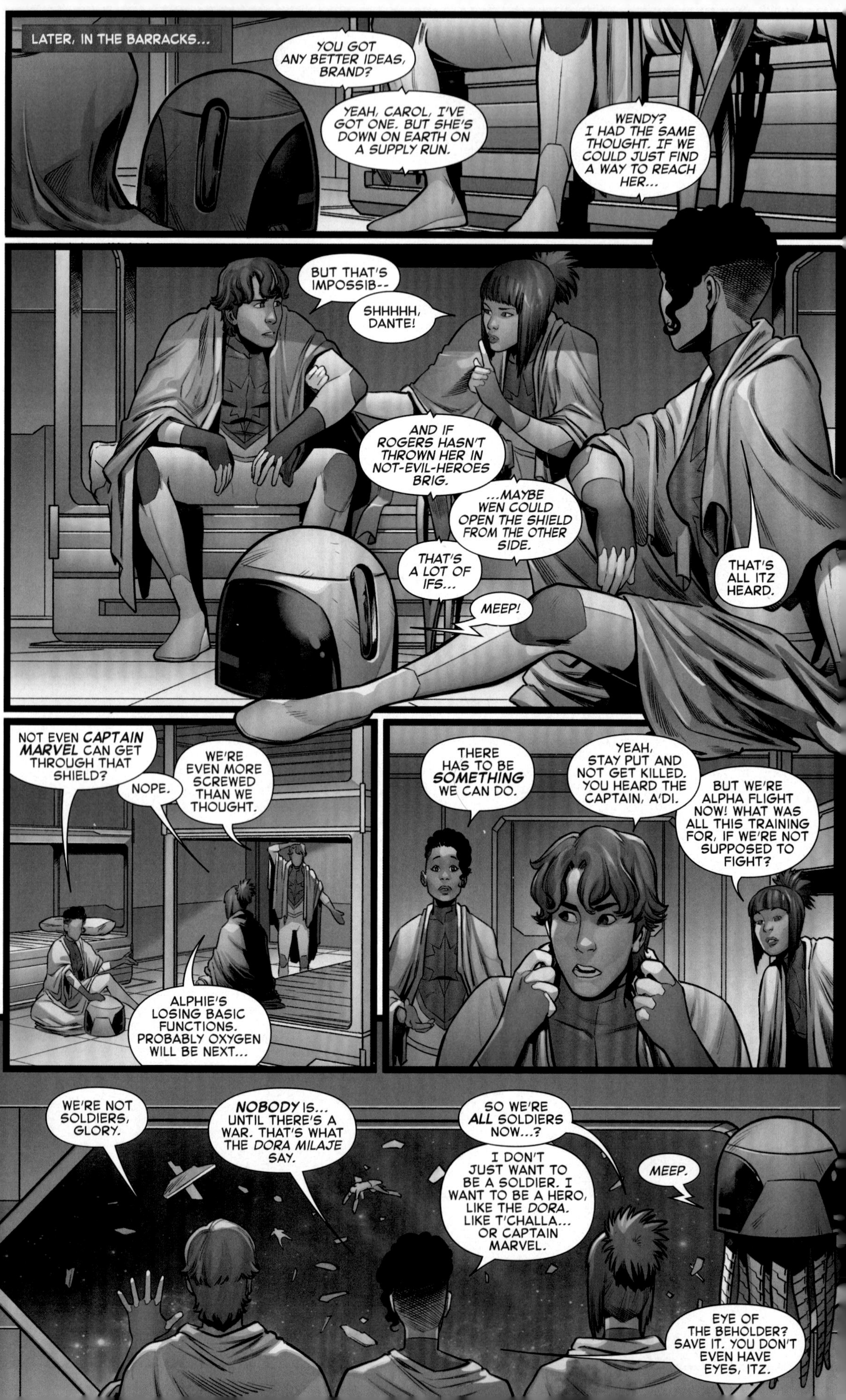
LATER, IN THE BARRACKS...
YOU GOT ANY BETTER IDEAS, BRAND?
YEAH, CAROL, I'VE GOT ONE. BUT SHE'S DOWN ON EARTH ON A SUPPLY RUN.
WENDY? I HAD THE SAME THOUGHT. IF WE COULD JUST FIND A WAY TO REACH HER...
BUT THAT'S IMPOSSIB--
SHHHHH, DANTE!
AND IF ROGERS HASN'T THROWN HER IN NOT-EVIL-HEROES BRIG.
...MAYBE WEN COULD OPEN THE SHIELD FROM THE OTHER SIDE.
THAT'S A LOT OF IFS...
MEEP!
THAT'S ALL ITZ HEARD.
NOT EVEN CAPTAIN MARVEL CAN GET THROUGH THAT SHIELD?
NOPE.
WE'RE EVEN MORE SCREWED THAN WE THOUGHT.
ALPHIE'S LOSING BASIC FUNCTIONS. PROBABLY OXYGEN WILL BE NEXT...
THERE HAS TO BE SOMETHING WE CAN DO.
YEAH, STAY PUT AND NOT GET KILLED. YOU HEARD THE CAPTAIN, A'DI.
BUT WE'RE ALPHA FLIGHT NOW! WHAT WAS ALL THIS TRAINING FOR, IF WE'RE NOT SUPPOSED TO FIGHT?
WE'RE NOT SOLDIERS, GLORY.
NOBODY IS... UNTIL THERE'S A WAR. THAT'S WHAT THE DORA MILAJE SAY.
SO WE'RE ALL SOLDIERS NOW...?
I DON'T JUST WANT TO BE A SOLDIER. I WANT TO BE A HERO, LIKE THE DORA. LIKE T'CHALLA... OR CAPTAIN MARVEL.
MEEP.
EYE OF THE BEHOLDER? SAVE IT. YOU DON'T EVEN HAVE EYES, ITZ.

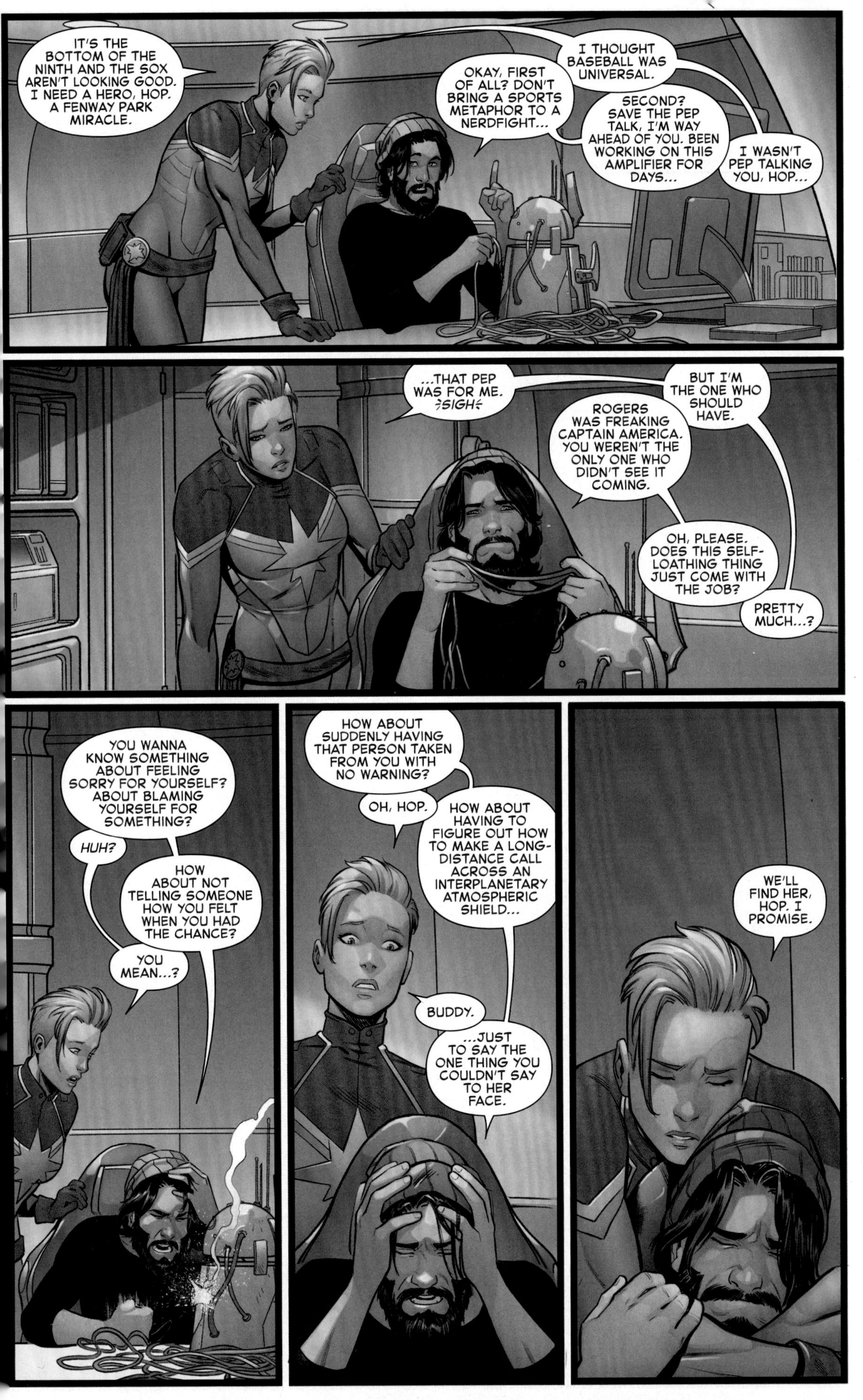
IT'S THE BOTTOM OF THE NINTH AND THE SOX AREN'T LOOKING GOOD. I NEED A HERO, HOP. A FENWAY PARK MIRACLE.
OKAY, FIRST OF ALL? DON'T BRING A SPORTS METAPHOR TO A NERDFIGHT...
I THOUGHT BASEBALL WAS UNIVERSAL.
SECOND? SAVE THE PEP TALK, I'M WAY AHEAD OF YOU. BEEN WORKING ON THIS AMPLIFIER FOR DAYS...
I WASN'T PEP TALKING YOU, HOP...
...THAT PEP WAS FOR ME. *SIGH*
BUT I'M THE ONE WHO SHOULD HAVE.
ROGERS WAS FREAKING CAPTAIN AMERICA. YOU WEREN'T THE ONLY ONE WHO DIDN'T SEE IT COMING.
OH, PLEASE. DOES THIS SELF-LOATHING THING JUST COME WITH THE JOB?
PRETTY MUCH...?
YOU WANNA KNOW SOMETHING ABOUT FEELING SORRY FOR YOURSELF? ABOUT BLAMING YOURSELF FOR SOMETHING?
HUH?
HOW ABOUT NOT TELLING SOMEONE HOW YOU FELT WHEN YOU HAD THE CHANCE?
YOU MEAN...?
HOW ABOUT SUDDENLY HAVING THAT PERSON TAKEN FROM YOU WITH NO WARNING?
OH, HOP.
HOW ABOUT HAVING TO FIGURE OUT HOW TO MAKE A LONG-DISTANCE CALL ACROSS AN INTERPLANETARY ATMOSPHERIC SHIELD...
BUDDY.
...JUST TO SAY THE ONE THING YOU COULDN'T SAY TO HER FACE.
WE'LL FIND HER, HOP. I PROMISE.

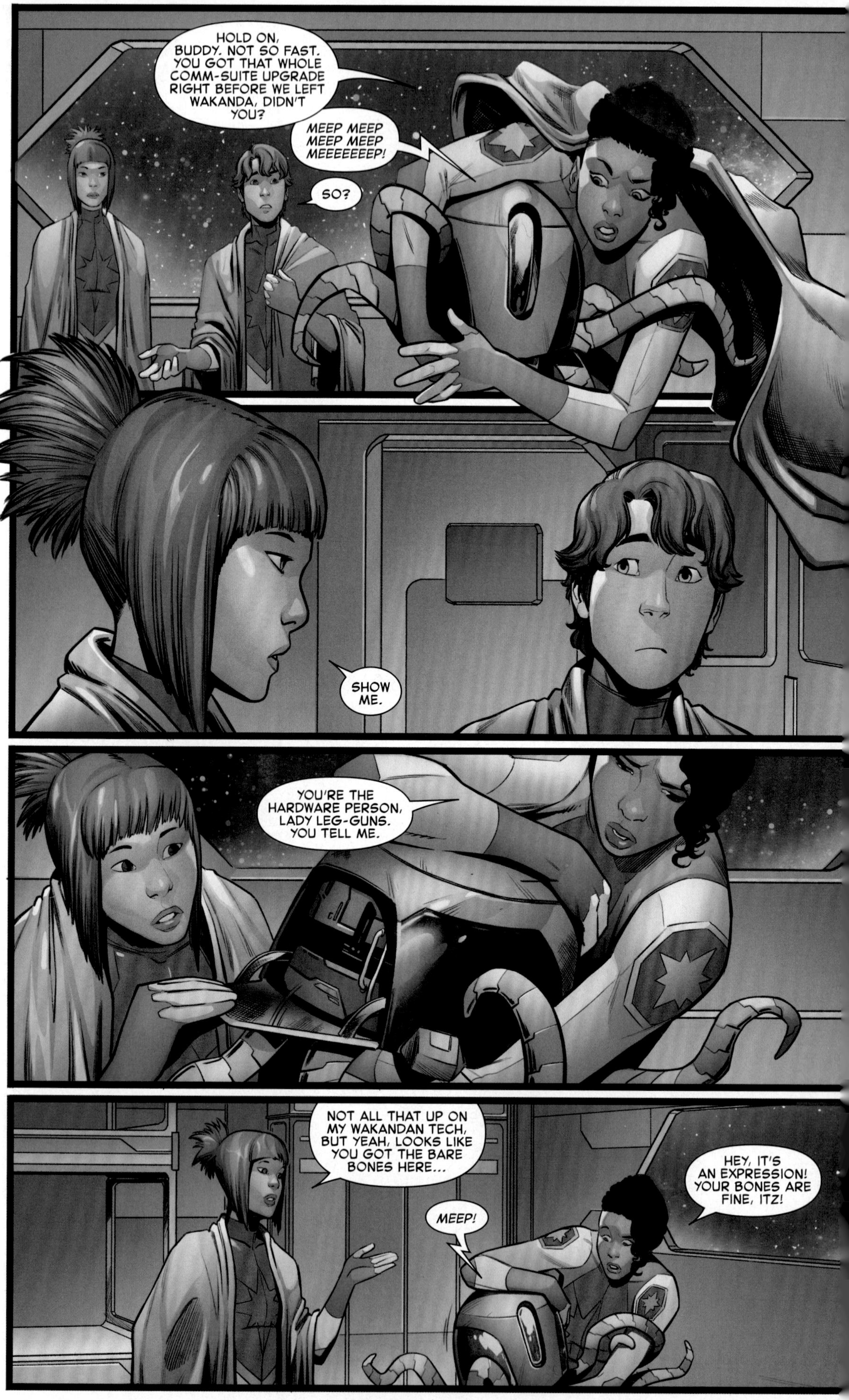
HOLD ON, BUDDY. NOT SO FAST. YOU GOT THAT WHOLE COMM-SUITE UPGRADE RIGHT BEFORE WE LEFT WAKANDA, DIDN'T YOU?
MEEP MEEP MEEP MEEP MEEEEEEEP!
SO?
SHOW ME.
YOU'RE THE HARDWARE PERSON, LADY LEG-GUNS. YOU TELL ME.
NOT ALL THAT UP ON MY WAKANDAN TECH, BUT YEAH, LOOKS LIKE YOU GOT THE BARE BONES HERE...
MEEP!
HEY, IT'S AN EXPRESSION! YOUR BONES ARE FINE, ITZ!

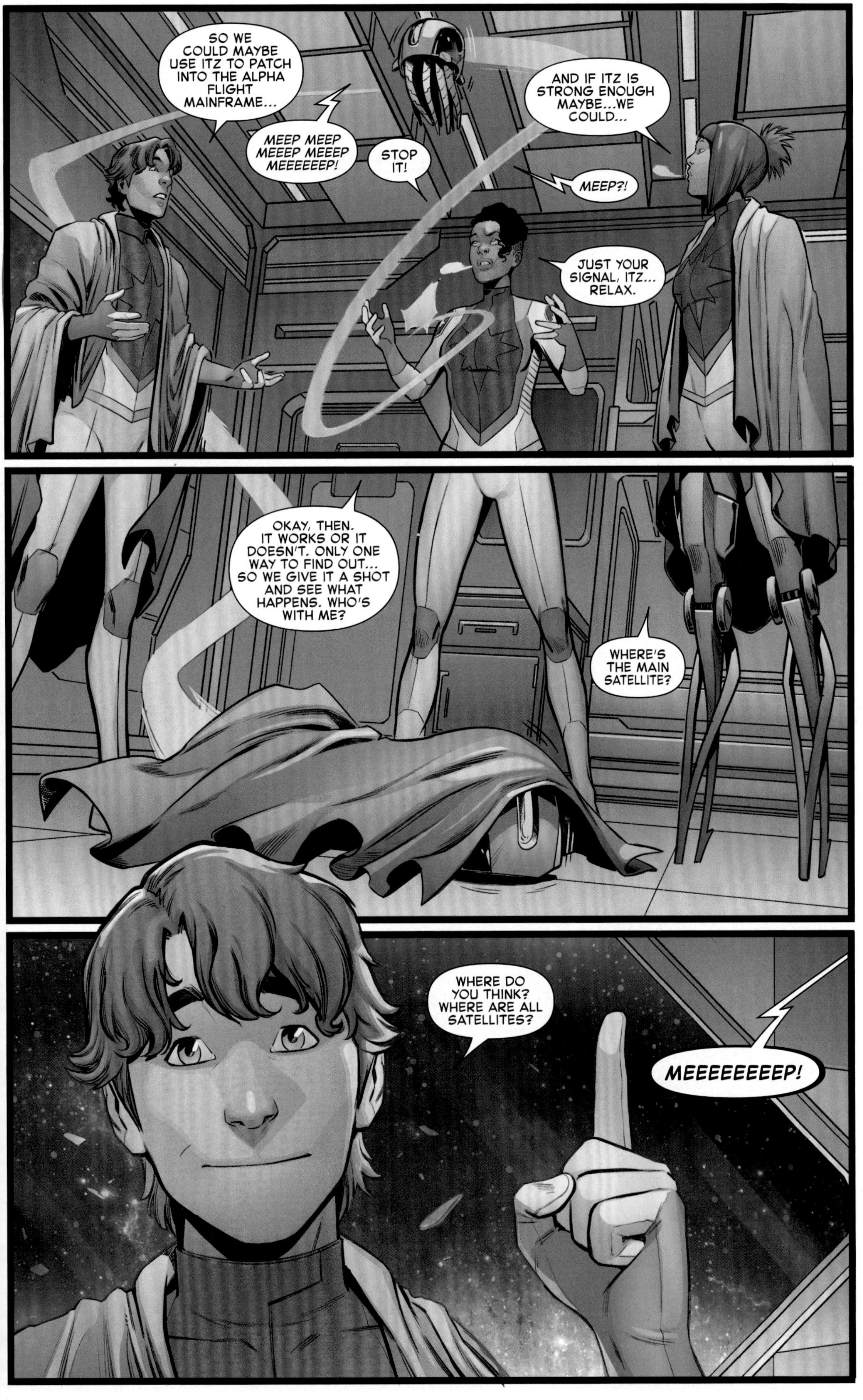
SO WE COULD MAYBE USE ITZ TO PATCH INTO THE ALPHA FLIGHT MAINFRAME...
MEEP MEEP MEEEP MEEEP MEEEEEEP!
STOP IT!
AND IF ITZ IS STRONG ENOUGH MAYBE...WE COULD...
MEEP?!
JUST YOUR SIGNAL, ITZ... RELAX.
OKAY, THEN. IT WORKS OR IT DOESN'T. ONLY ONE WAY TO FIND OUT... SO WE GIVE IT A SHOT AND SEE WHAT HAPPENS. WHO'S WITH ME?
WHERE'S THE MAIN SATELLITE?
WHERE DO YOU THINK? WHERE ARE ALL SATELLITES?
MEEEEEEEEP!

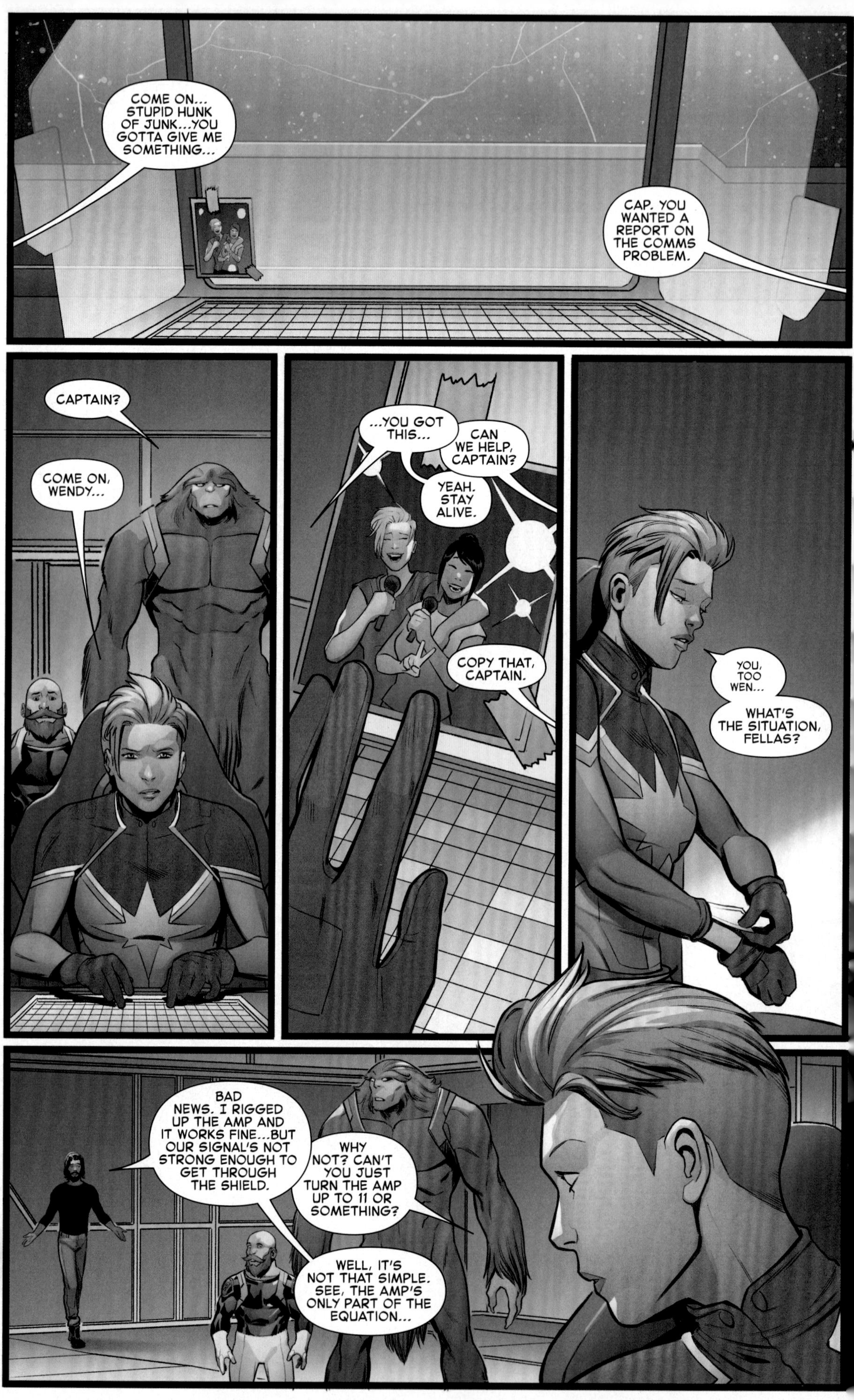
COME ON... STUPID HUNK OF JUNK...YOU GOTTA GIVE ME SOMETHING...
CAP. YOU WANTED A REPORT ON THE COMMS PROBLEM.
CAPTAIN?
COME ON, WENDY...
...YOU GOT THIS...
CAN WE HELP, CAPTAIN?
YEAH. STAY ALIVE.
COPY THAT, CAPTAIN.
YOU, TOO WEN...
WHAT'S THE SITUATION, FELLAS?
BAD NEWS. I RIGGED UP THE AMP AND IT WORKS FINE...BUT OUR SIGNAL'S NOT STRONG ENOUGH TO GET THROUGH THE SHIELD.
WHY NOT? CAN'T YOU JUST TURN THE AMP UP TO 11 OR SOMETHING?
WELL, IT'S NOT THAT SIMPLE. SEE, THE AMP'S ONLY PART OF THE EQUATION...

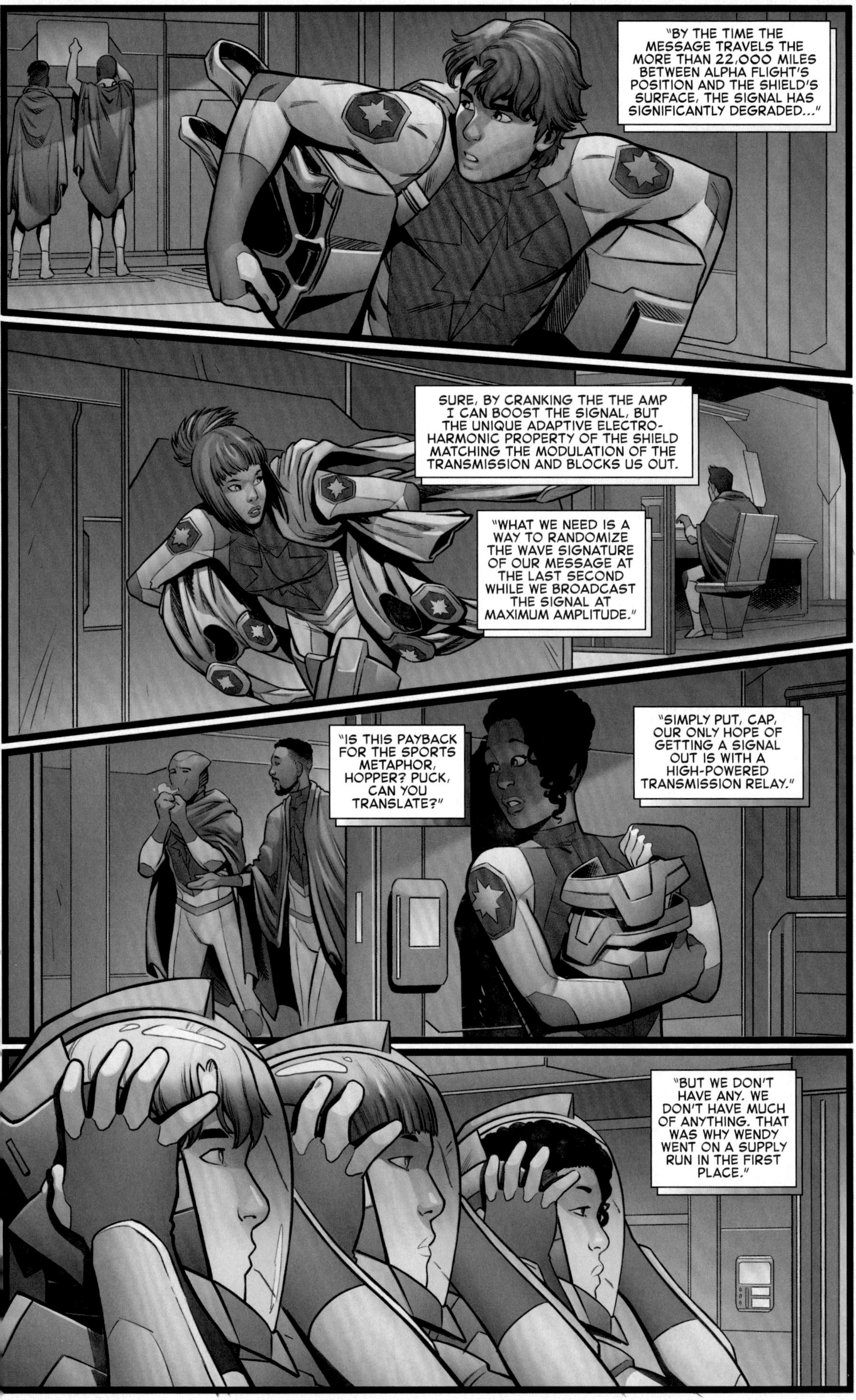
"BY THE TIME THE MESSAGE TRAVELS THE MORE THAN 22,000 MILES BETWEEN ALPHA FLIGHT'S POSITION AND THE SHIELD'S SURFACE, THE SIGNAL HAS SIGNIFICANTLY DEGRADED..."
SURE, BY CRANKING THE THE AMP I CAN BOOST THE SIGNAL, BUT THE UNIQUE ADAPTIVE ELECTRO-HARMONIC PROPERTY OF THE SHIELD MATCHING THE MODULATION OF THE TRANSMISSION AND BLOCKS US OUT.
"WHAT WE NEED IS A WAY TO RANDOMIZE THE WAVE SIGNATURE OF OUR MESSAGE AT THE LAST SECOND WHILE WE BROADCAST THE SIGNAL AT MAXIMUM AMPLITUDE."
"IS THIS PAYBACK FOR THE SPORTS METAPHOR, HOPPER? PUCK, CAN YOU TRANSLATE?"
"SIMPLY PUT, CAP, OUR ONLY HOPE OF GETTING A SIGNAL OUT IS WITH A HIGH-POWERED TRANSMISSION RELAY."
"BUT WE DON'T HAVE ANY. WE DON'T HAVE MUCH OF ANYTHING. THAT WAS WHY WENDY WENT ON A SUPPLY RUN IN THE FIRST PLACE."

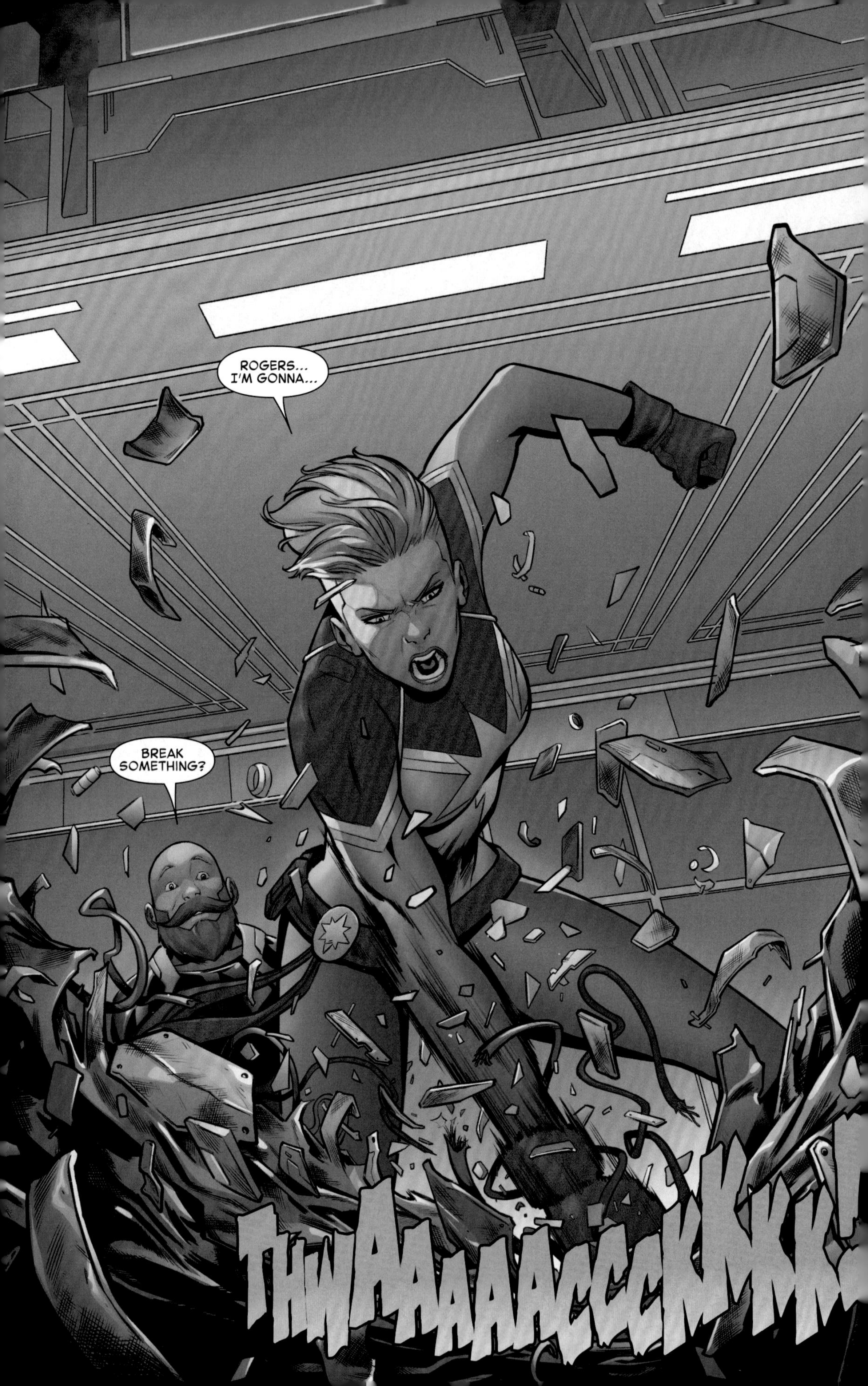
ROGERS... I'M GONNA...
BREAK SOMETHING?
THWAAAAACCCKKKK!

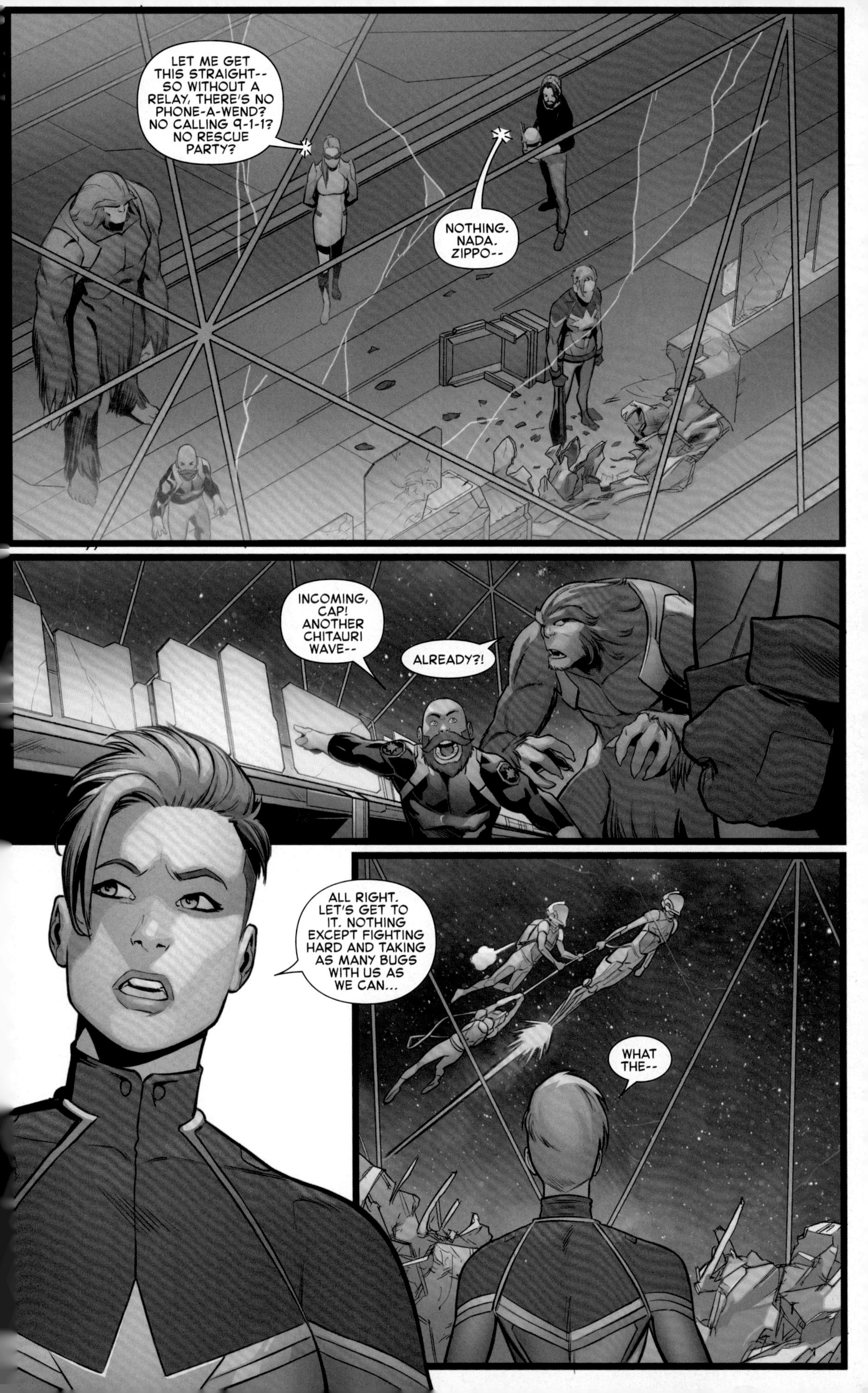
LET ME GET THIS STRAIGHT-- SO WITHOUT A RELAY, THERE'S NO PHONE-A-WEND? NO CALLING 9-1-1? NO RESCUE PARTY?
NOTHING. NADA. ZIPPO--
INCOMING, CAP! ANOTHER CHITAURI WAVE--
ALREADY?!
ALL RIGHT. LET'S GET TO IT. NOTHING EXCEPT FIGHTING HARD AND TAKING AS MANY BUGS WITH US AS WE CAN...
WHAT THE--

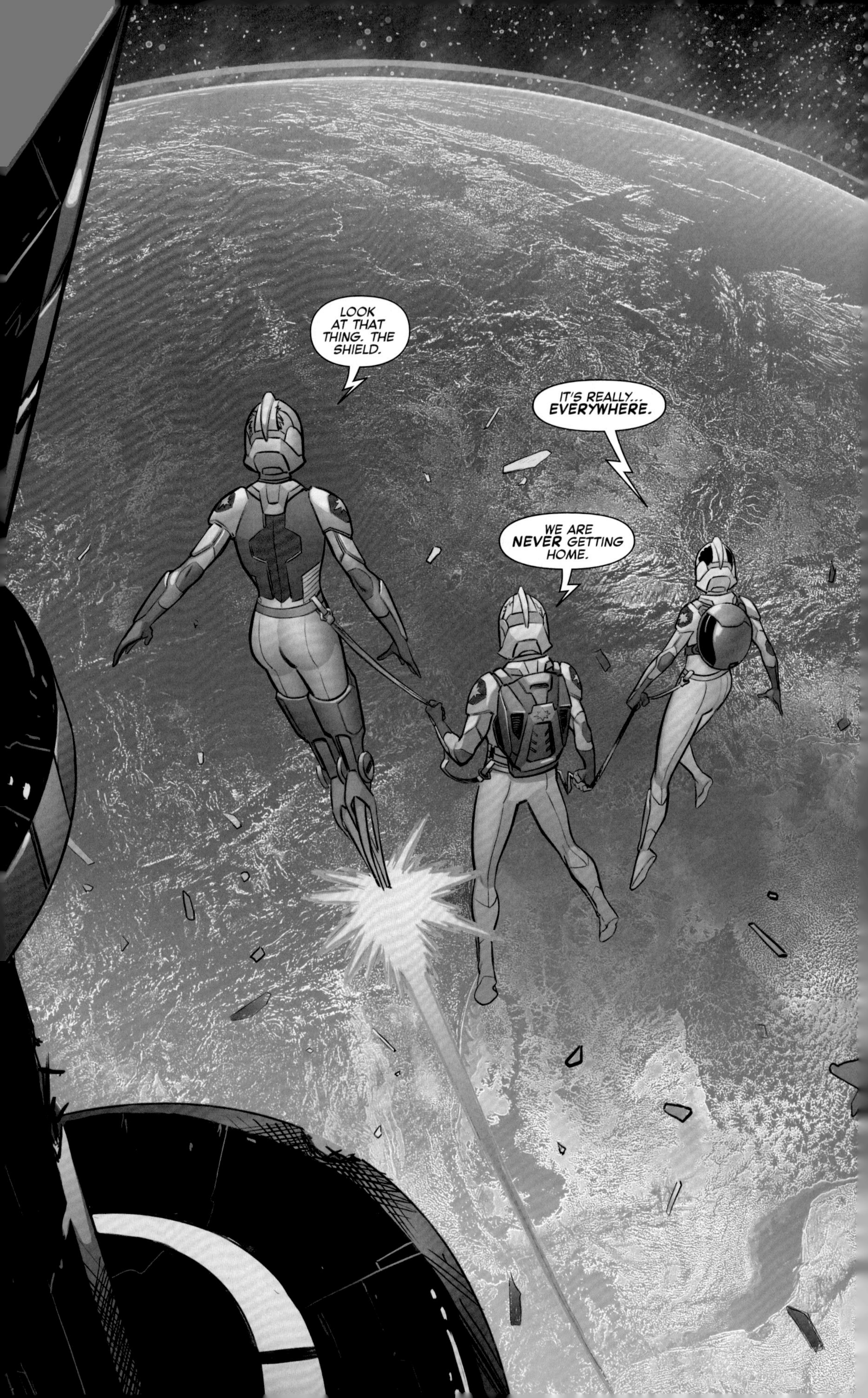
LOOK AT THAT THING. THE SHIELD.
IT'S REALLY... **EVERYWHERE.**
WE ARE **NEVER** GETTING HOME.

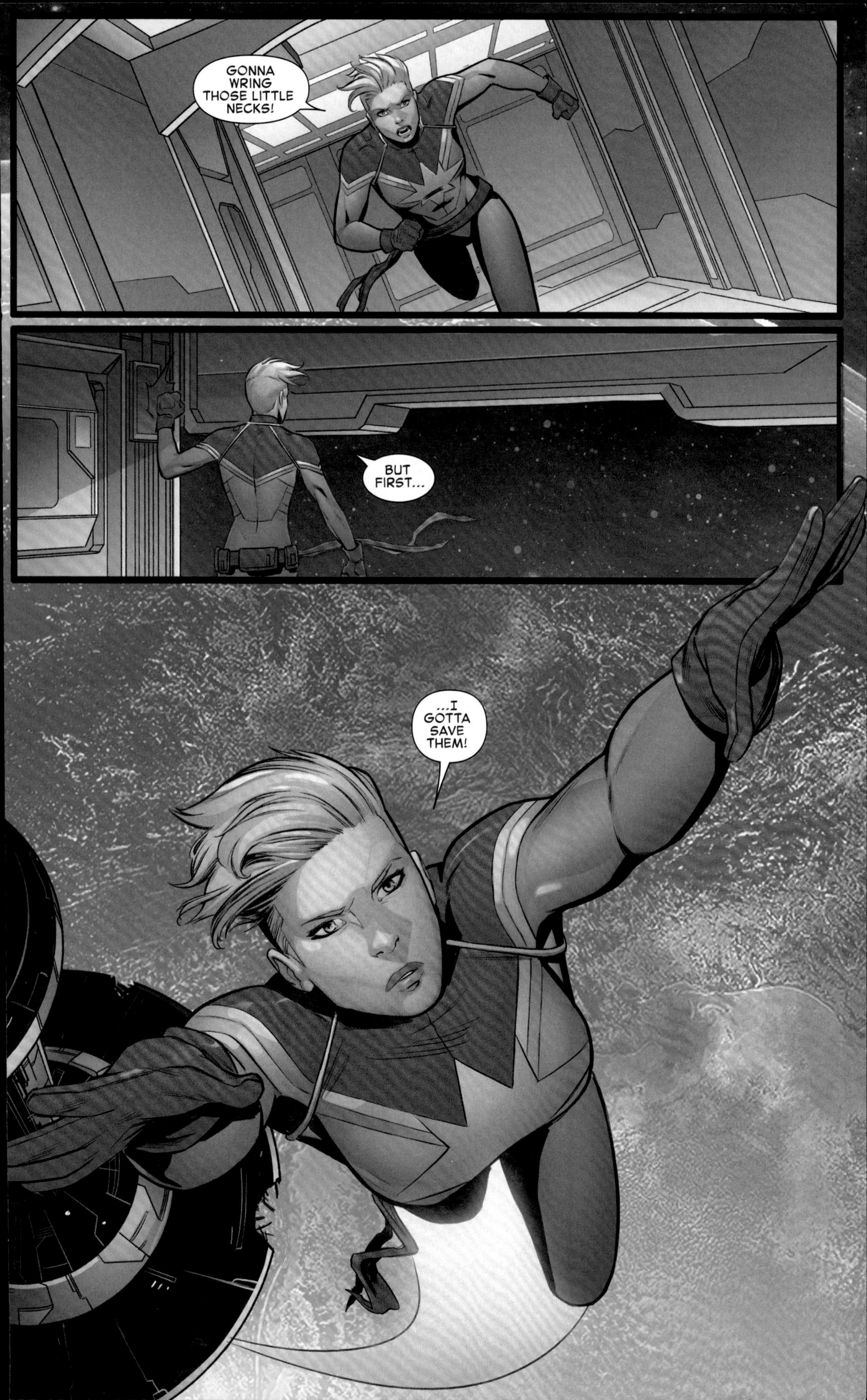
GONNA WRING THOSE LITTLE NECKS!
BUT FIRST...
...I GOTTA SAVE THEM!

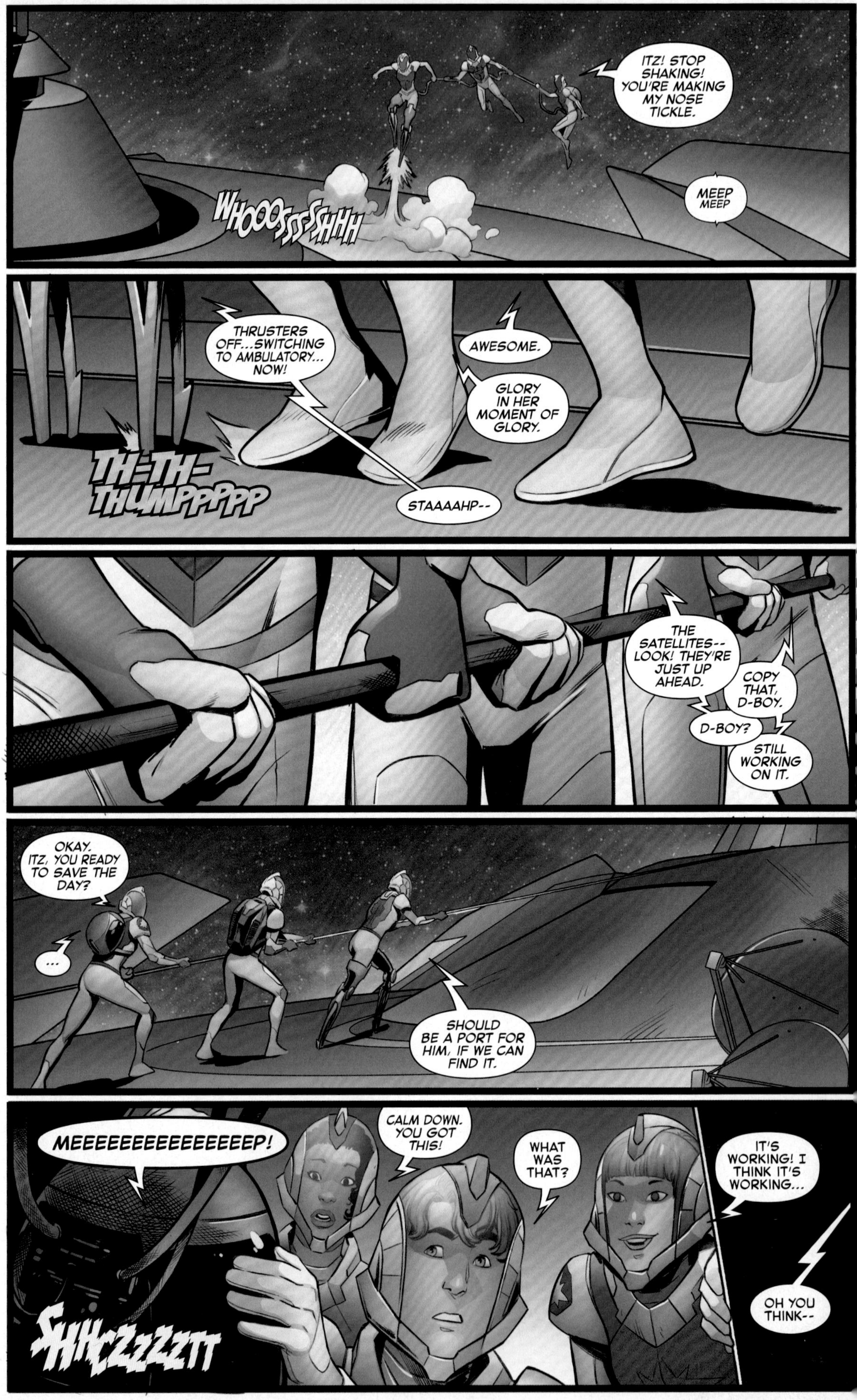
ITZ! STOP SHAKING! YOU'RE MAKING MY NOSE TICKLE.
WHOOOSSSSSHHH
MEEP MEEP
THRUSTERS OFF...SWITCHING TO AMBULATORY... NOW!
AWESOME.
GLORY IN HER MOMENT OF GLORY.
TH-TH-THUMPPPPP
STAAAAHP--
THE SATELLITES-- LOOK! THEY'RE JUST UP AHEAD.
COPY THAT, D-BOY.
D-BOY?
STILL WORKING ON IT.
OKAY. ITZ, YOU READY TO SAVE THE DAY?
...
SHOULD BE A PORT FOR HIM, IF WE CAN FIND IT.
MEEEEEEEEEEEEEEEP!
CALM DOWN. YOU GOT THIS!
WHAT WAS THAT?
IT'S WORKING! I THINK IT'S WORKING...
OH YOU THINK--
SHHCZZZZTT

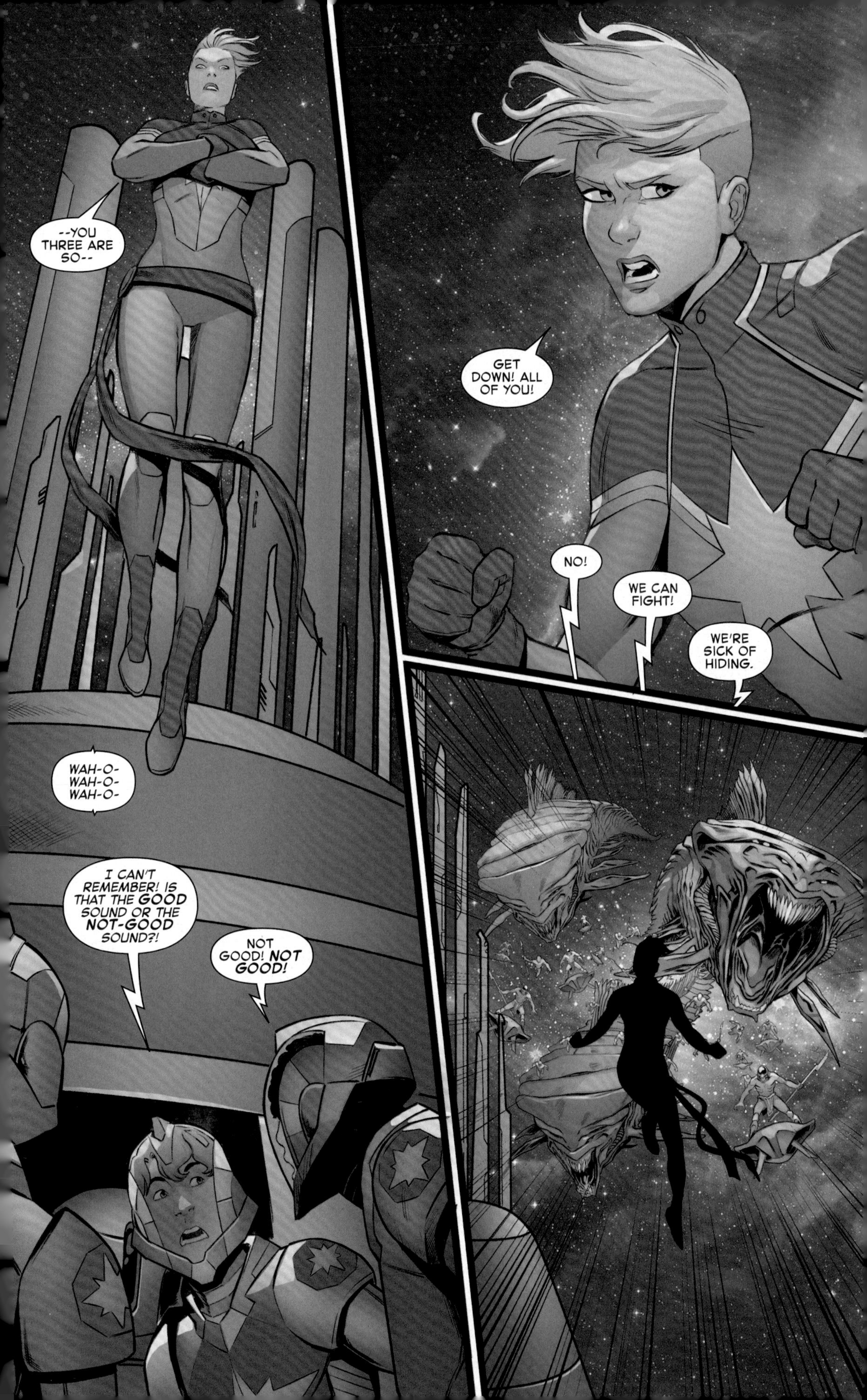
--YOU THREE ARE SO--
WAH-O-WAH-O-WAH-O-
I CAN'T REMEMBER! IS THAT THE **GOOD** SOUND OR THE **NOT-GOOD** SOUND?!
NOT GOOD! **NOT GOOD!**
GET DOWN! ALL OF YOU!
NO!
WE CAN FIGHT!
WE'RE SICK OF HIDING.

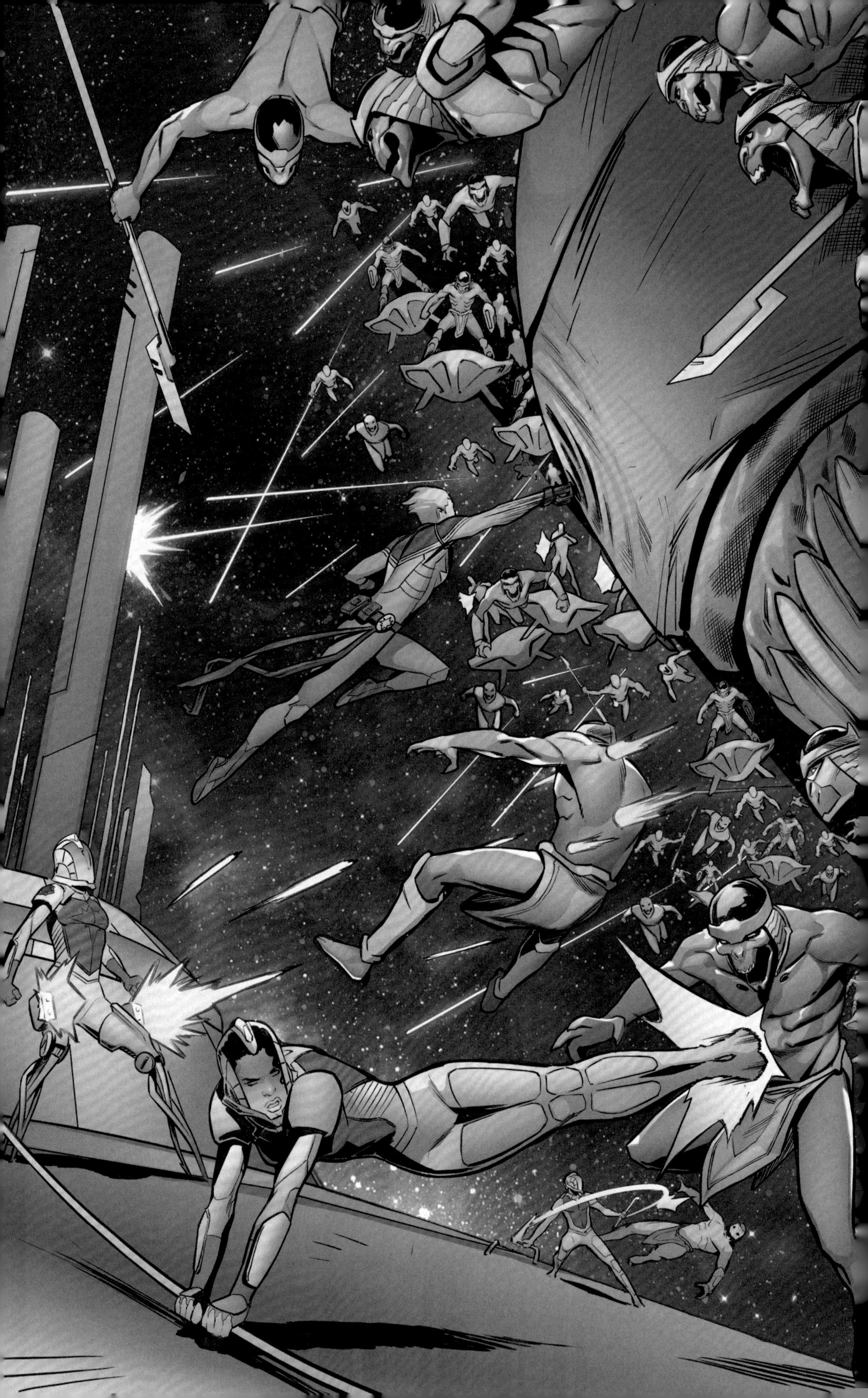

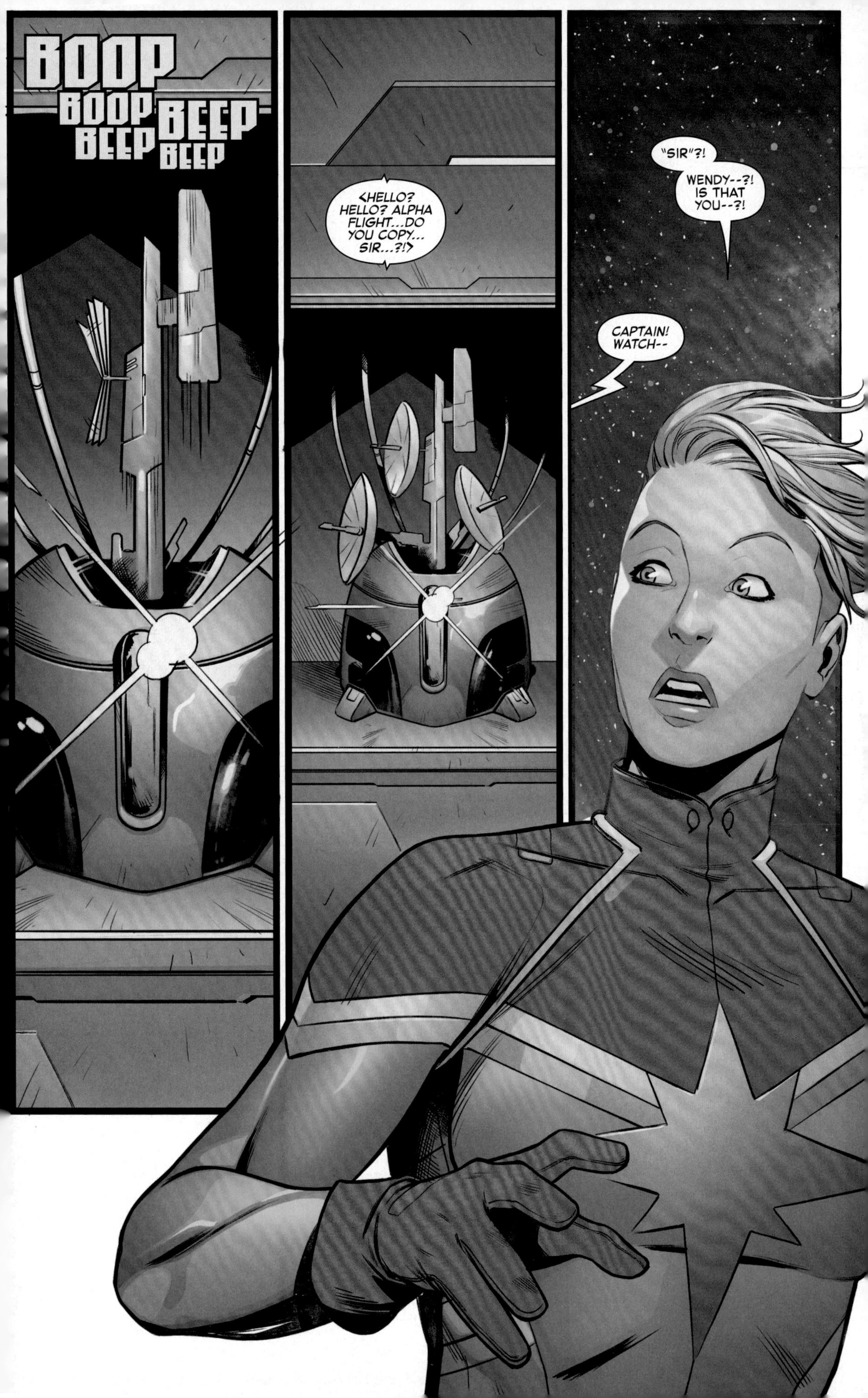
BOOP
BOOP BEEP BEEP BEEP
<HELLO? HELLO? ALPHA FLIGHT...DO YOU COPY... SIR...?!>
"SIR"?!
WENDY--?! IS THAT YOU--?!
CAPTAIN! WATCH--

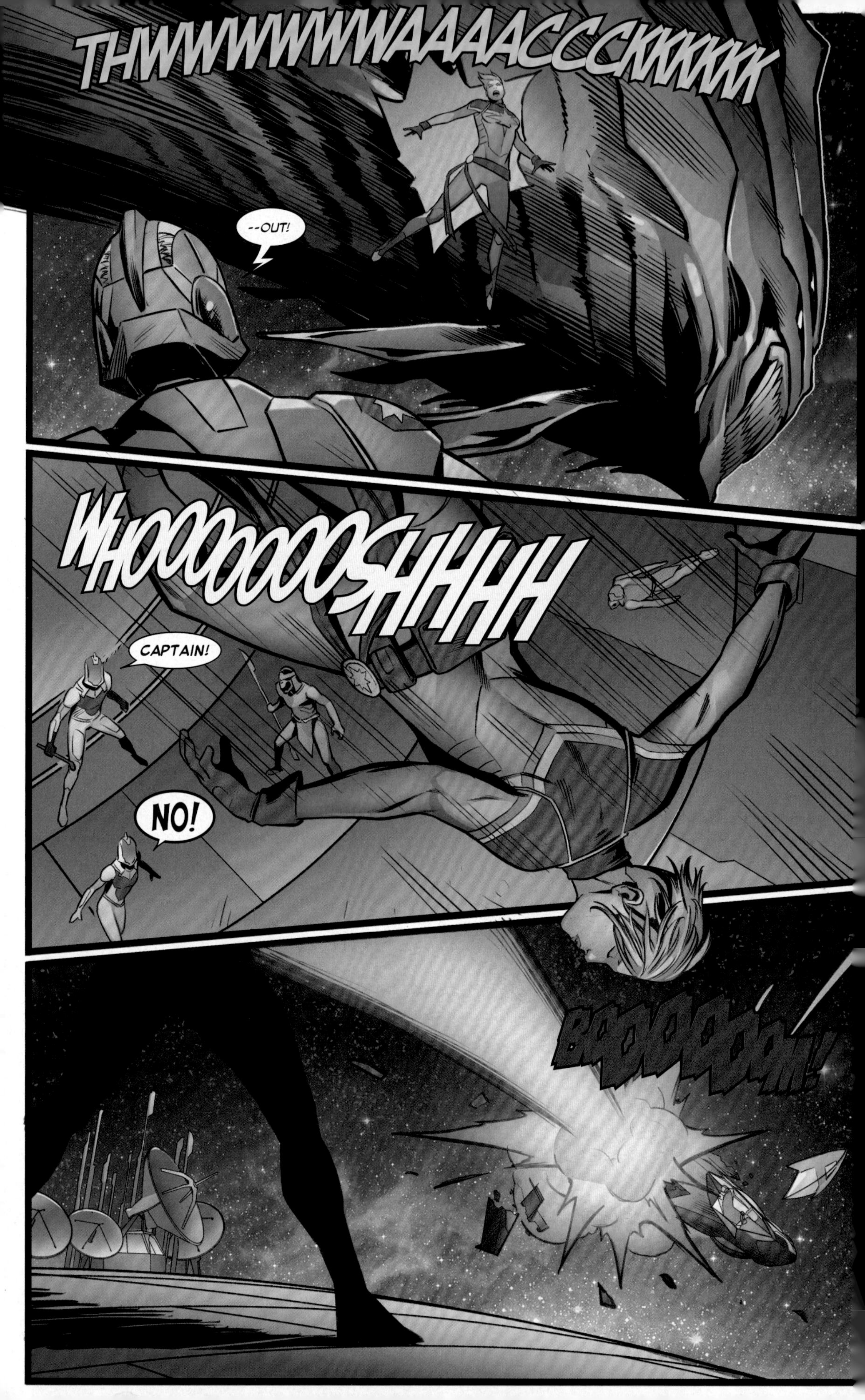
THWWWWWWAAAACCCKKKKKK
--OUT!
WHOOOOOOOSHHHH
CAPTAIN!
NO!

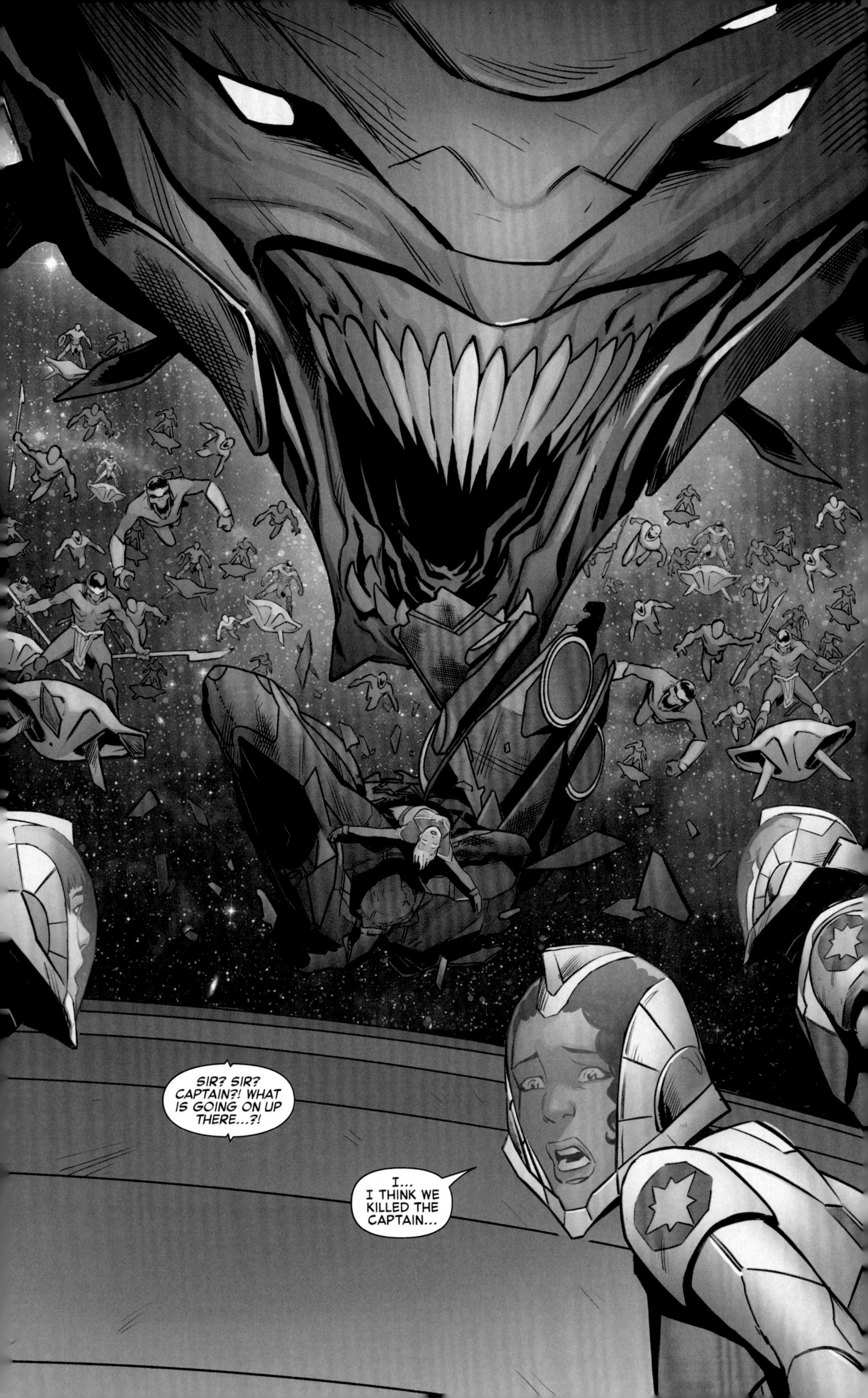
SIR? SIR? CAPTAIN?! WHAT IS GOING ON UP THERE...?!
I... I THINK WE KILLED THE CAPTAIN...

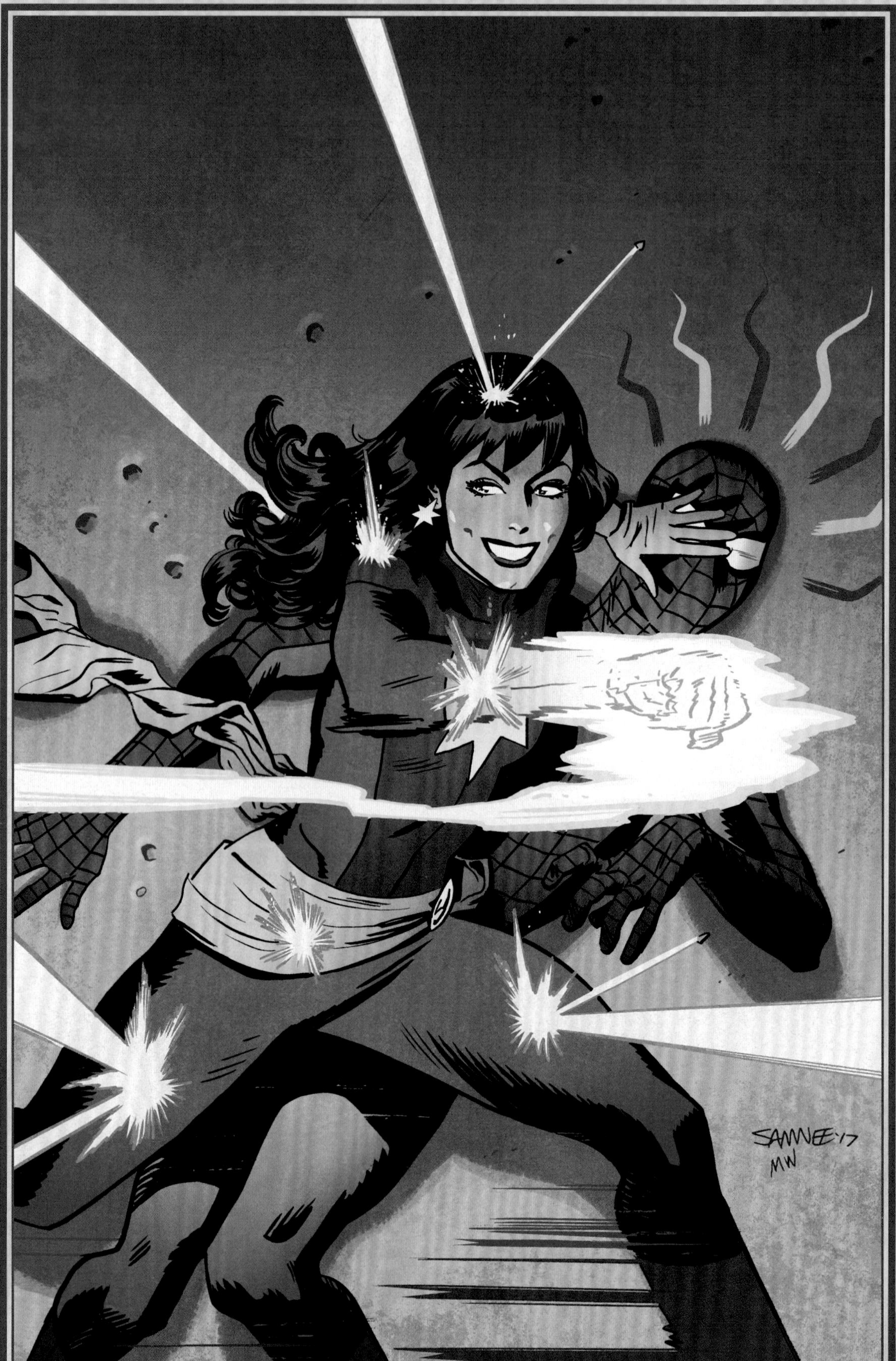
SAMNEE '17
MW

#6 MARY JANE VARIANT BY
CHRIS SAMNEE & MATTHEW WILSON

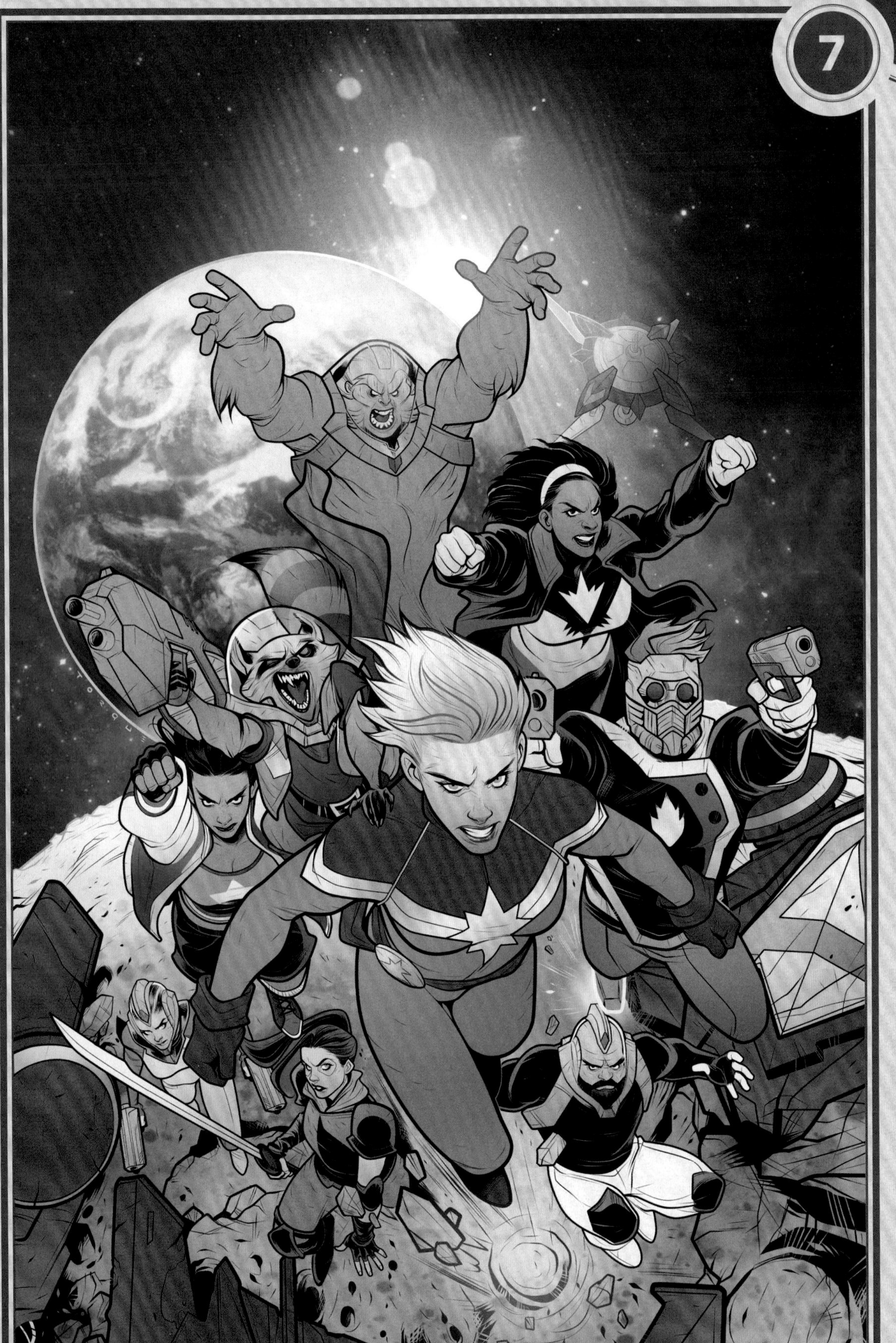
7

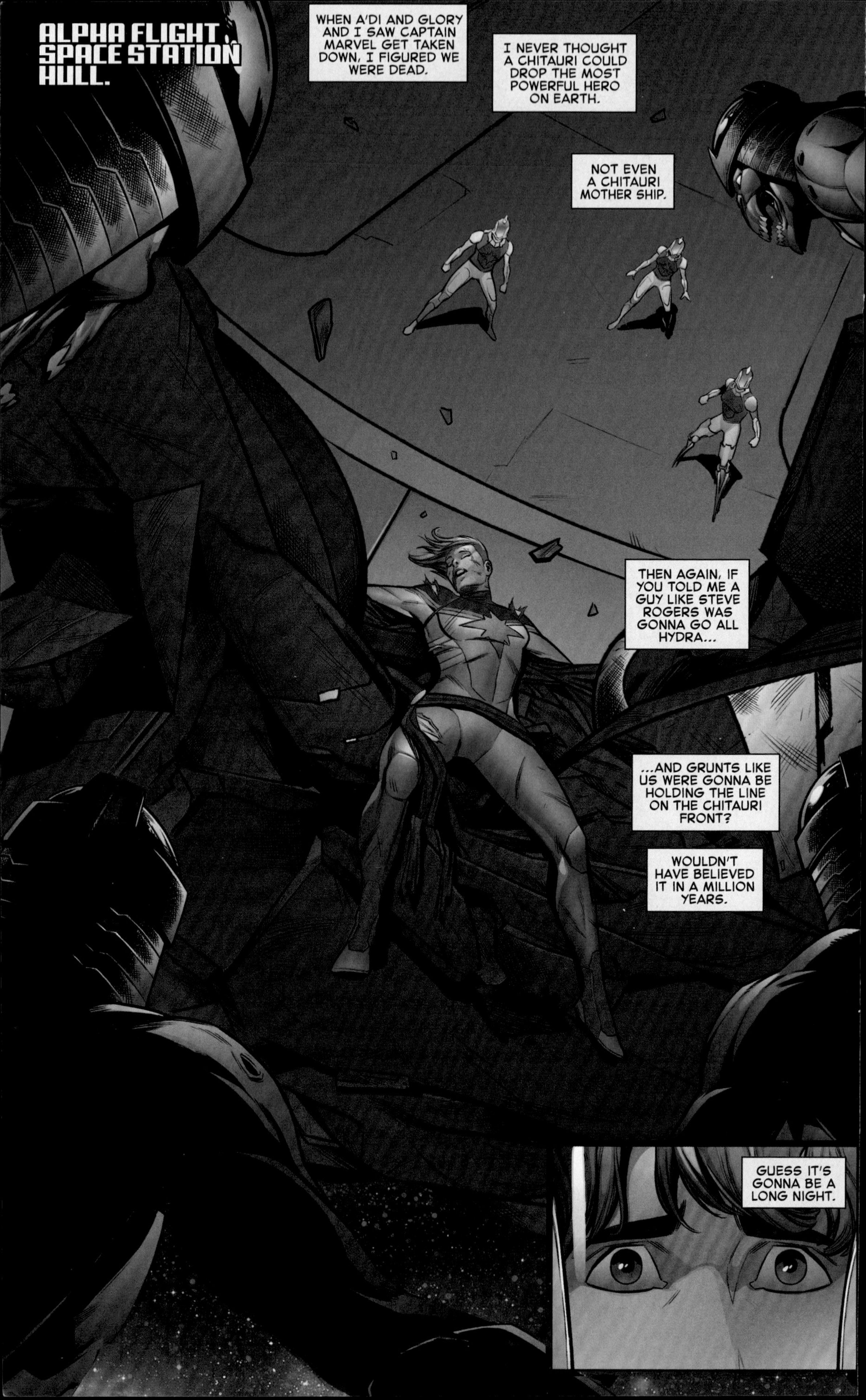
ALPHA FLIGHT SPACE STATION HULL.
WHEN A'DI AND GLORY AND I SAW CAPTAIN MARVEL GET TAKEN DOWN, I FIGURED WE WERE DEAD.
I NEVER THOUGHT A CHITAURI COULD DROP THE MOST POWERFUL HERO ON EARTH.
NOT EVEN A CHITAURI MOTHER SHIP.
THEN AGAIN, IF YOU TOLD ME A GUY LIKE STEVE ROGERS WAS GONNA GO ALL HYDRA...
...AND GRUNTS LIKE US WERE GONNA BE HOLDING THE LINE ON THE CHITAURI FRONT?
WOULDN'T HAVE BELIEVED IT IN A MILLION YEARS.
GUESS IT'S GONNA BE A LONG NIGHT.

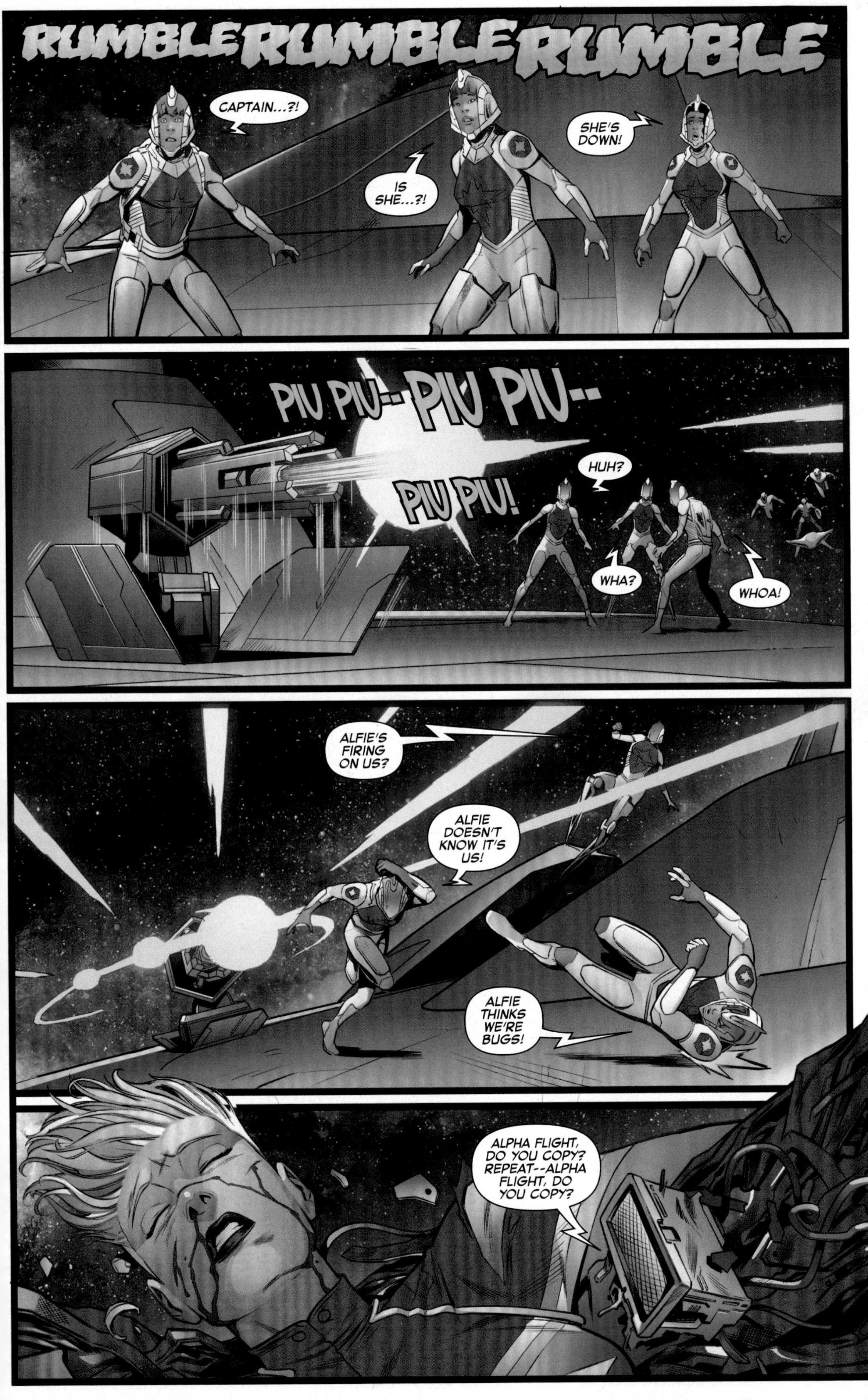
RUMBLE RUMBLE RUMBLE
CAPTAIN...?!
IS SHE...?!
SHE'S DOWN!
PIU PIU-- PIU PIU--
PIU PIU!
HUH?
WHA?
WHOA!
ALFIE'S FIRING ON US?
ALFIE DOESN'T KNOW IT'S US!
ALFIE THINKS WE'RE BUGS!
ALPHA FLIGHT, DO YOU COPY? REPEAT--ALPHA FLIGHT, DO YOU COPY?

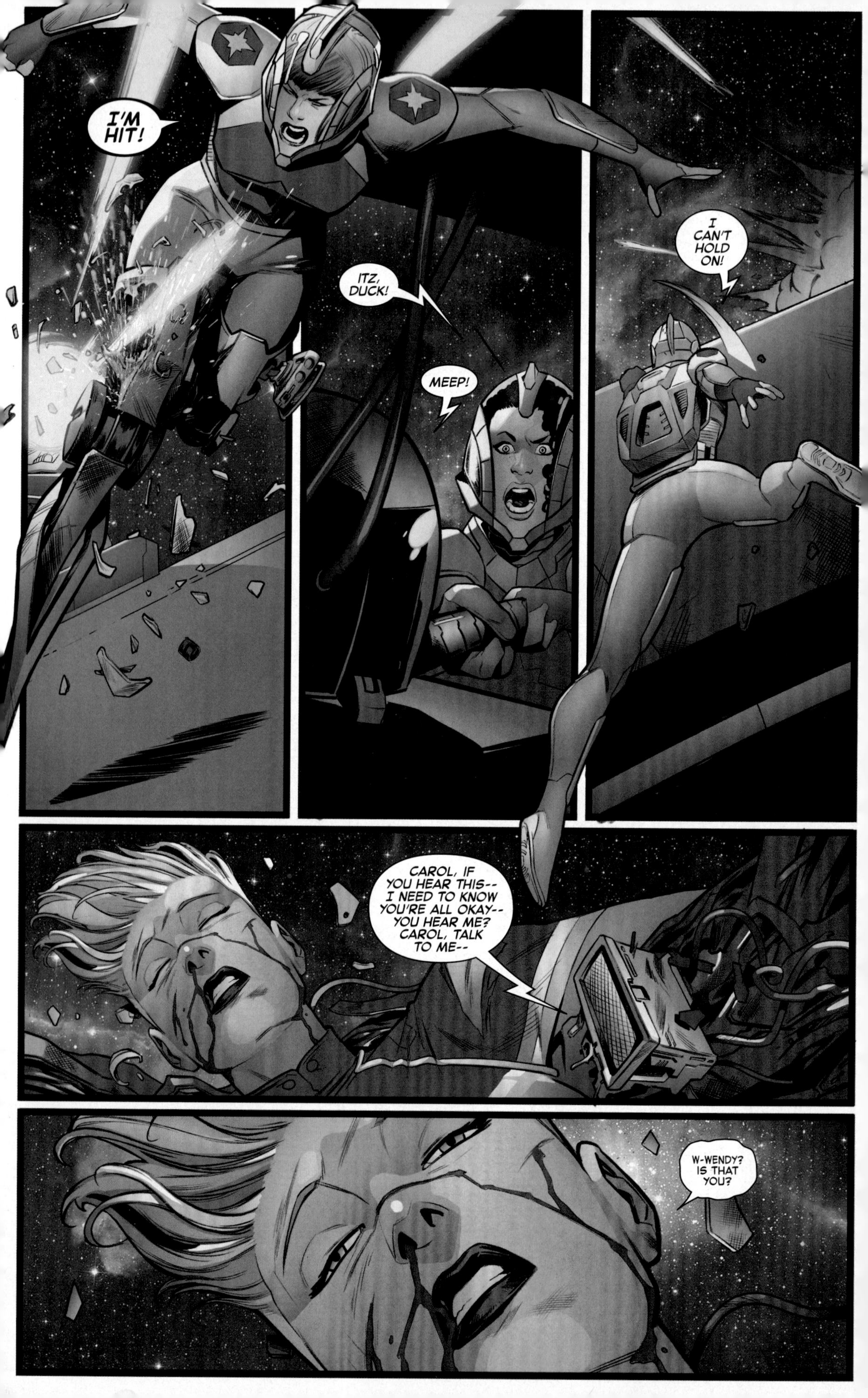
I'M HIT!
ITZ, DUCK!
MEEP!
I CAN'T HOLD ON!
CAROL, IF YOU HEAR THIS-- I NEED TO KNOW YOU'RE ALL OKAY-- YOU HEAR ME? CAROL, TALK TO ME--
W-WENDY? IS THAT YOU?

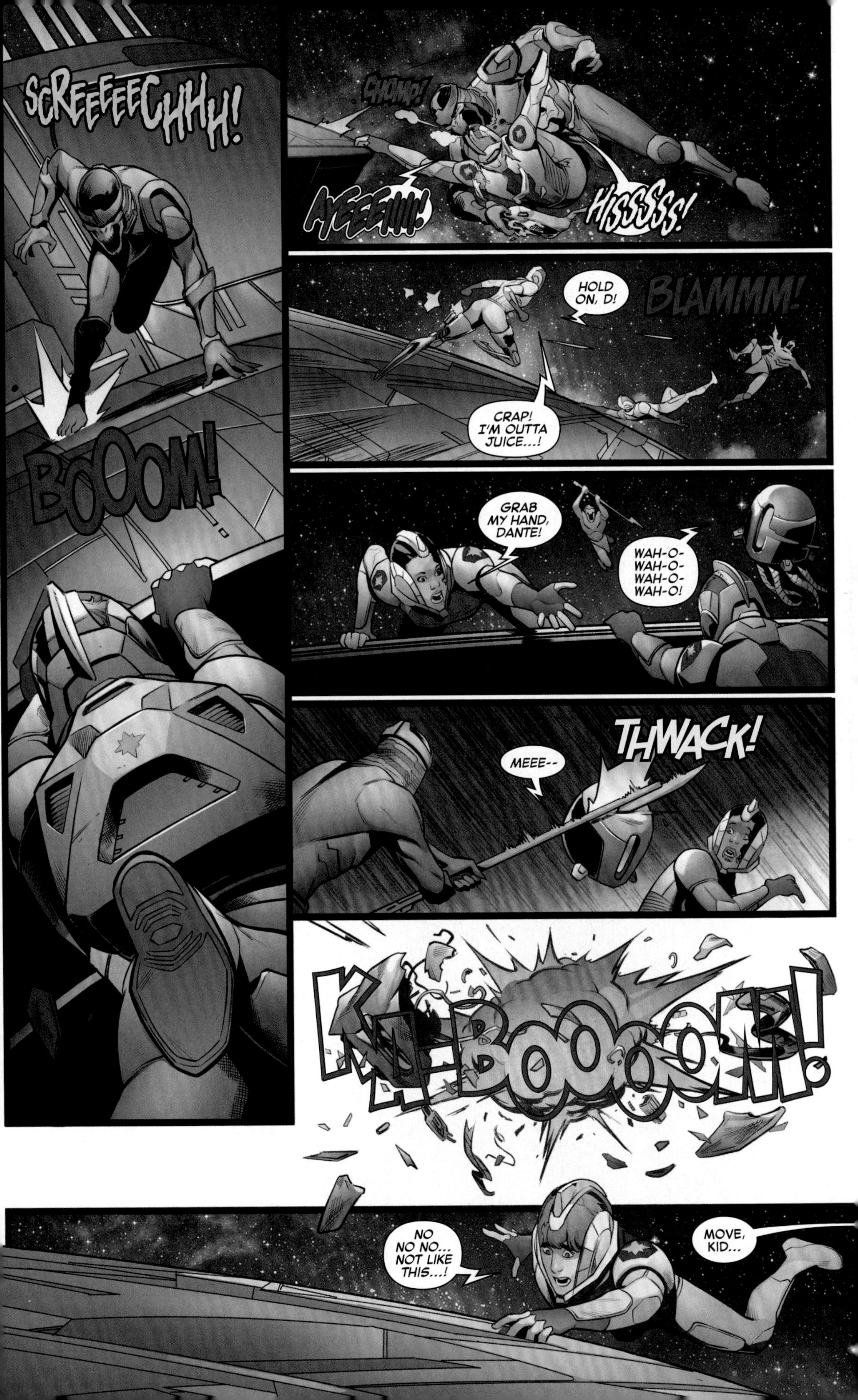
SCREEEEEECHHH!
BOOOM!
CHOMP!
AYEEEIIII!
HISSSSS!
HOLD ON, D!
BLAMMM!
CRAP! I'M OUTTA JUICE...!
GRAB MY HAND, DANTE!
WAH-O-WAH-O-WAH-O-WAH-O!
MEEE--
THWACK!
NO NO NO... NOT LIKE THIS...!
MOVE, KID...

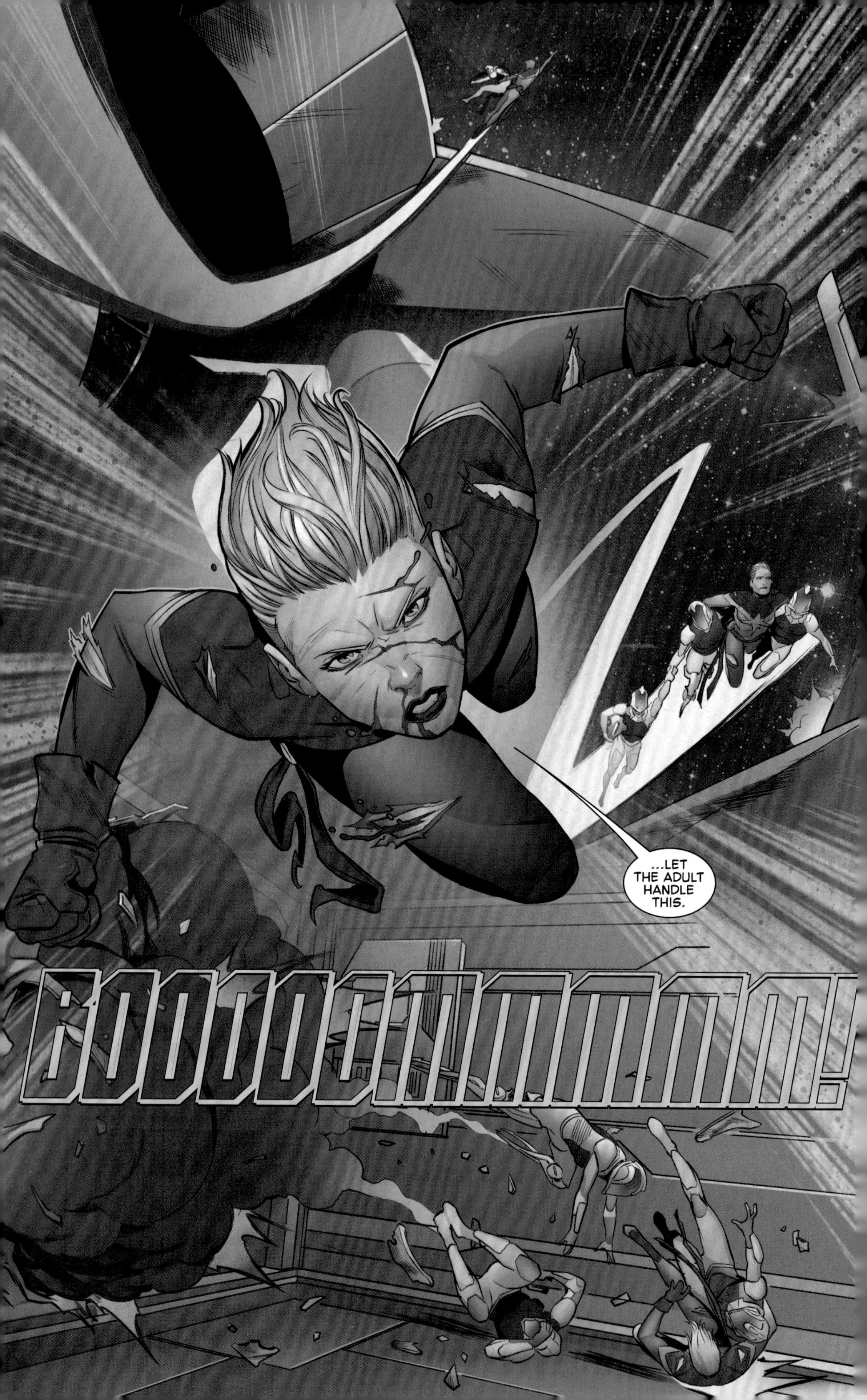
...LET THE ADULT HANDLE THIS.

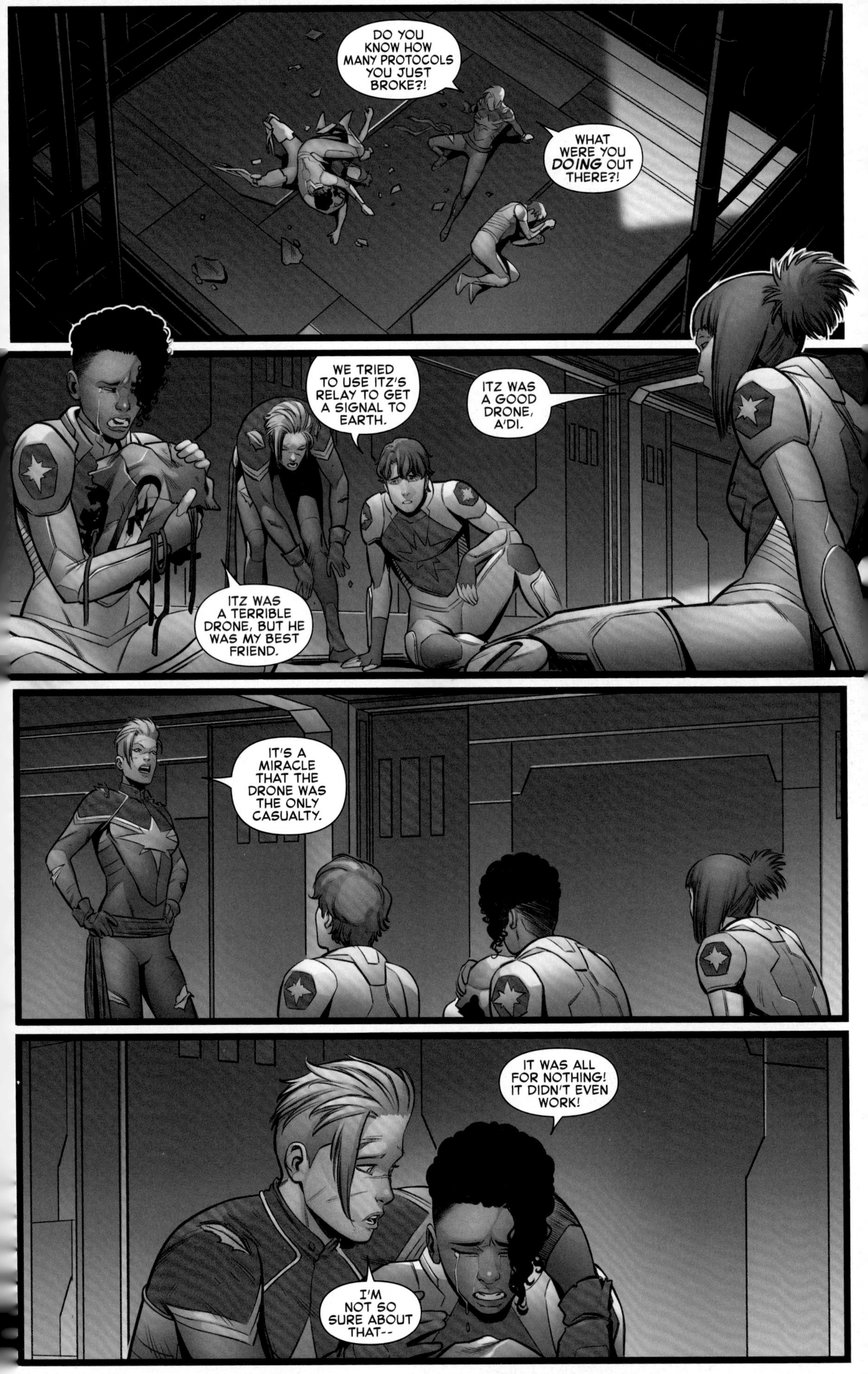
DO YOU KNOW HOW MANY PROTOCOLS YOU JUST BROKE?!
WHAT WERE YOU DOING OUT THERE?!
WE TRIED TO USE ITZ'S RELAY TO GET A SIGNAL TO EARTH.
ITZ WAS A GOOD DRONE, A'DI.
ITZ WAS A TERRIBLE DRONE, BUT HE WAS MY BEST FRIEND.
IT'S A MIRACLE THAT THE DRONE WAS THE ONLY CASUALTY.
IT WAS ALL FOR NOTHING! IT DIDN'T EVEN WORK!
I'M NOT SO SURE ABOUT THAT--

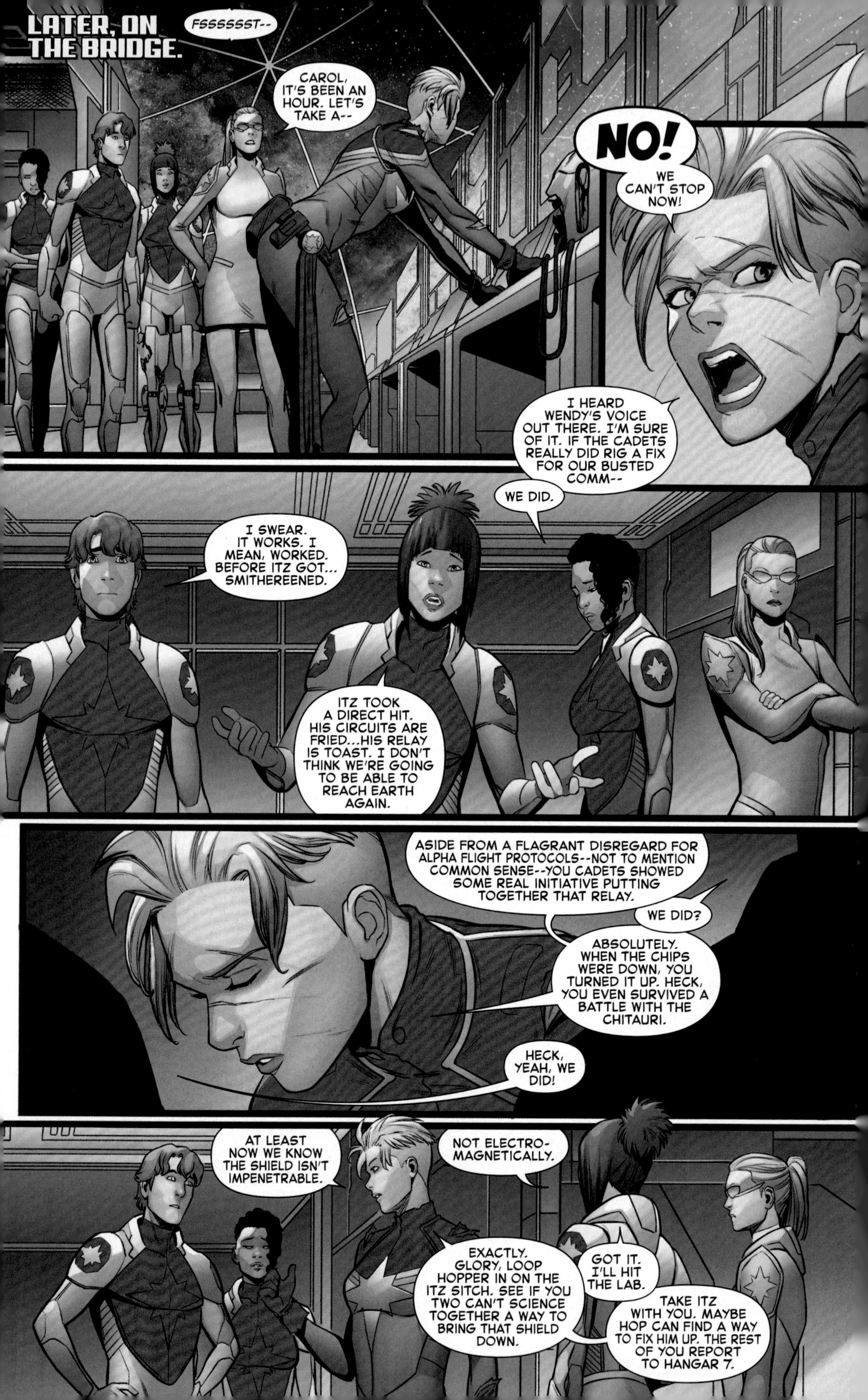
LATER, ON THE BRIDGE.
FSSSSSST--
CAROL, IT'S BEEN AN HOUR. LET'S TAKE A--
NO!
WE CAN'T STOP NOW!
I HEARD WENDY'S VOICE OUT THERE. I'M SURE OF IT. IF THE CADETS REALLY DID RIG A FIX FOR OUR BUSTED COMM--
WE DID.
I SWEAR. IT WORKS. I MEAN, WORKED. BEFORE ITZ GOT... SMITHEREENED.
ITZ TOOK A DIRECT HIT. HIS CIRCUITS ARE FRIED...HIS RELAY IS TOAST. I DON'T THINK WE'RE GOING TO BE ABLE TO REACH EARTH AGAIN.
ASIDE FROM A FLAGRANT DISREGARD FOR ALPHA FLIGHT PROTOCOLS--NOT TO MENTION COMMON SENSE--YOU CADETS SHOWED SOME REAL INITIATIVE PUTTING TOGETHER THAT RELAY.
WE DID?
ABSOLUTELY. WHEN THE CHIPS WERE DOWN, YOU TURNED IT UP. HECK, YOU EVEN SURVIVED A BATTLE WITH THE CHITAURI.
HECK, YEAH, WE DID!
AT LEAST NOW WE KNOW THE SHIELD ISN'T IMPENETRABLE.
NOT ELECTRO-MAGNETICALLY.
EXACTLY. GLORY, LOOP HOPPER IN ON THE ITZ SITCH. SEE IF YOU TWO CAN'T SCIENCE TOGETHER A WAY TO BRING THAT SHIELD DOWN.
GOT IT. I'LL HIT THE LAB.
TAKE ITZ WITH YOU. MAYBE HOP CAN FIND A WAY TO FIX HIM UP. THE REST OF YOU REPORT TO HANGAR 7.

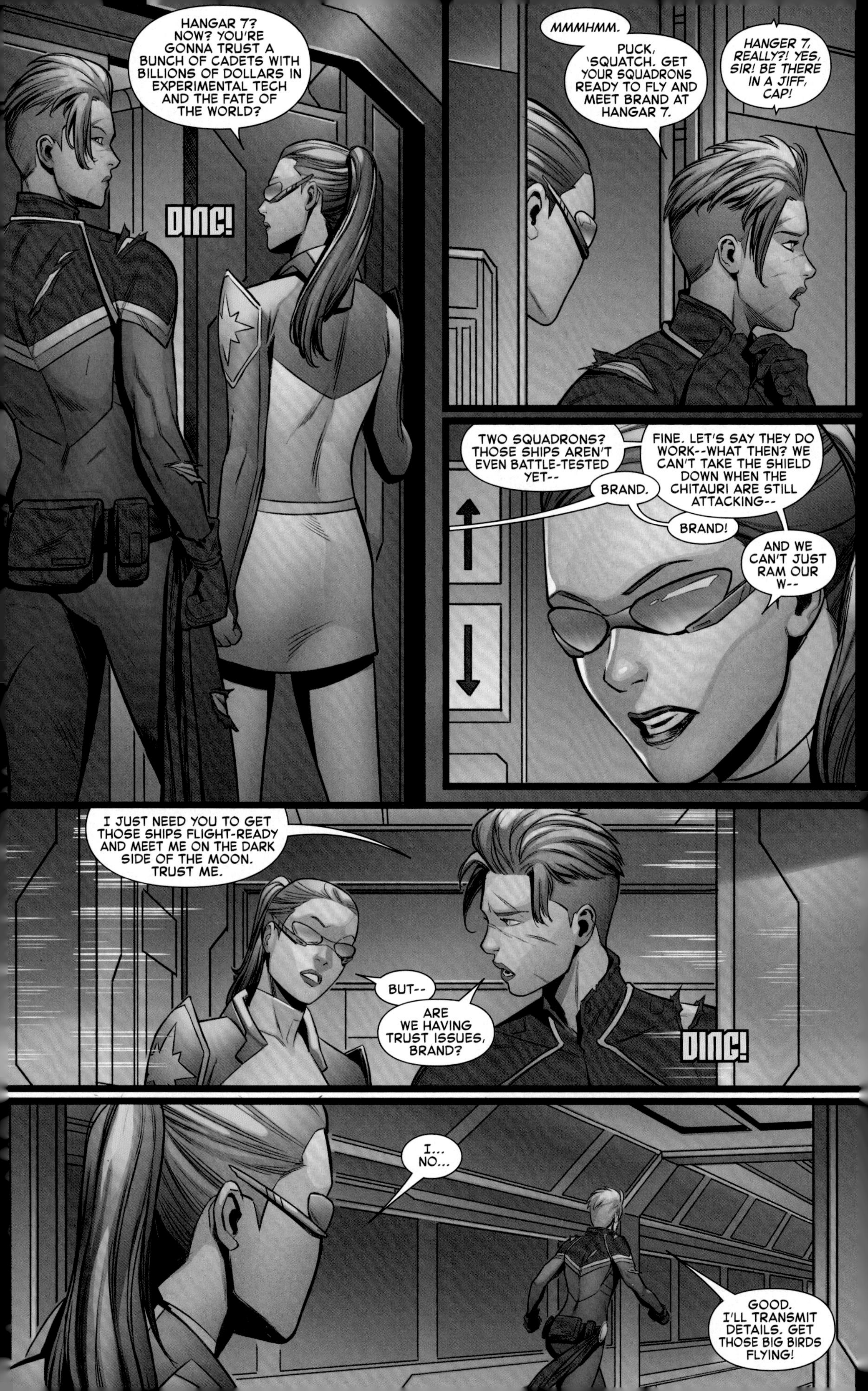
HANGAR 7? NOW? YOU'RE GONNA TRUST A BUNCH OF CADETS WITH BILLIONS OF DOLLARS IN EXPERIMENTAL TECH AND THE FATE OF THE WORLD?
DING!
MMMHMM.
PUCK, 'SQUATCH. GET YOUR SQUADRONS READY TO FLY AND MEET BRAND AT HANGAR 7.
HANGER 7, REALLY?! YES, SIR! BE THERE IN A JIFF, CAP!
TWO SQUADRONS? THOSE SHIPS AREN'T EVEN BATTLE-TESTED YET--
BRAND.
FINE. LET'S SAY THEY DO WORK--WHAT THEN? WE CAN'T TAKE THE SHIELD DOWN WHEN THE CHITAURI ARE STILL ATTACKING--
BRAND!
AND WE CAN'T JUST RAM OUR W--
I JUST NEED YOU TO GET THOSE SHIPS FLIGHT-READY AND MEET ME ON THE DARK SIDE OF THE MOON. TRUST ME.
BUT--
ARE WE HAVING TRUST ISSUES, BRAND?
DING!
I... NO...
GOOD. I'LL TRANSMIT DETAILS. GET THOSE BIG BIRDS FLYING!

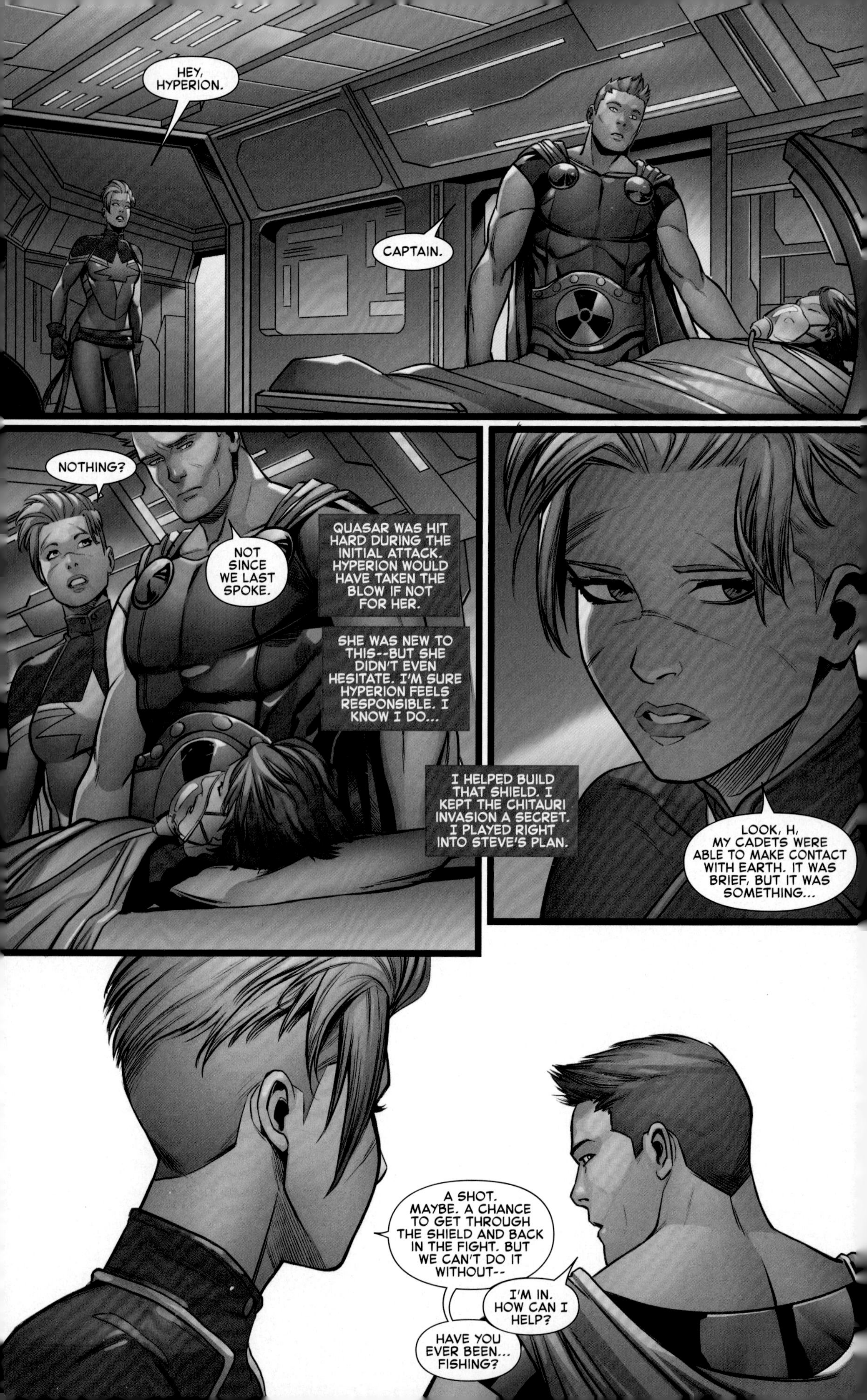
HEY, HYPERION.
CAPTAIN.
NOTHING?
NOT SINCE WE LAST SPOKE.
QUASAR WAS HIT HARD DURING THE INITIAL ATTACK. HYPERION WOULD HAVE TAKEN THE BLOW IF NOT FOR HER.
SHE WAS NEW TO THIS--BUT SHE DIDN'T EVEN HESITATE. I'M SURE HYPERION FEELS RESPONSIBLE. I KNOW I DO...
I HELPED BUILD THAT SHIELD. I KEPT THE CHITAURI INVASION A SECRET. I PLAYED RIGHT INTO STEVE'S PLAN.
LOOK, H, MY CADETS WERE ABLE TO MAKE CONTACT WITH EARTH. IT WAS BRIEF, BUT IT WAS SOMETHING...
A SHOT. MAYBE. A CHANCE TO GET THROUGH THE SHIELD AND BACK IN THE FIGHT. BUT WE CAN'T DO IT WITHOUT--
I'M IN. HOW CAN I HELP?
HAVE YOU EVER BEEN... FISHING?

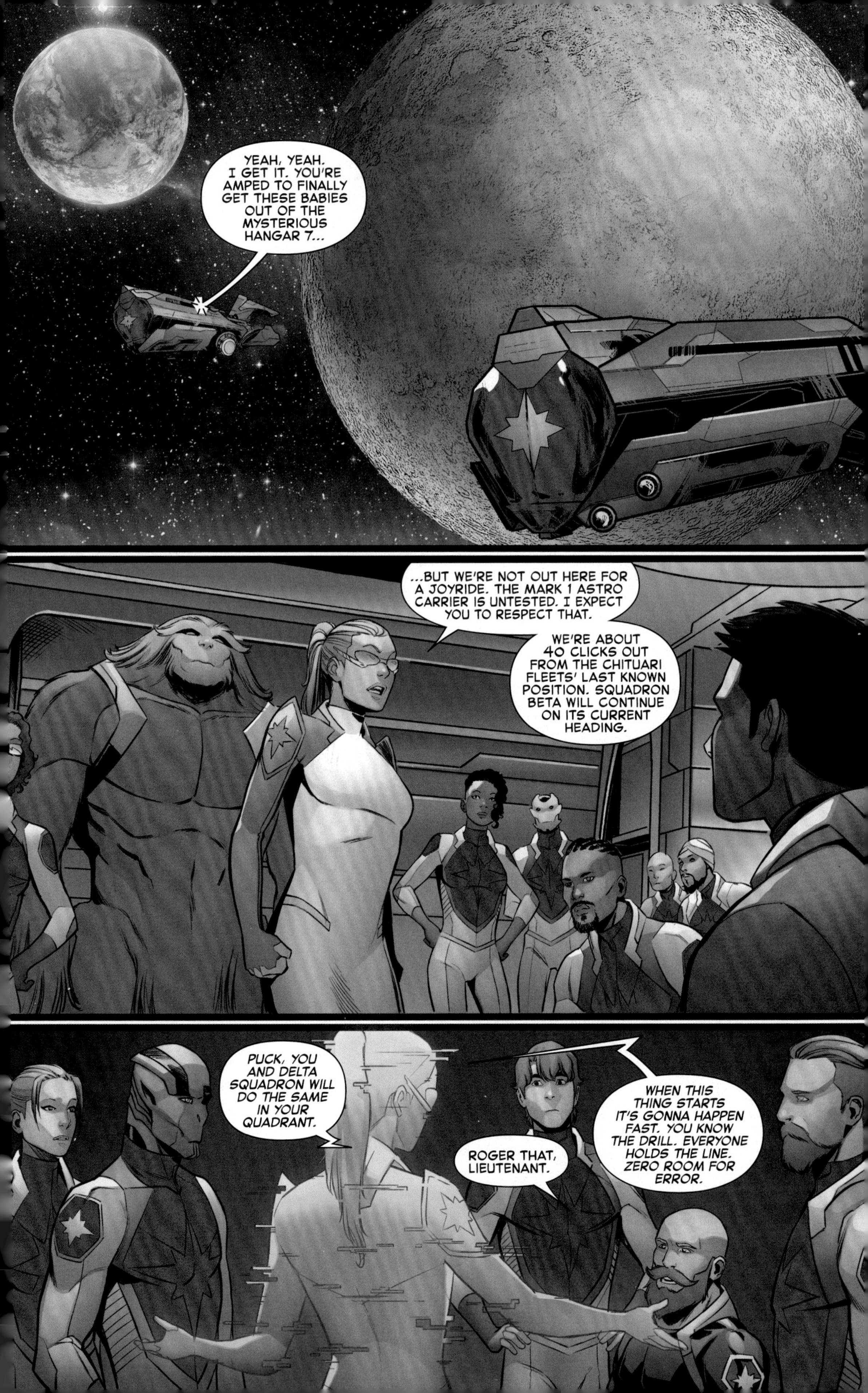
YEAH, YEAH. I GET IT. YOU'RE AMPED TO FINALLY GET THESE BABIES OUT OF THE MYSTERIOUS HANGAR 7...
...BUT WE'RE NOT OUT HERE FOR A JOYRIDE. THE MARK 1 ASTRO CARRIER IS UNTESTED. I EXPECT YOU TO RESPECT THAT.
WE'RE ABOUT 40 CLICKS OUT FROM THE CHITUARI FLEETS' LAST KNOWN POSITION. SQUADRON BETA WILL CONTINUE ON ITS CURRENT HEADING.
PUCK, YOU AND DELTA SQUADRON WILL DO THE SAME IN YOUR QUADRANT.
ROGER THAT, LIEUTENANT.
WHEN THIS THING STARTS IT'S GONNA HAPPEN FAST. YOU KNOW THE DRILL. EVERYONE HOLDS THE LINE. ZERO ROOM FOR ERROR.

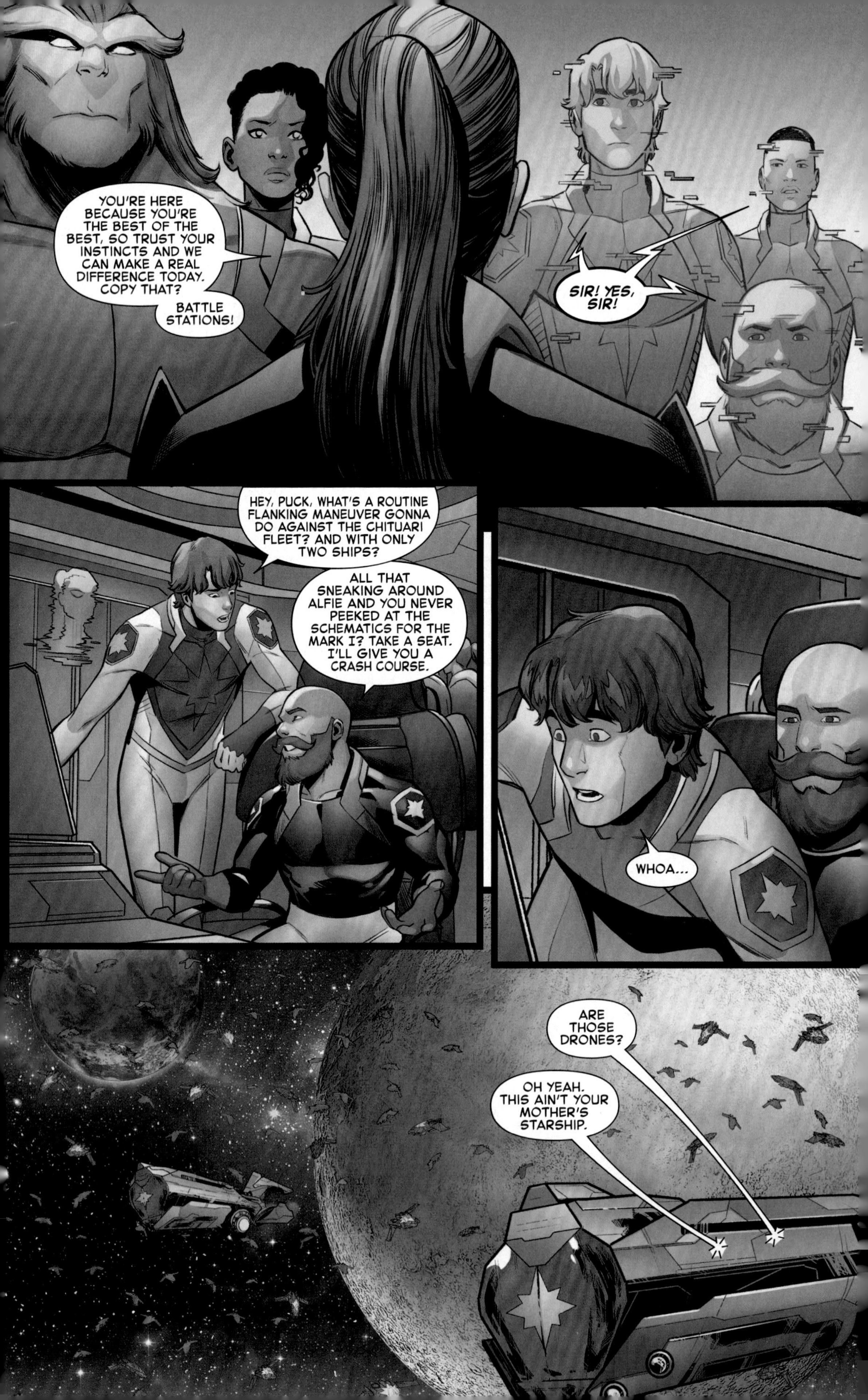
YOU'RE HERE BECAUSE YOU'RE THE BEST OF THE BEST, SO TRUST YOUR INSTINCTS AND WE CAN MAKE A REAL DIFFERENCE TODAY. COPY THAT?
BATTLE STATIONS!
SIR! YES, SIR!
HEY, PUCK, WHAT'S A ROUTINE FLANKING MANEUVER GONNA DO AGAINST THE CHITUARI FLEET? AND WITH ONLY TWO SHIPS?
ALL THAT SNEAKING AROUND ALFIE AND YOU NEVER PEEKED AT THE SCHEMATICS FOR THE MARK I? TAKE A SEAT. I'LL GIVE YOU A CRASH COURSE.
WHOA...
ARE THOSE DRONES?
OH YEAH. THIS AIN'T YOUR MOTHER'S STARSHIP.

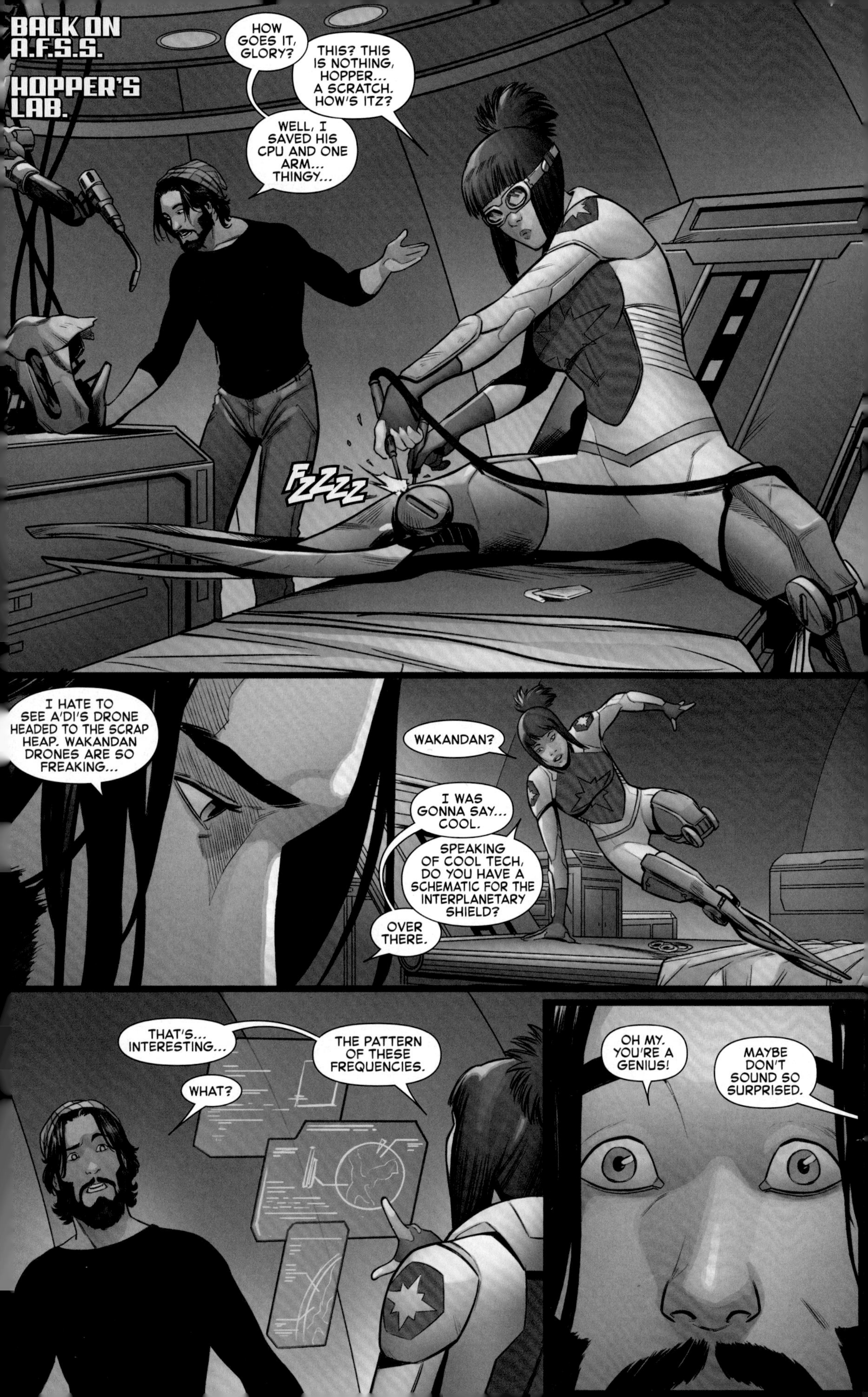
BACK ON A.F.S.S.
HOPPER'S LAB.
HOW GOES IT, GLORY?
THIS? THIS IS NOTHING, HOPPER... A SCRATCH. HOW'S ITZ?
WELL, I SAVED HIS CPU AND ONE ARM... THINGY...
FZZZZ
I HATE TO SEE A'DI'S DRONE HEADED TO THE SCRAP HEAP. WAKANDAN DRONES ARE SO FREAKING...
WAKANDAN?
I WAS GONNA SAY... COOL.
SPEAKING OF COOL TECH, DO YOU HAVE A SCHEMATIC FOR THE INTERPLANETARY SHIELD?
OVER THERE.
THAT'S... INTERESTING...
THE PATTERN OF THESE FREQUENCIES.
WHAT?
OH MY. YOU'RE A GENIUS!
MAYBE DON'T SOUND SO SURPRISED.

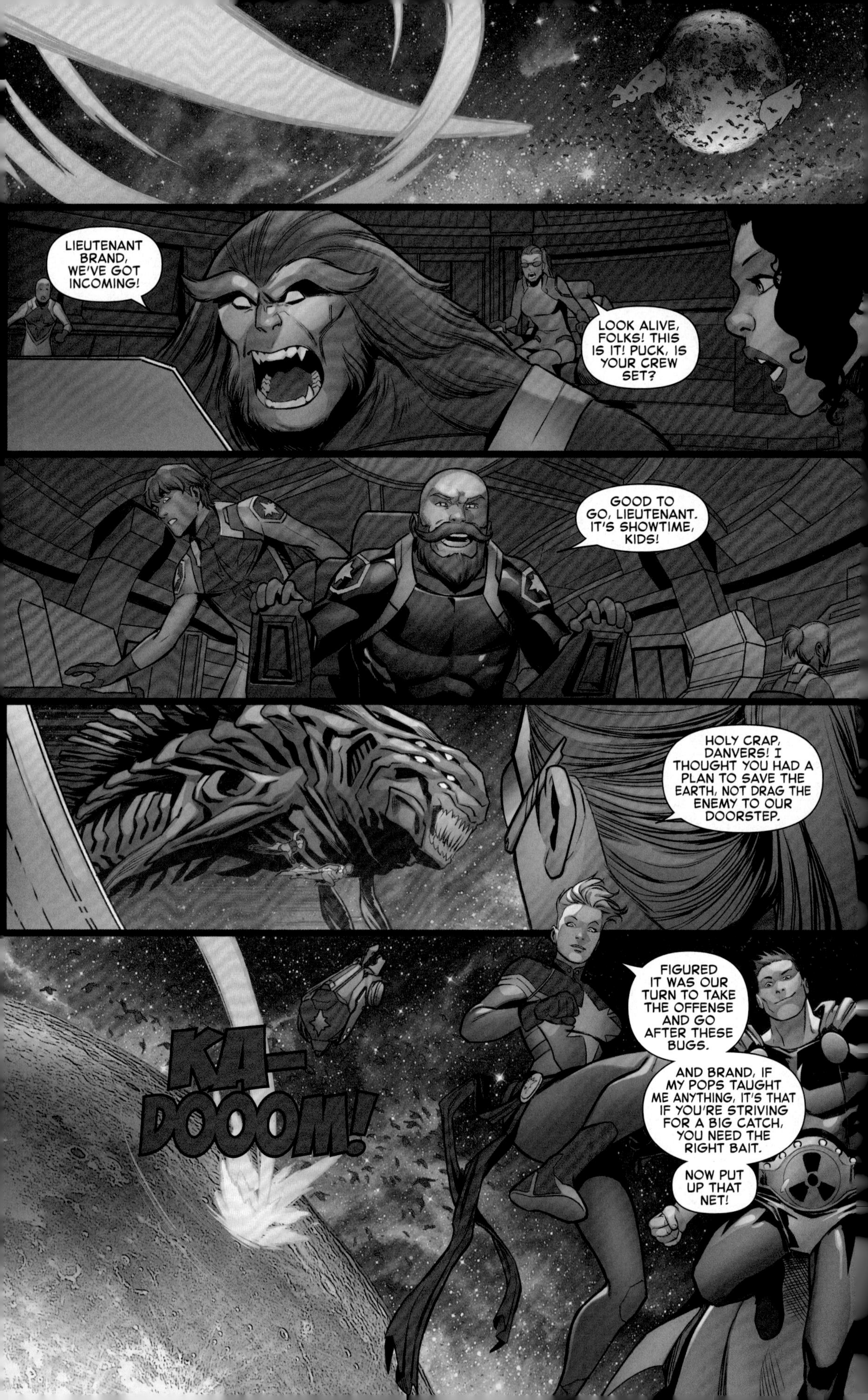
LIEUTENANT BRAND, WE'VE GOT INCOMING!
LOOK ALIVE, FOLKS! THIS IS IT! PUCK, IS YOUR CREW SET?
GOOD TO GO, LIEUTENANT. IT'S SHOWTIME, KIDS!
HOLY CRAP, DANVERS! I THOUGHT YOU HAD A PLAN TO SAVE THE EARTH, NOT DRAG THE ENEMY TO OUR DOORSTEP.
KA-DOOOM!
FIGURED IT WAS OUR TURN TO TAKE THE OFFENSE AND GO AFTER THESE BUGS.
AND BRAND, IF MY POPS TAUGHT ME ANYTHING, IT'S THAT IF YOU'RE STRIVING FOR A BIG CATCH, YOU NEED THE RIGHT BAIT.
NOW PUT UP THAT NET!

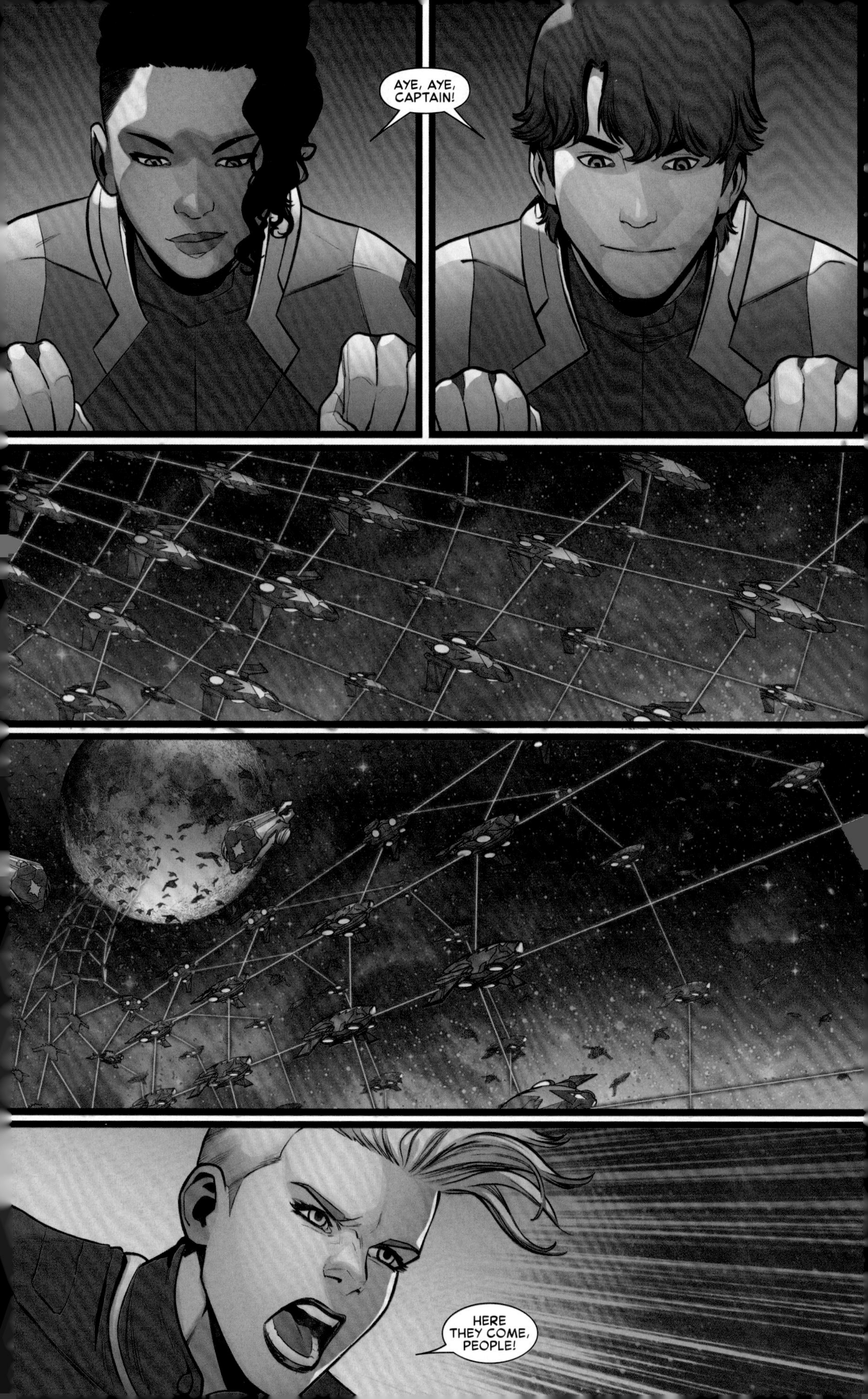
AYE, AYE, CAPTAIN!
HERE THEY COME, PEOPLE!

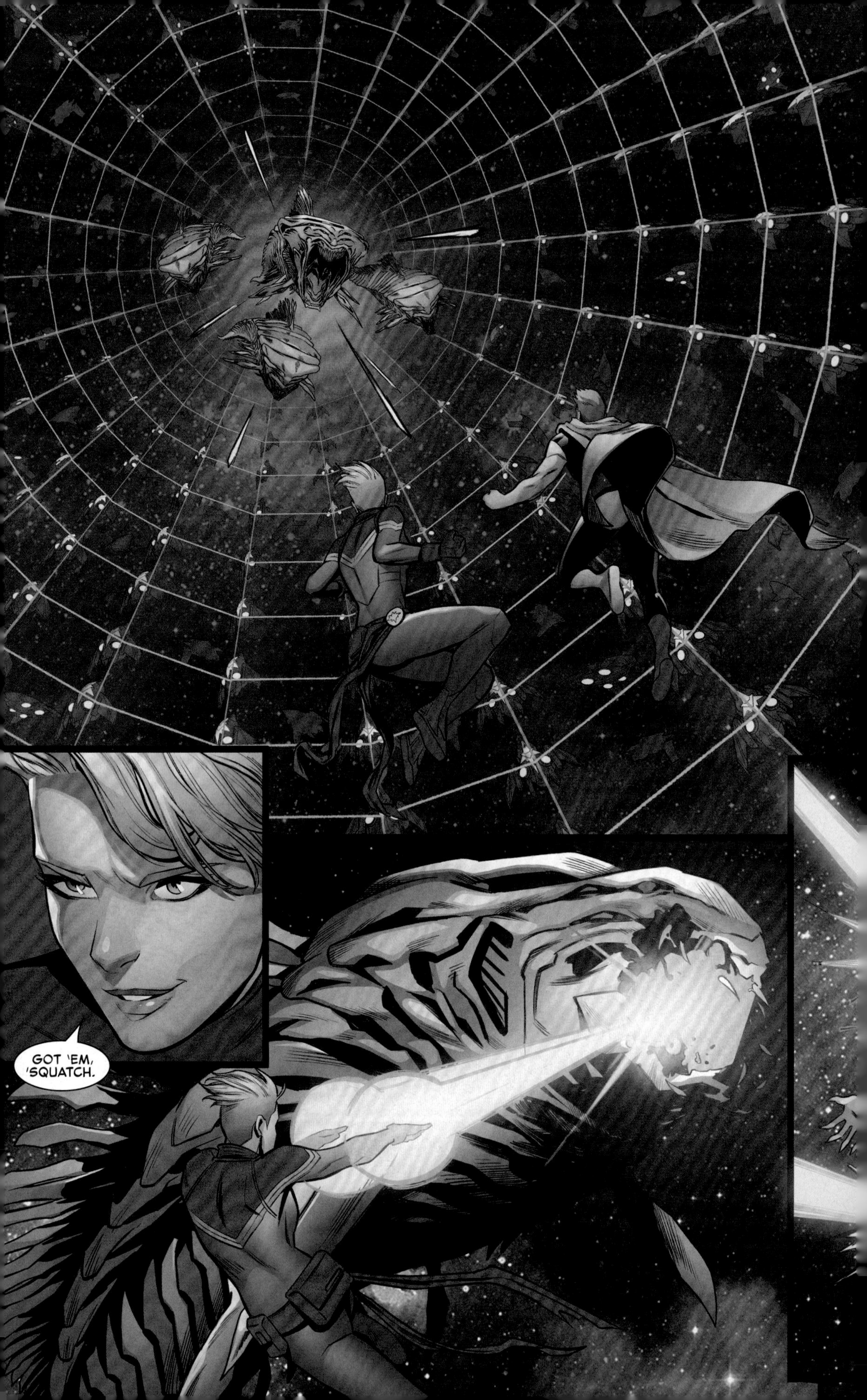
GOT 'EM, 'SQUATCH.

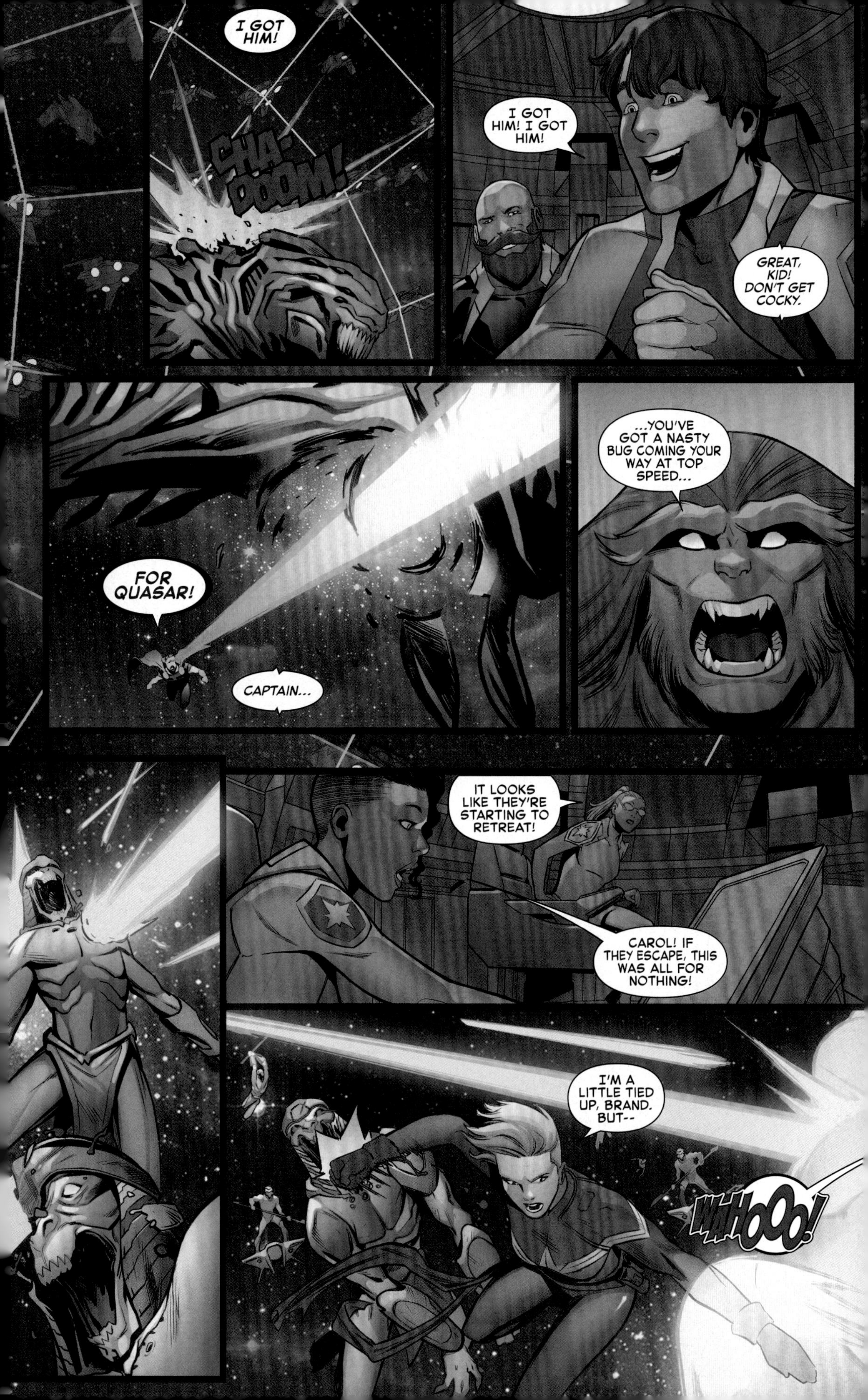
I GOT HIM!
CHA-DOOM!
I GOT HIM! I GOT HIM!
GREAT, KID! DON'T GET COCKY.
FOR QUASAR!
CAPTAIN...
...YOU'VE GOT A NASTY BUG COMING YOUR WAY AT TOP SPEED...
IT LOOKS LIKE THEY'RE STARTING TO RETREAT!
CAROL! IF THEY ESCAPE, THIS WAS ALL FOR NOTHING!
I'M A LITTLE TIED UP, BRAND. BUT--
WAHOOO!

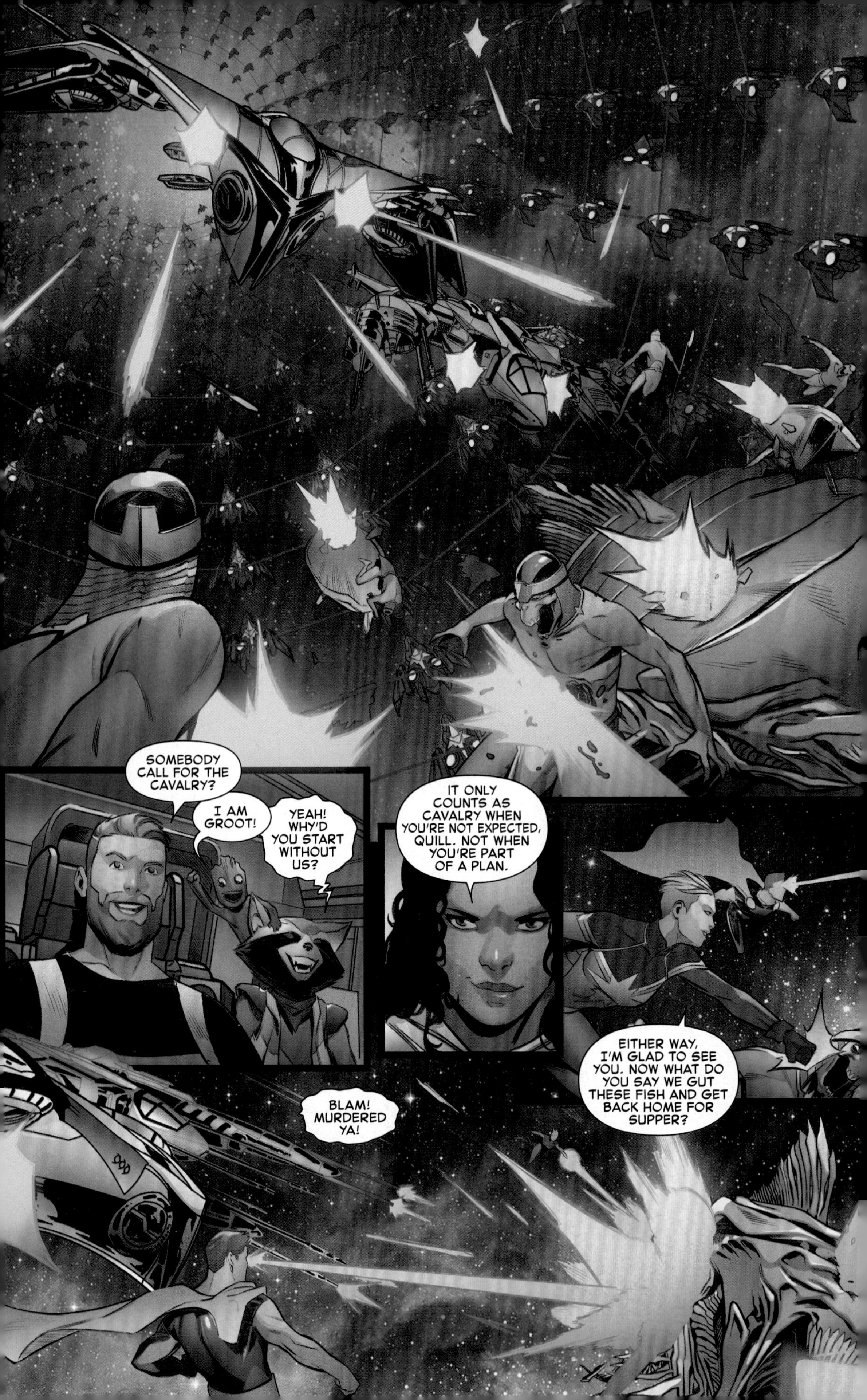

SOMEBODY CALL FOR THE CAVALRY?
I AM GROOT!
YEAH! WHY'D YOU START WITHOUT US?
IT ONLY COUNTS AS CAVALRY WHEN YOU'RE NOT EXPECTED, QUILL. NOT WHEN YOU'RE PART OF A PLAN.
EITHER WAY, I'M GLAD TO SEE YOU. NOW WHAT DO YOU SAY WE GUT THESE FISH AND GET BACK HOME FOR SUPPER?
BLAM! MURDERED YA!

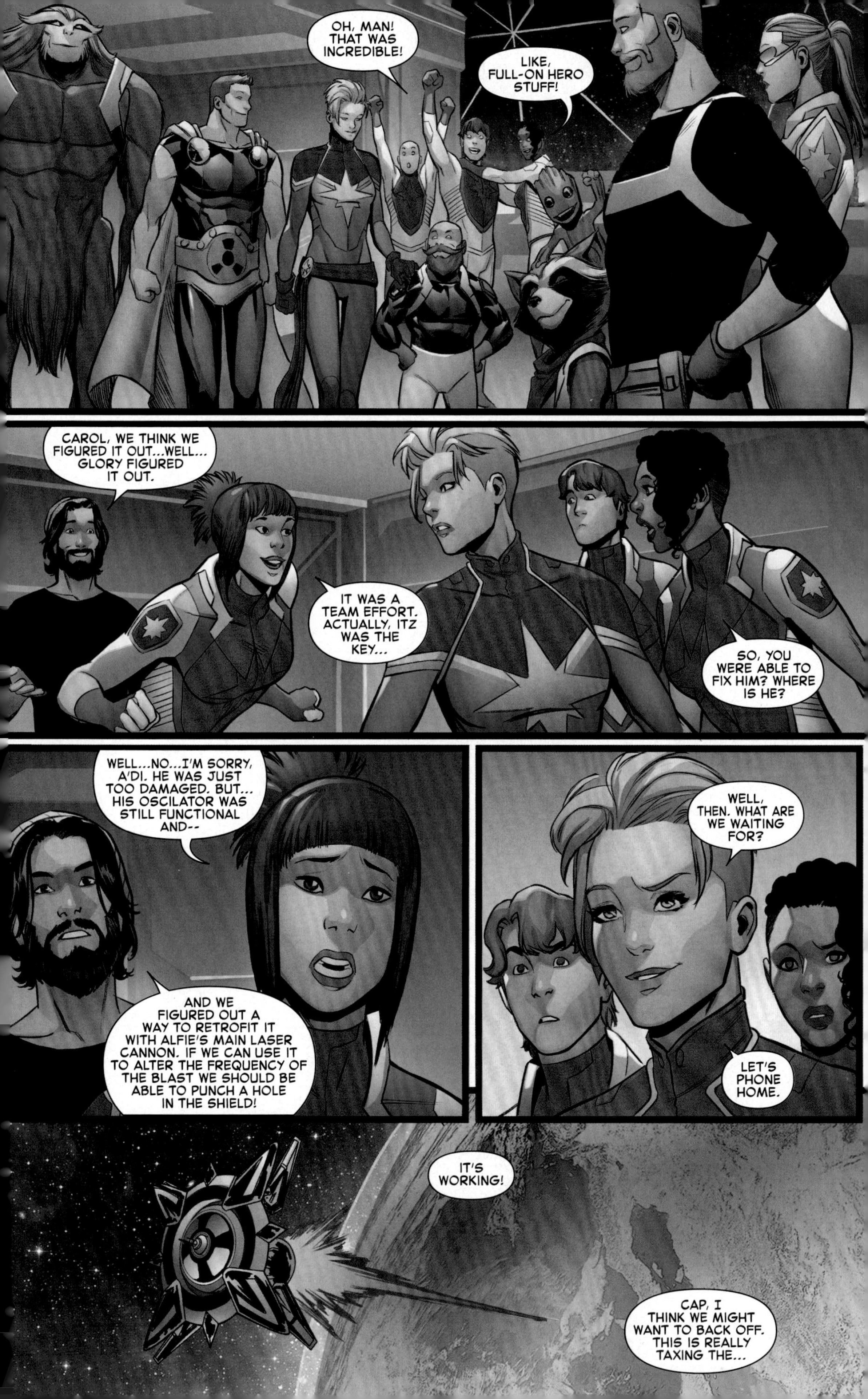
OH, MAN! THAT WAS INCREDIBLE!
LIKE, FULL-ON HERO STUFF!
CAROL, WE THINK WE FIGURED IT OUT...WELL... GLORY FIGURED IT OUT.
IT WAS A TEAM EFFORT. ACTUALLY, ITZ WAS THE KEY...
SO, YOU WERE ABLE TO FIX HIM? WHERE IS HE?
WELL...NO...I'M SORRY, A'DI. HE WAS JUST TOO DAMAGED. BUT... HIS OSCILATOR WAS STILL FUNCTIONAL AND--
AND WE FIGURED OUT A WAY TO RETROFIT IT WITH ALFIE'S MAIN LASER CANNON. IF WE CAN USE IT TO ALTER THE FREQUENCY OF THE BLAST WE SHOULD BE ABLE TO PUNCH A HOLE IN THE SHIELD!
WELL, THEN. WHAT ARE WE WAITING FOR?
LET'S PHONE HOME.
IT'S WORKING!
CAP, I THINK WE MIGHT WANT TO BACK OFF. THIS IS REALLY TAXING THE...

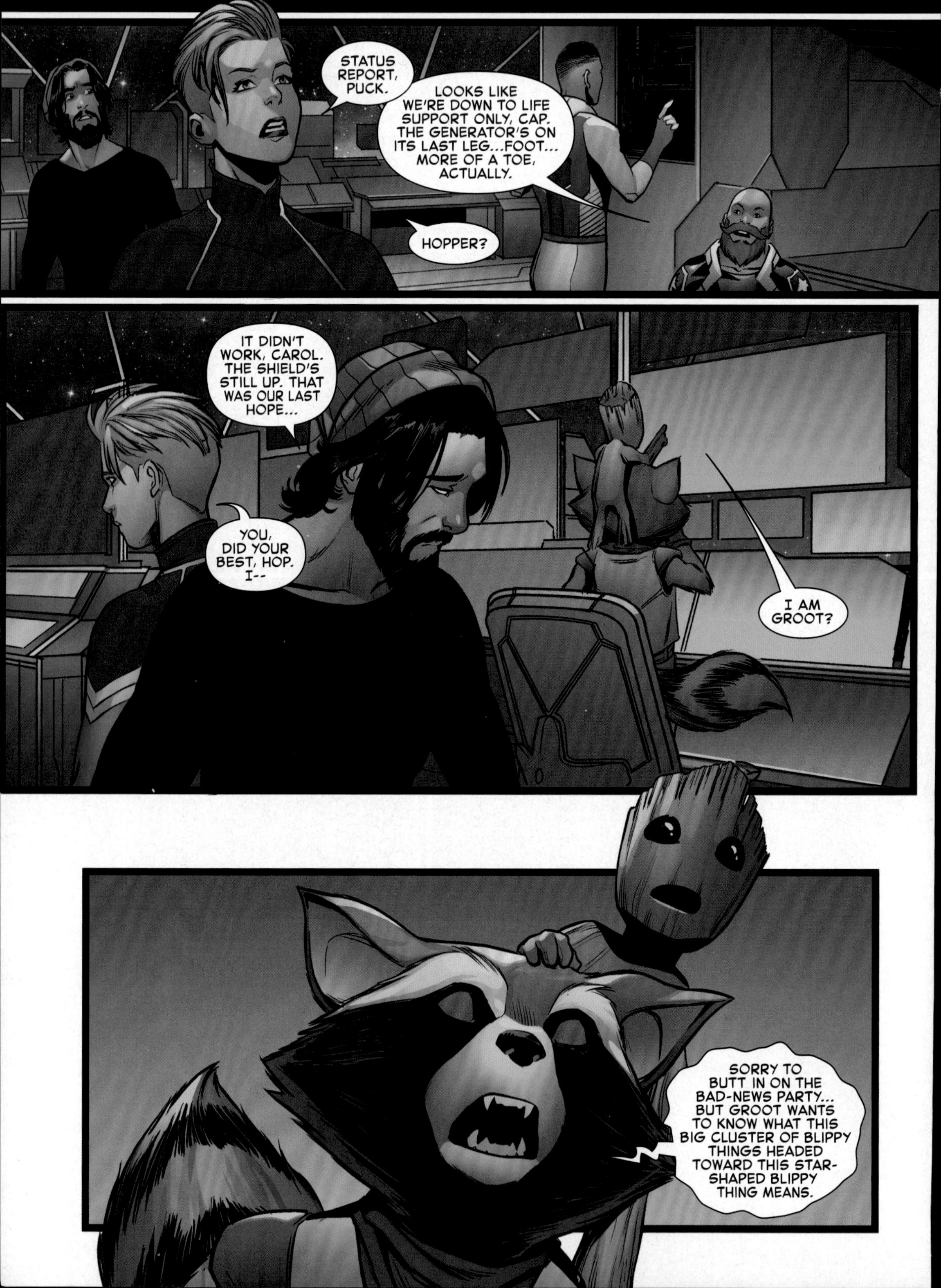
STATUS REPORT, PUCK.
LOOKS LIKE WE'RE DOWN TO LIFE SUPPORT ONLY, CAP. THE GENERATOR'S ON ITS LAST LEG...FOOT... MORE OF A TOE, ACTUALLY.
HOPPER?
IT DIDN'T WORK, CAROL. THE SHIELD'S STILL UP. THAT WAS OUR LAST HOPE...
YOU, DID YOUR BEST, HOP. I--
I AM GROOT?
SORRY TO BUTT IN ON THE BAD-NEWS PARTY... BUT GROOT WANTS TO KNOW WHAT THIS BIG CLUSTER OF BLIPPY THINGS HEADED TOWARD THIS STAR-SHAPED BLIPPY THING MEANS.

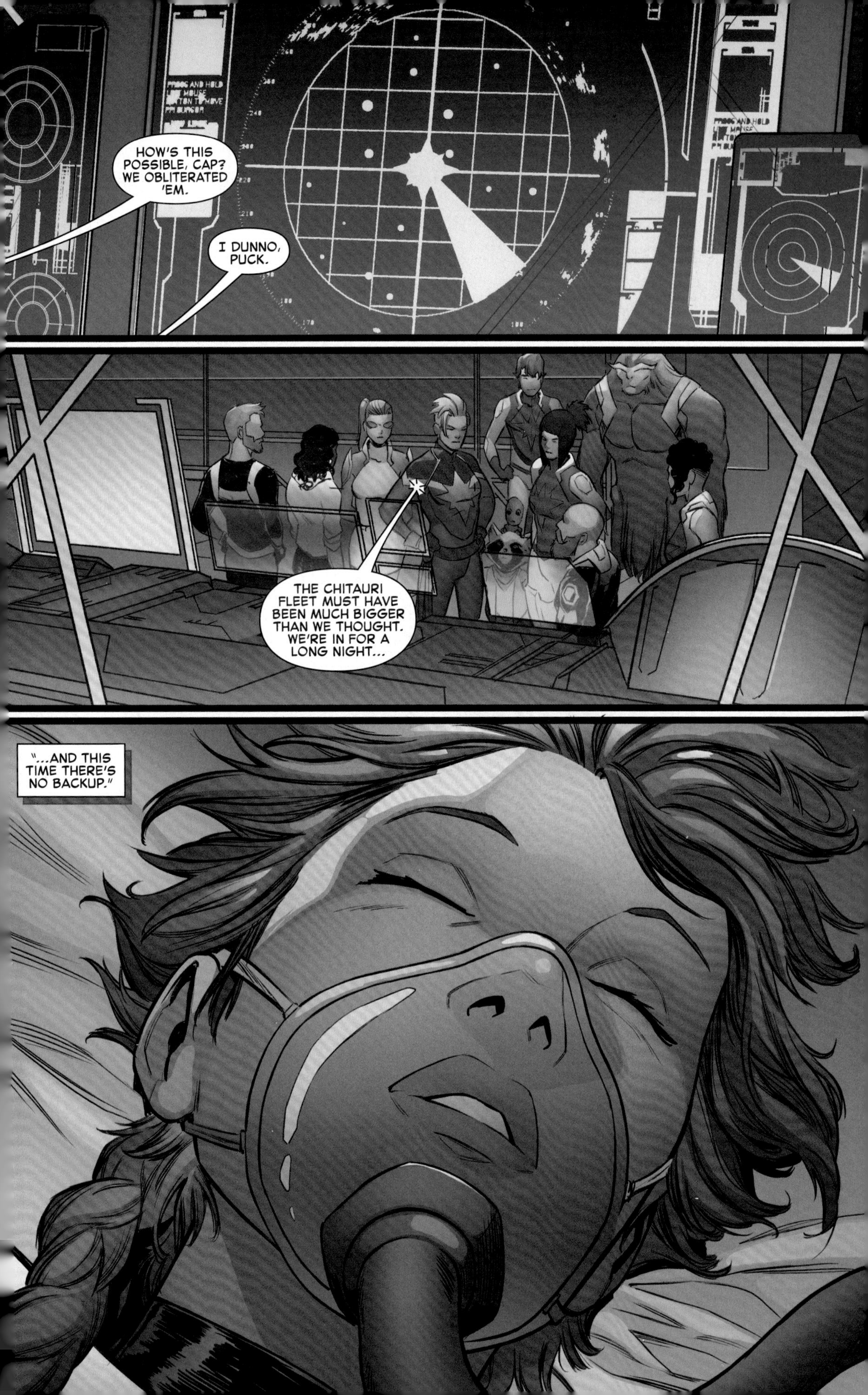
HOW'S THIS POSSIBLE, CAP? WE OBLITERATED 'EM.
I DUNNO, PUCK.
THE CHITAURI FLEET MUST HAVE BEEN MUCH BIGGER THAN WE THOUGHT. WE'RE IN FOR A LONG NIGHT...
"...AND THIS TIME THERE'S NO BACKUP."

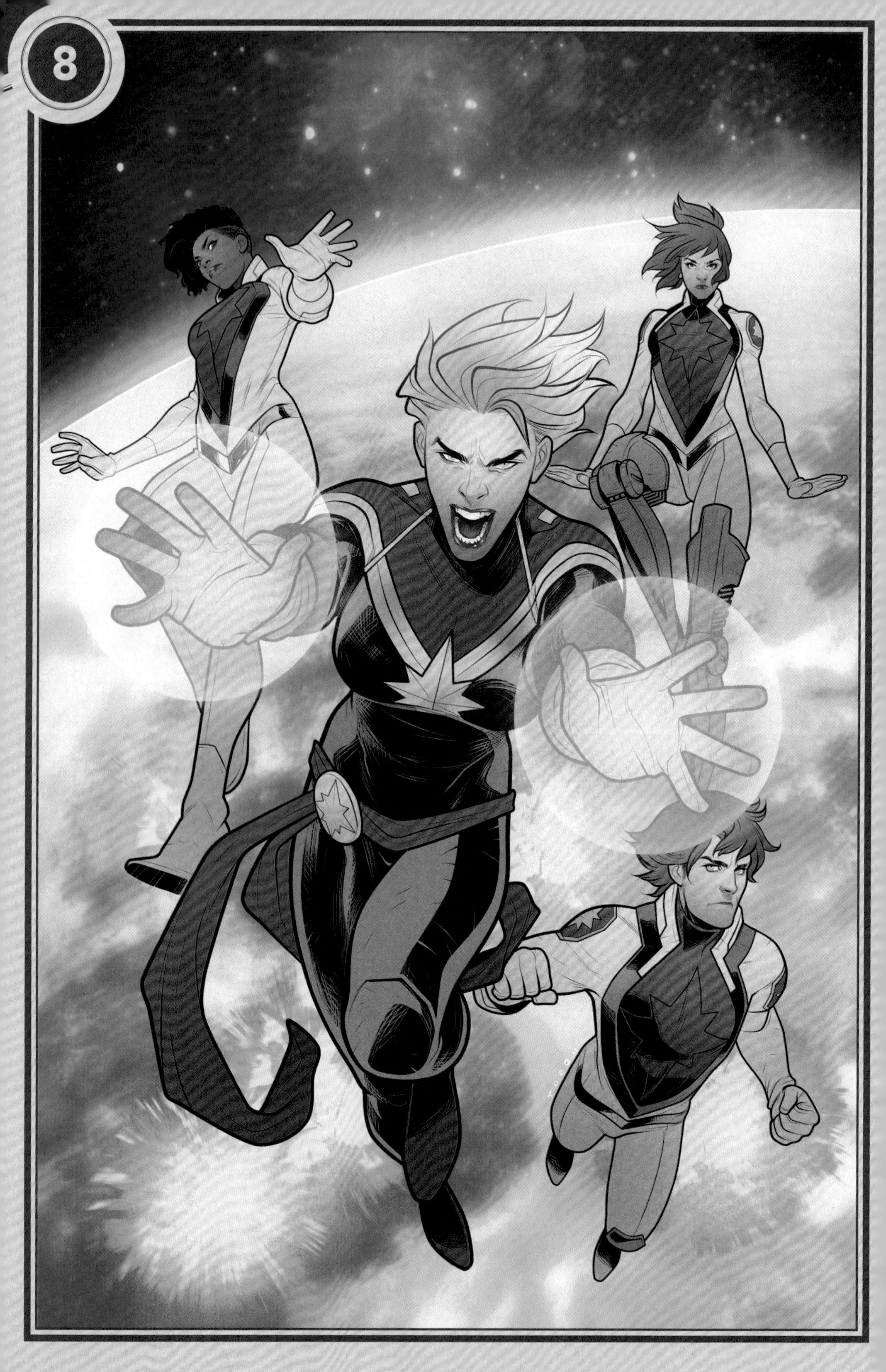
8

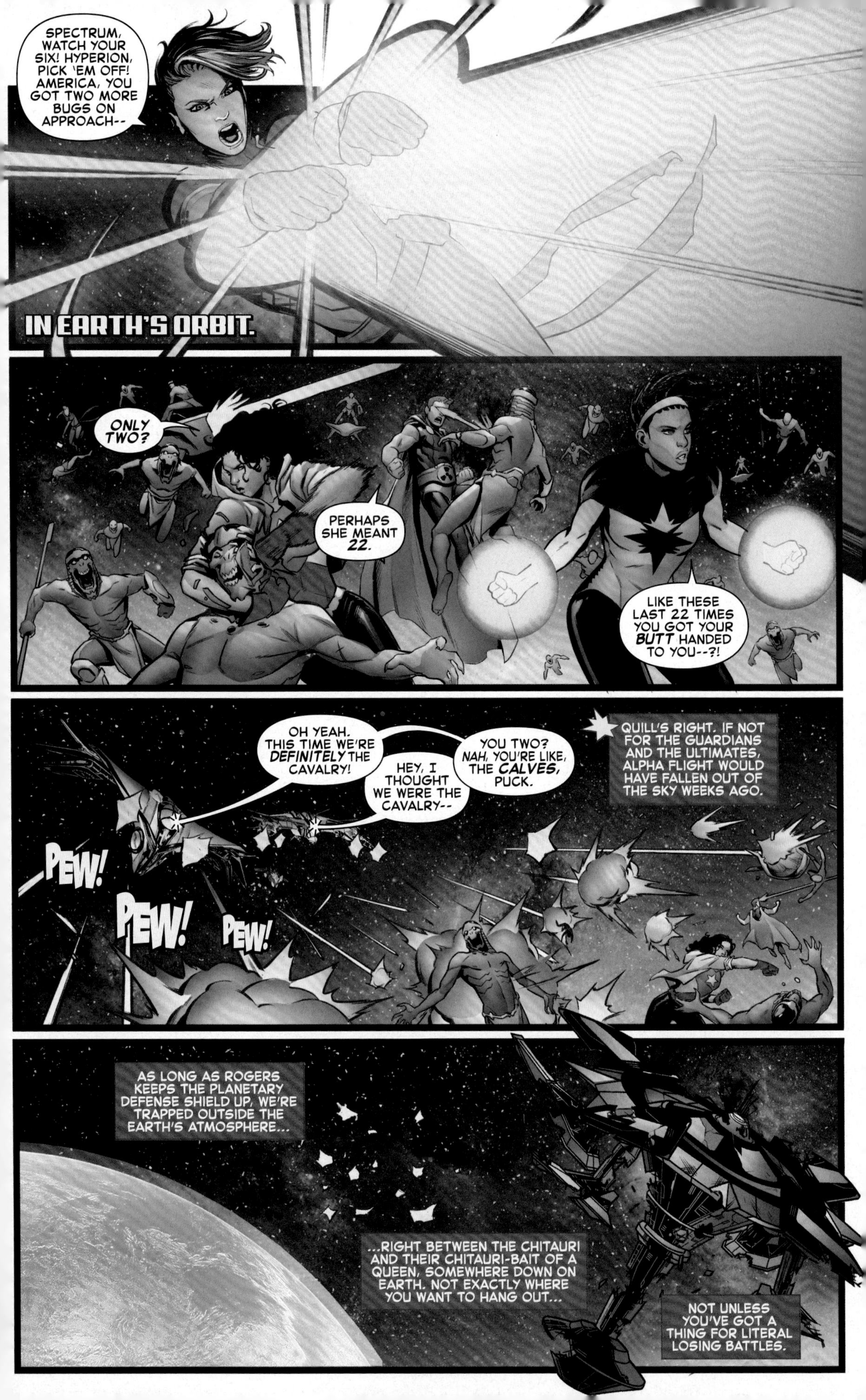
SPECTRUM, WATCH YOUR SIX! HYPERION, PICK 'EM OFF! AMERICA, YOU GOT TWO MORE BUGS ON APPROACH--
IN EARTH'S ORBIT.
ONLY TWO?
PERHAPS SHE MEANT 22.
LIKE THESE LAST 22 TIMES YOU GOT YOUR BUTT HANDED TO YOU--?!
OH YEAH. THIS TIME WE'RE DEFINITELY THE CAVALRY!
HEY, I THOUGHT WE WERE THE CAVALRY--
YOU TWO? NAH, YOU'RE LIKE, THE CALVES, PUCK.
QUILL'S RIGHT. IF NOT FOR THE GUARDIANS AND THE ULTIMATES, ALPHA FLIGHT WOULD HAVE FALLEN OUT OF THE SKY WEEKS AGO.
PEW!
PEW!
PEW!
AS LONG AS ROGERS KEEPS THE PLANETARY DEFENSE SHIELD UP, WE'RE TRAPPED OUTSIDE THE EARTH'S ATMOSPHERE...
...RIGHT BETWEEN THE CHITAURI AND THEIR CHITAURI-BAIT OF A QUEEN, SOMEWHERE DOWN ON EARTH. NOT EXACTLY WHERE YOU WANT TO HANG OUT...
NOT UNLESS YOU'VE GOT A THING FOR LITERAL LOSING BATTLES.

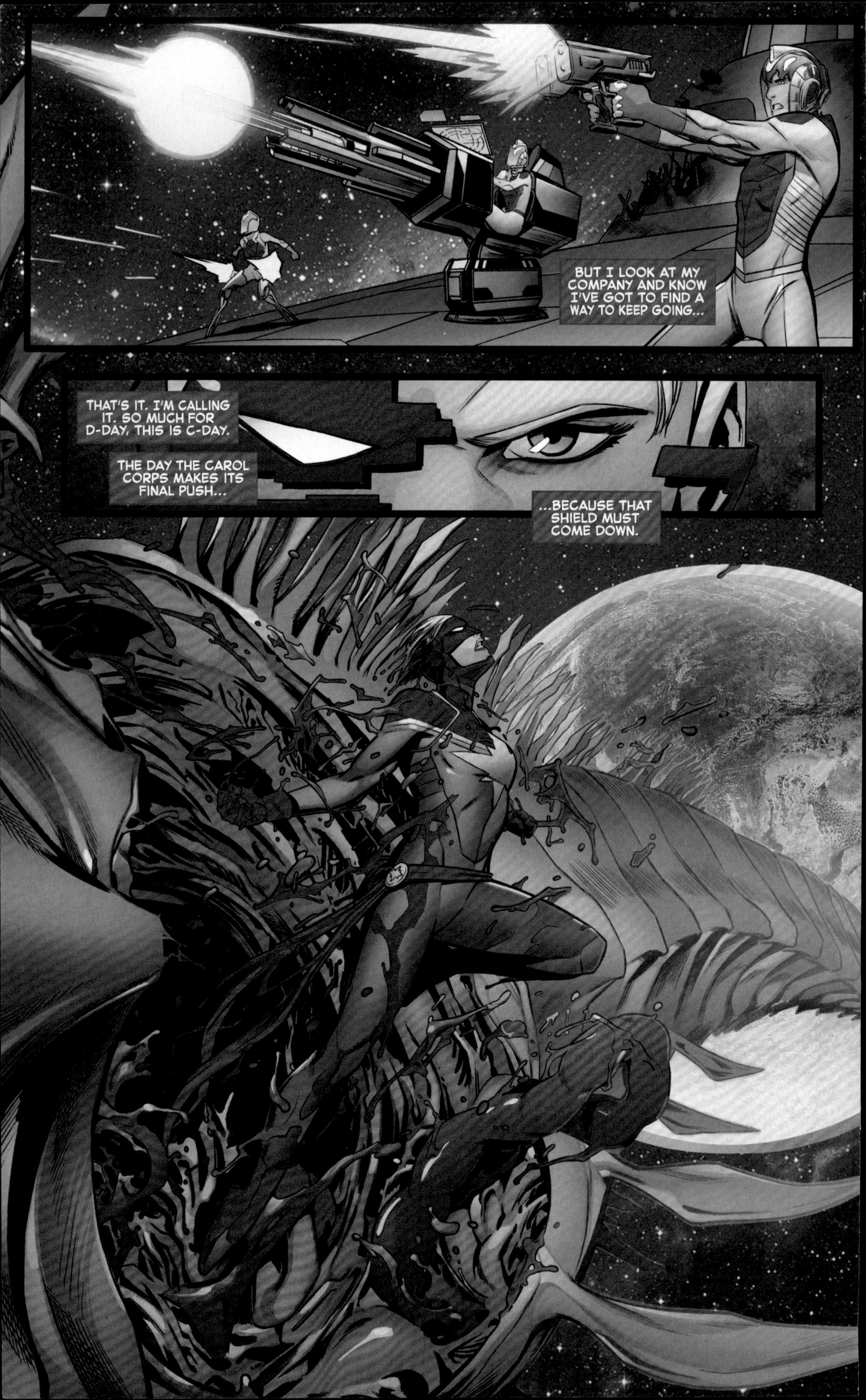
BUT I LOOK AT MY COMPANY AND KNOW I'VE GOT TO FIND A WAY TO KEEP GOING...
THAT'S IT. I'M CALLING IT. SO MUCH FOR D-DAY, THIS IS C-DAY.
THE DAY THE CAROL CORPS MAKES ITS FINAL PUSH...
...BECAUSE THAT SHIELD MUST COME DOWN.

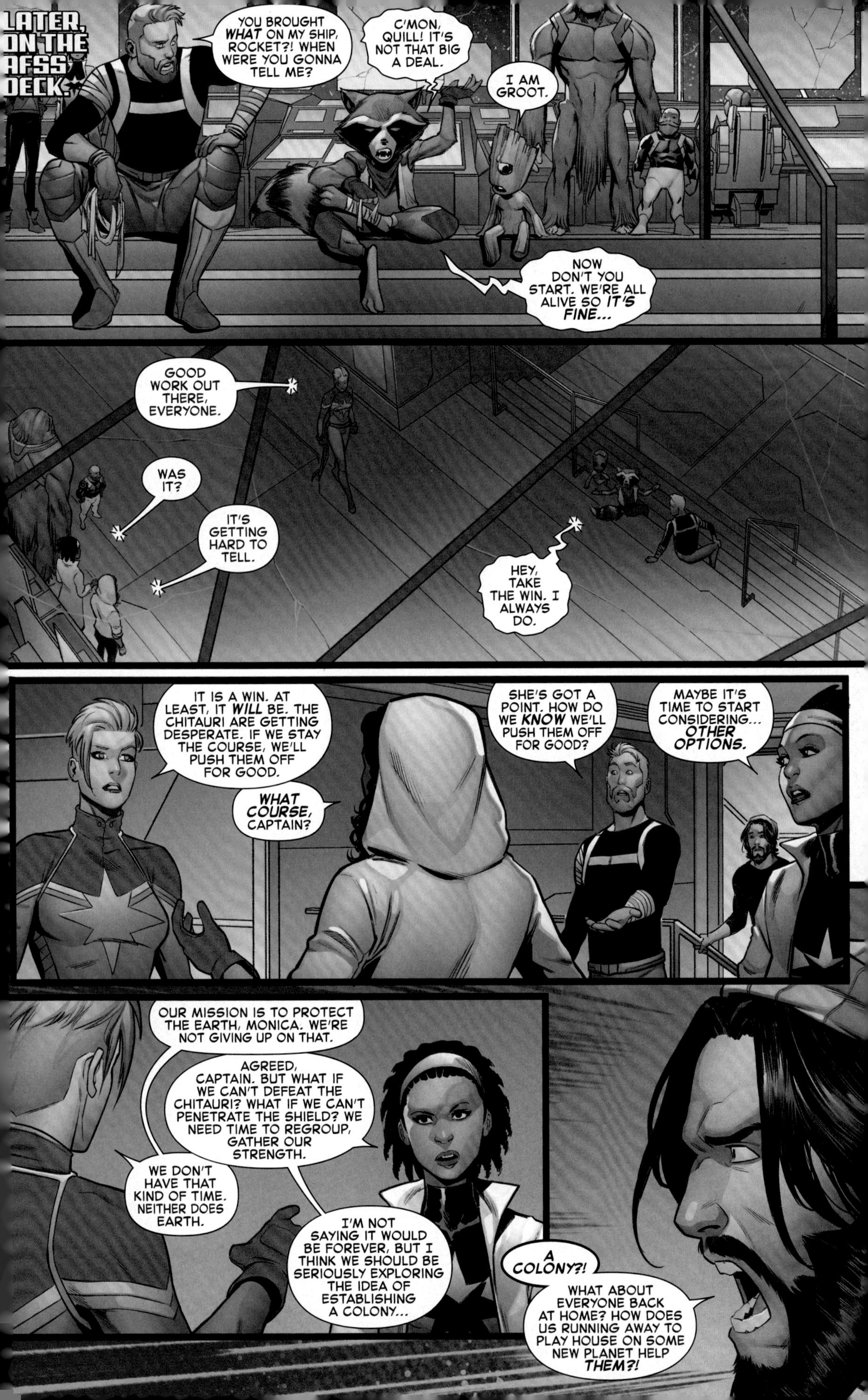
LATER, ON THE AFSS DECK:
YOU BROUGHT WHAT ON MY SHIP, ROCKET?! WHEN WERE YOU GONNA TELL ME?
C'MON, QUILL! IT'S NOT THAT BIG A DEAL.
I AM GROOT.
NOW DON'T YOU START. WE'RE ALL ALIVE SO IT'S FINE...
GOOD WORK OUT THERE, EVERYONE.
WAS IT?
IT'S GETTING HARD TO TELL.
HEY, TAKE THE WIN. I ALWAYS DO.
IT IS A WIN. AT LEAST, IT WILL BE. THE CHITAURI ARE GETTING DESPERATE. IF WE STAY THE COURSE, WE'LL PUSH THEM OFF FOR GOOD.
WHAT COURSE, CAPTAIN?
SHE'S GOT A POINT. HOW DO WE KNOW WE'LL PUSH THEM OFF FOR GOOD?
MAYBE IT'S TIME TO START CONSIDERING... OTHER OPTIONS.
OUR MISSION IS TO PROTECT THE EARTH, MONICA. WE'RE NOT GIVING UP ON THAT.
AGREED, CAPTAIN. BUT WHAT IF WE CAN'T DEFEAT THE CHITAURI? WHAT IF WE CAN'T PENETRATE THE SHIELD? WE NEED TIME TO REGROUP, GATHER OUR STRENGTH.
WE DON'T HAVE THAT KIND OF TIME. NEITHER DOES EARTH.
I'M NOT SAYING IT WOULD BE FOREVER, BUT I THINK WE SHOULD BE SERIOUSLY EXPLORING THE IDEA OF ESTABLISHING A COLONY...
A COLONY?!
WHAT ABOUT EVERYONE BACK AT HOME? HOW DOES US RUNNING AWAY TO PLAY HOUSE ON SOME NEW PLANET HELP THEM?!

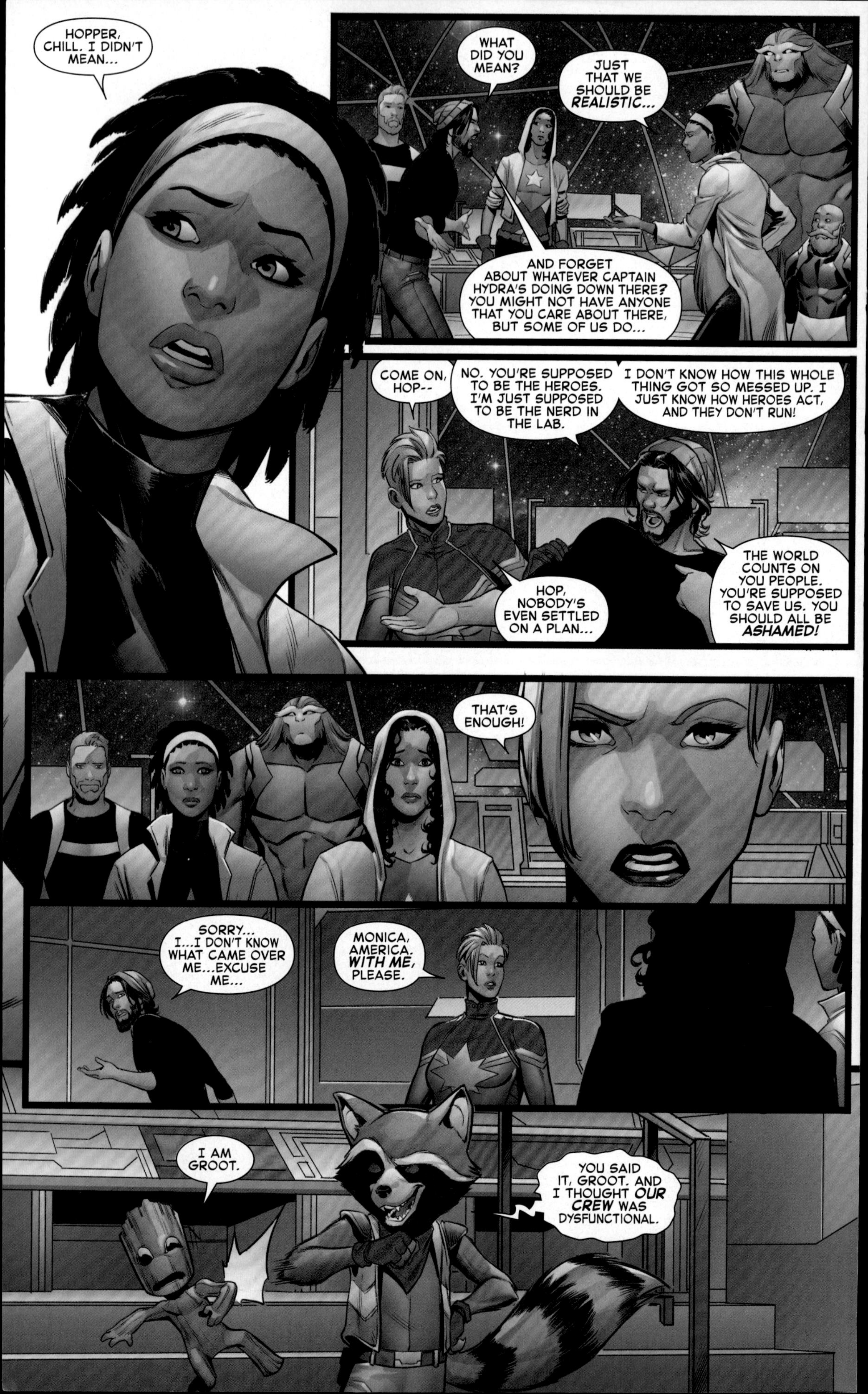
HOPPER, CHILL. I DIDN'T MEAN...
WHAT DID YOU MEAN?
JUST THAT WE SHOULD BE REALISTIC...
AND FORGET ABOUT WHATEVER CAPTAIN HYDRA'S DOING DOWN THERE? YOU MIGHT NOT HAVE ANYONE THAT YOU CARE ABOUT THERE, BUT SOME OF US DO...
COME ON, HOP--
NO. YOU'RE SUPPOSED TO BE THE HEROES. I'M JUST SUPPOSED TO BE THE NERD IN THE LAB.
I DON'T KNOW HOW THIS WHOLE THING GOT SO MESSED UP. I JUST KNOW HOW HEROES ACT, AND THEY DON'T RUN!
HOP, NOBODY'S EVEN SETTLED ON A PLAN...
THE WORLD COUNTS ON YOU PEOPLE. YOU'RE SUPPOSED TO SAVE US. YOU SHOULD ALL BE ASHAMED!
THAT'S ENOUGH!
SORRY... I...I DON'T KNOW WHAT CAME OVER ME...EXCUSE ME...
MONICA, AMERICA. WITH ME, PLEASE.
I AM GROOT.
YOU SAID IT, GROOT. AND I THOUGHT OUR CREW WAS DYSFUNCTIONAL.

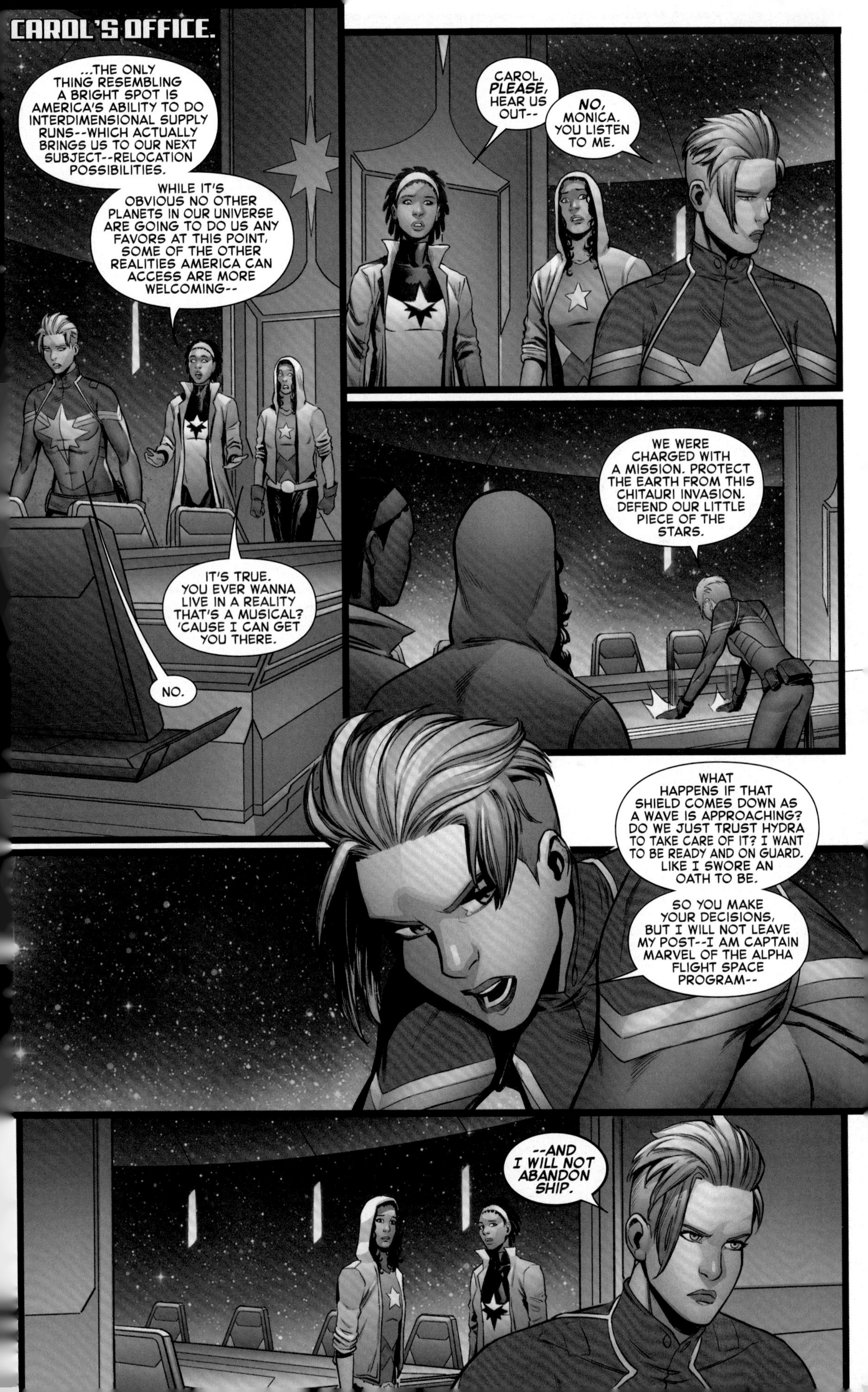
CAROL'S OFFICE.
...THE ONLY THING RESEMBLING A BRIGHT SPOT IS AMERICA'S ABILITY TO DO INTERDIMENSIONAL SUPPLY RUNS--WHICH ACTUALLY BRINGS US TO OUR NEXT SUBJECT--RELOCATION POSSIBILITIES.
WHILE IT'S OBVIOUS NO OTHER PLANETS IN OUR UNIVERSE ARE GOING TO DO US ANY FAVORS AT THIS POINT, SOME OF THE OTHER REALITIES AMERICA CAN ACCESS ARE MORE WELCOMING--
IT'S TRUE. YOU EVER WANNA LIVE IN A REALITY THAT'S A MUSICAL? 'CAUSE I CAN GET YOU THERE.
NO.
CAROL, PLEASE, HEAR US OUT--
NO, MONICA. YOU LISTEN TO ME.
WE WERE CHARGED WITH A MISSION. PROTECT THE EARTH FROM THIS CHITAURI INVASION. DEFEND OUR LITTLE PIECE OF THE STARS.
WHAT HAPPENS IF THAT SHIELD COMES DOWN AS A WAVE IS APPROACHING? DO WE JUST TRUST HYDRA TO TAKE CARE OF IT? I WANT TO BE READY AND ON GUARD. LIKE I SWORE AN OATH TO BE.
SO YOU MAKE YOUR DECISIONS, BUT I WILL NOT LEAVE MY POST--I AM CAPTAIN MARVEL OF THE ALPHA FLIGHT SPACE PROGRAM--
--AND I WILL NOT ABANDON SHIP.

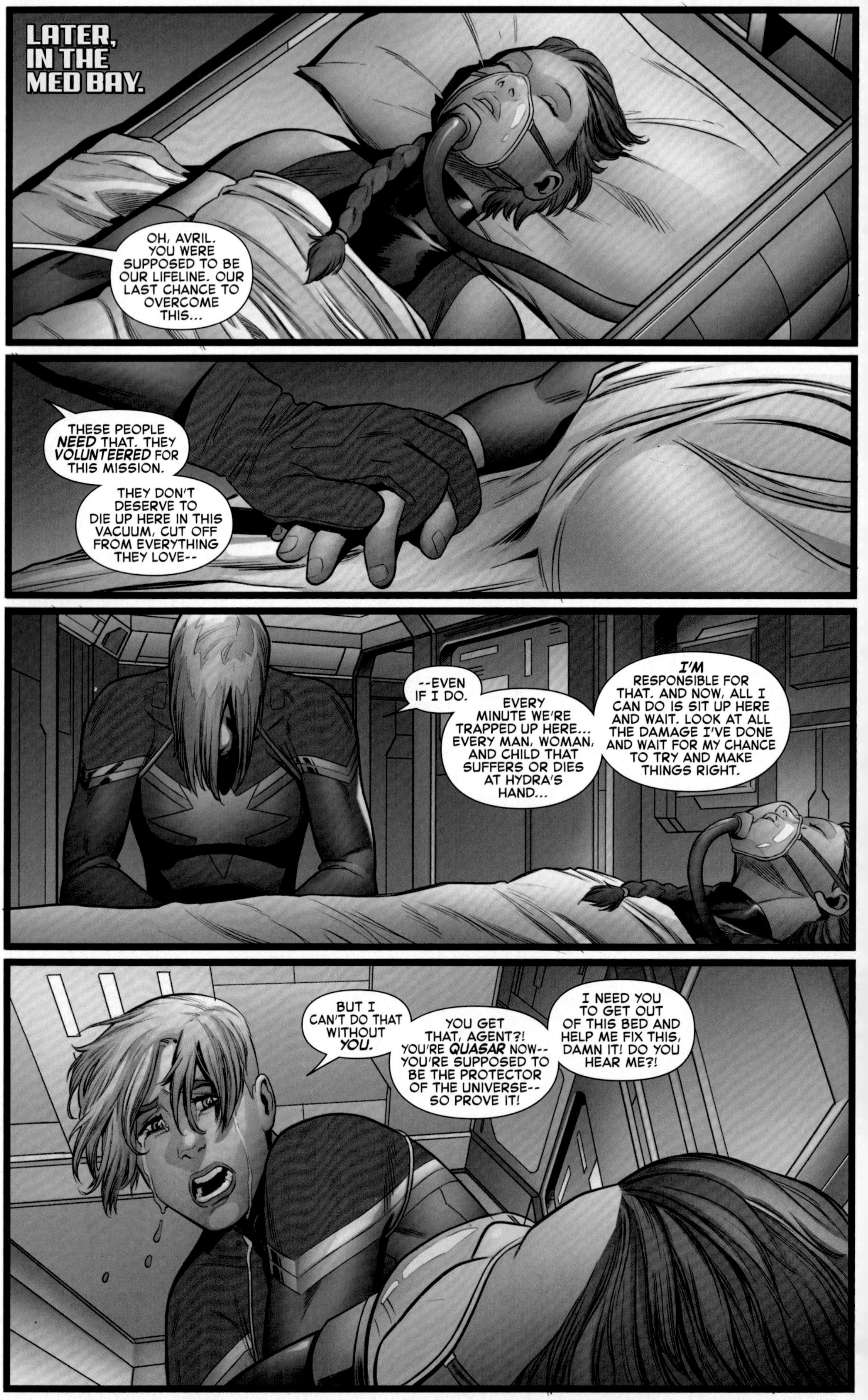
LATER, IN THE MED BAY.
OH, AVRIL. YOU WERE SUPPOSED TO BE OUR LIFELINE. OUR LAST CHANCE TO OVERCOME THIS...
THESE PEOPLE NEED THAT. THEY VOLUNTEERED FOR THIS MISSION.
THEY DON'T DESERVE TO DIE UP HERE IN THIS VACUUM, CUT OFF FROM EVERYTHING THEY LOVE--
--EVEN IF I DO.
EVERY MINUTE WE'RE TRAPPED UP HERE... EVERY MAN, WOMAN, AND CHILD THAT SUFFERS OR DIES AT HYDRA'S HAND...
I'M RESPONSIBLE FOR THAT. AND NOW, ALL I CAN DO IS SIT UP HERE AND WAIT. LOOK AT ALL THE DAMAGE I'VE DONE AND WAIT FOR MY CHANCE TO TRY AND MAKE THINGS RIGHT.
BUT I CAN'T DO THAT WITHOUT YOU.
YOU GET THAT, AGENT?! YOU'RE QUASAR NOW-- YOU'RE SUPPOSED TO BE THE PROTECTOR OF THE UNIVERSE-- SO PROVE IT!
I NEED YOU TO GET OUT OF THIS BED AND HELP ME FIX THIS, DAMN IT! DO YOU HEAR ME?!

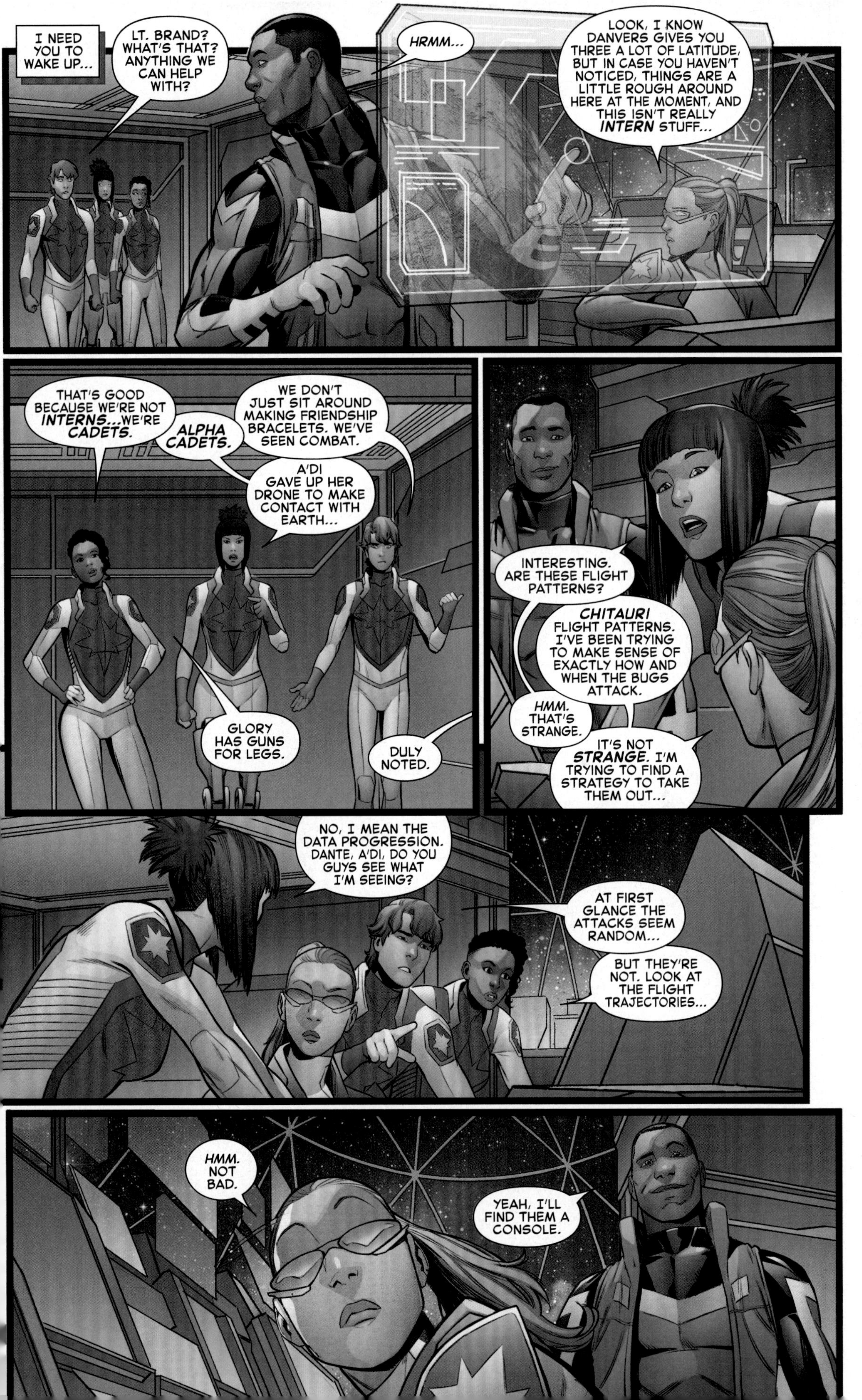
I NEED YOU TO WAKE UP...
LT. BRAND? WHAT'S THAT? ANYTHING WE CAN HELP WITH?
HRMM...
LOOK, I KNOW DANVERS GIVES YOU THREE A LOT OF LATITUDE, BUT IN CASE YOU HAVEN'T NOTICED, THINGS ARE A LITTLE ROUGH AROUND HERE AT THE MOMENT, AND THIS ISN'T REALLY INTERN STUFF...
THAT'S GOOD BECAUSE WE'RE NOT INTERNS...WE'RE CADETS.
ALPHA CADETS.
WE DON'T JUST SIT AROUND MAKING FRIENDSHIP BRACELETS. WE'VE SEEN COMBAT.
A'DI GAVE UP HER DRONE TO MAKE CONTACT WITH EARTH...
GLORY HAS GUNS FOR LEGS.
DULY NOTED.
INTERESTING. ARE THESE FLIGHT PATTERNS?
CHITAURI FLIGHT PATTERNS. I'VE BEEN TRYING TO MAKE SENSE OF EXACTLY HOW AND WHEN THE BUGS ATTACK.
HMM. THAT'S STRANGE.
IT'S NOT STRANGE. I'M TRYING TO FIND A STRATEGY TO TAKE THEM OUT...
NO, I MEAN THE DATA PROGRESSION. DANTE, A'DI, DO YOU GUYS SEE WHAT I'M SEEING?
AT FIRST GLANCE THE ATTACKS SEEM RANDOM...
BUT THEY'RE NOT. LOOK AT THE FLIGHT TRAJECTORIES...
HMM. NOT BAD.
YEAH, I'LL FIND THEM A CONSOLE.

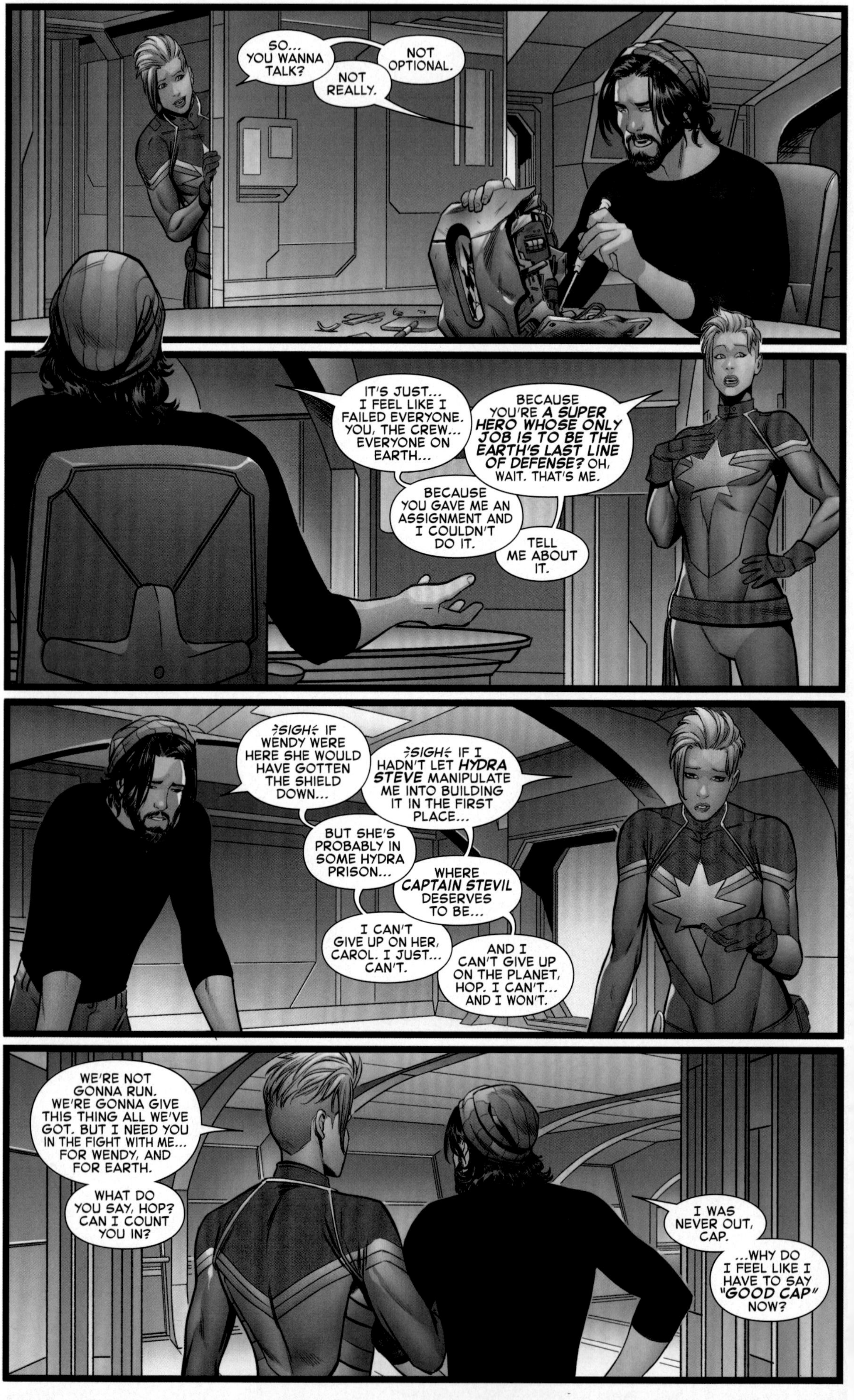
SO... YOU WANNA TALK?
NOT REALLY.
NOT OPTIONAL.
IT'S JUST... I FEEL LIKE I FAILED EVERYONE. YOU, THE CREW... EVERYONE ON EARTH...
BECAUSE YOU GAVE ME AN ASSIGNMENT AND I COULDN'T DO IT.
BECAUSE YOU'RE A SUPER HERO WHOSE ONLY JOB IS TO BE THE EARTH'S LAST LINE OF DEFENSE? OH, WAIT. THAT'S ME.
TELL ME ABOUT IT.
SIGH IF WENDY WERE HERE SHE WOULD HAVE GOTTEN THE SHIELD DOWN...
BUT SHE'S PROBABLY IN SOME HYDRA PRISON...
SIGH IF I HADN'T LET HYDRA STEVE MANIPULATE ME INTO BUILDING IT IN THE FIRST PLACE...
WHERE CAPTAIN STEVIL DESERVES TO BE...
I CAN'T GIVE UP ON HER, CAROL. I JUST... CAN'T.
AND I CAN'T GIVE UP ON THE PLANET, HOP. I CAN'T... AND I WON'T.
WE'RE NOT GONNA RUN. WE'RE GONNA GIVE THIS THING ALL WE'VE GOT. BUT I NEED YOU IN THE FIGHT WITH ME... FOR WENDY, AND FOR EARTH.
WHAT DO YOU SAY, HOP? CAN I COUNT YOU IN?
I WAS NEVER OUT, CAP.
...WHY DO I FEEL LIKE I HAVE TO SAY "GOOD CAP" NOW?

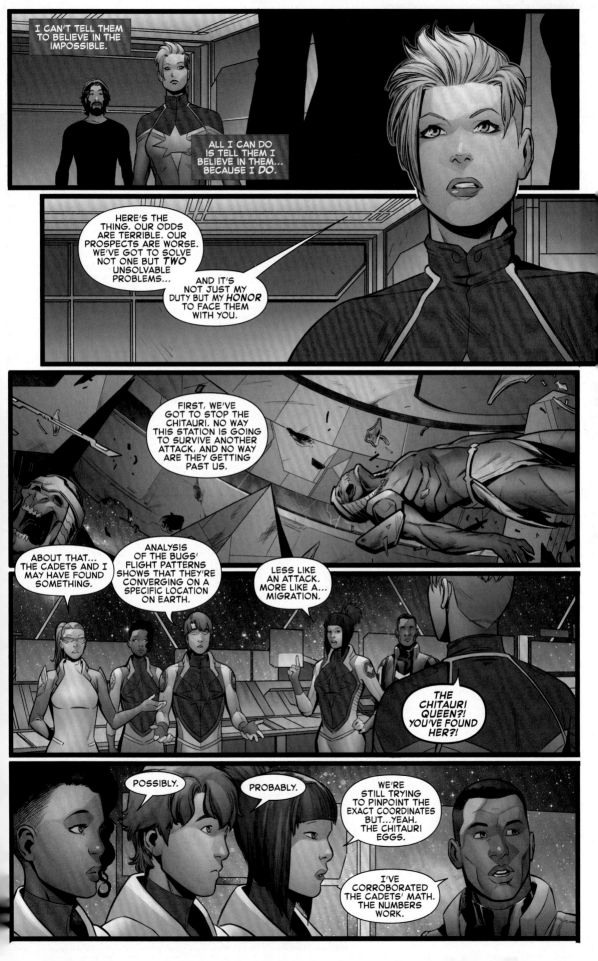

I CAN'T TELL THEM TO BELIEVE IN THE IMPOSSIBLE.

ALL I CAN DO IS TELL THEM I BELIEVE IN THEM... BECAUSE I *DO.*

HERE'S THE THING. OUR ODDS ARE TERRIBLE. OUR PROSPECTS ARE WORSE. WE'VE GOT TO SOLVE NOT ONE BUT *TWO* UNSOLVABLE PROBLEMS...

AND IT'S NOT JUST MY DUTY BUT MY *HONOR* TO FACE THEM WITH YOU.

FIRST, WE'VE GOT TO STOP THE CHITAURI. NO WAY THIS STATION IS GOING TO SURVIVE ANOTHER ATTACK, AND NO WAY ARE THEY GETTING PAST US.

ABOUT THAT... THE CADETS AND I MAY HAVE FOUND SOMETHING.

ANALYSIS OF THE BUGS' FLIGHT PATTERNS SHOWS THAT THEY'RE CONVERGING ON A SPECIFIC LOCATION ON EARTH.

LESS LIKE AN ATTACK. MORE LIKE A... MIGRATION.

THE CHITAURI QUEEN?! YOU'VE FOUND HER?!

POSSIBLY.

PROBABLY.

WE'RE STILL TRYING TO PINPOINT THE EXACT COORDINATES BUT...YEAH. THE CHITAURI EGGS.

I'VE CORROBORATED THE CADETS' MATH. THE NUMBERS WORK.

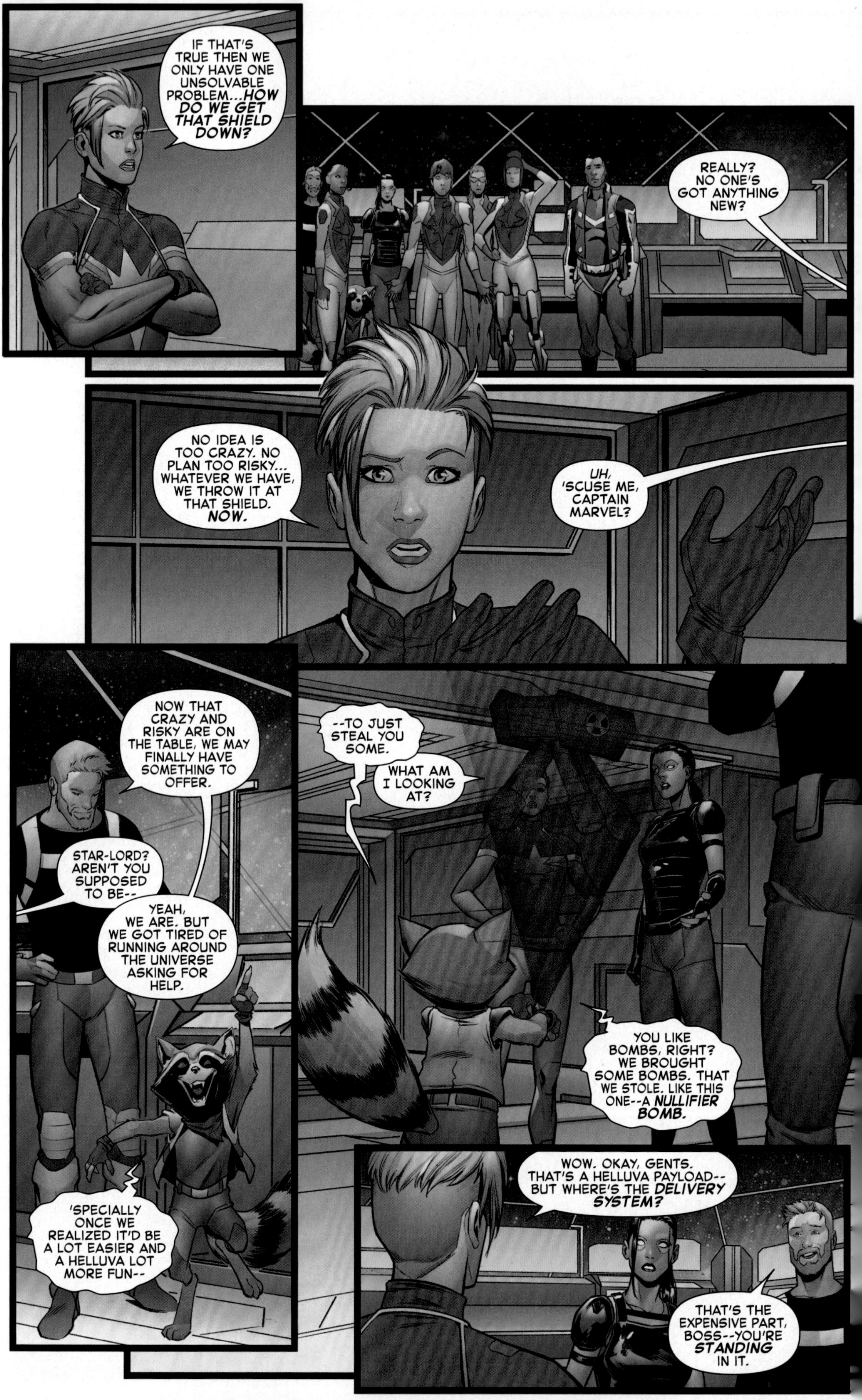
IF THAT'S TRUE THEN WE ONLY HAVE ONE UNSOLVABLE PROBLEM...HOW DO WE GET THAT SHIELD DOWN?
REALLY? NO ONE'S GOT ANYTHING NEW?
NO IDEA IS TOO CRAZY. NO PLAN TOO RISKY... WHATEVER WE HAVE, WE THROW IT AT THAT SHIELD. NOW.
UH, 'SCUSE ME, CAPTAIN MARVEL?
NOW THAT CRAZY AND RISKY ARE ON THE TABLE, WE MAY FINALLY HAVE SOMETHING TO OFFER.
STAR-LORD? AREN'T YOU SUPPOSED TO BE--
YEAH, WE ARE. BUT WE GOT TIRED OF RUNNING AROUND THE UNIVERSE ASKING FOR HELP.
'SPECIALLY ONCE WE REALIZED IT'D BE A LOT EASIER AND A HELLUVA LOT MORE FUN--
--TO JUST STEAL YOU SOME.
WHAT AM I LOOKING AT?
YOU LIKE BOMBS, RIGHT? WE BROUGHT SOME BOMBS. THAT WE STOLE. LIKE THIS ONE--A NULLIFIER BOMB.
WOW. OKAY, GENTS. THAT'S A HELLUVA PAYLOAD-- BUT WHERE'S THE DELIVERY SYSTEM?
THAT'S THE EXPENSIVE PART, BOSS--YOU'RE STANDING IN IT.

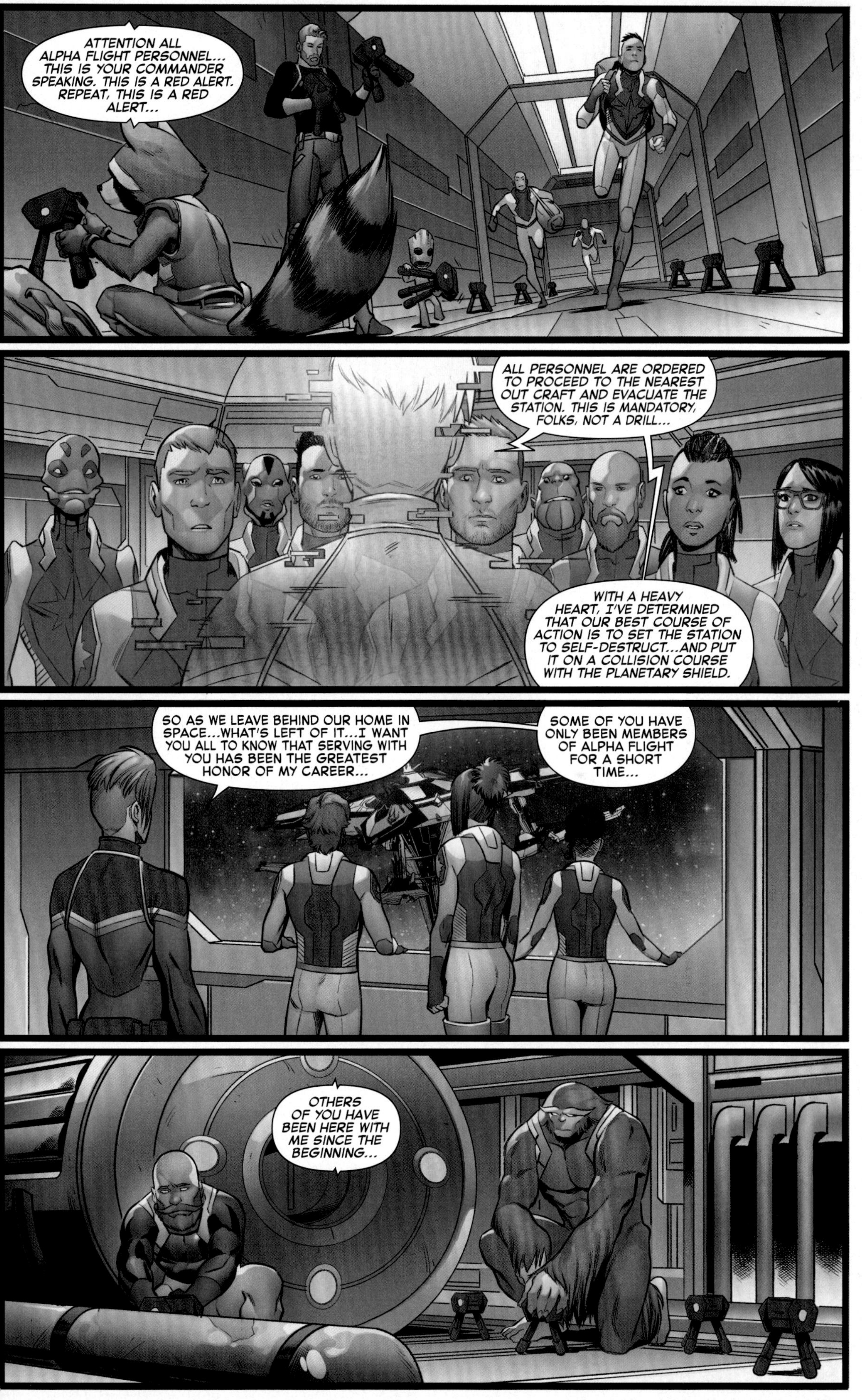
ATTENTION ALL ALPHA FLIGHT PERSONNEL... THIS IS YOUR COMMANDER SPEAKING. THIS IS A RED ALERT. REPEAT, THIS IS A RED ALERT...
ALL PERSONNEL ARE ORDERED TO PROCEED TO THE NEAREST OUT CRAFT AND EVACUATE THE STATION. THIS IS MANDATORY, FOLKS, NOT A DRILL...
WITH A HEAVY HEART, I'VE DETERMINED THAT OUR BEST COURSE OF ACTION IS TO SET THE STATION TO SELF-DESTRUCT...AND PUT IT ON A COLLISION COURSE WITH THE PLANETARY SHIELD.
SO AS WE LEAVE BEHIND OUR HOME IN SPACE...WHAT'S LEFT OF IT...I WANT YOU ALL TO KNOW THAT SERVING WITH YOU HAS BEEN THE GREATEST HONOR OF MY CAREER...
SOME OF YOU HAVE ONLY BEEN MEMBERS OF ALPHA FLIGHT FOR A SHORT TIME...
OTHERS OF YOU HAVE BEEN HERE WITH ME SINCE THE BEGINNING...

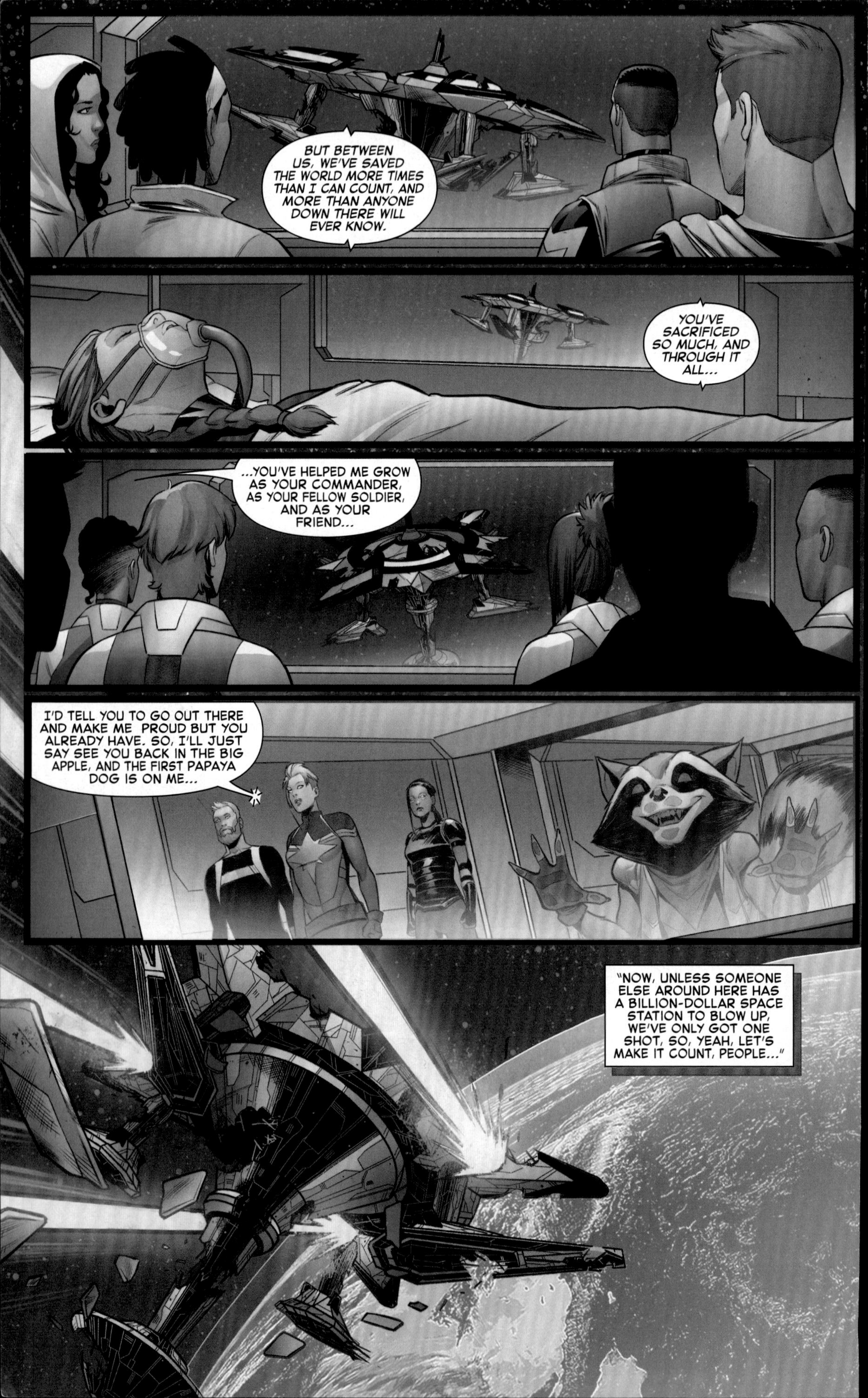
BUT BETWEEN US, WE'VE SAVED THE WORLD MORE TIMES THAN I CAN COUNT, AND MORE THAN ANYONE DOWN THERE WILL EVER KNOW.
YOU'VE SACRIFICED SO MUCH, AND THROUGH IT ALL...
...YOU'VE HELPED ME GROW AS YOUR COMMANDER, AS YOUR FELLOW SOLDIER, AND AS YOUR FRIEND...
I'D TELL YOU TO GO OUT THERE AND MAKE ME PROUD BUT YOU ALREADY HAVE. SO, I'LL JUST SAY SEE YOU BACK IN THE BIG APPLE, AND THE FIRST PAPAYA DOG IS ON ME...
"NOW, UNLESS SOMEONE ELSE AROUND HERE HAS A BILLION-DOLLAR SPACE STATION TO BLOW UP, WE'VE ONLY GOT ONE SHOT, SO, YEAH, LET'S MAKE IT COUNT, PEOPLE..."

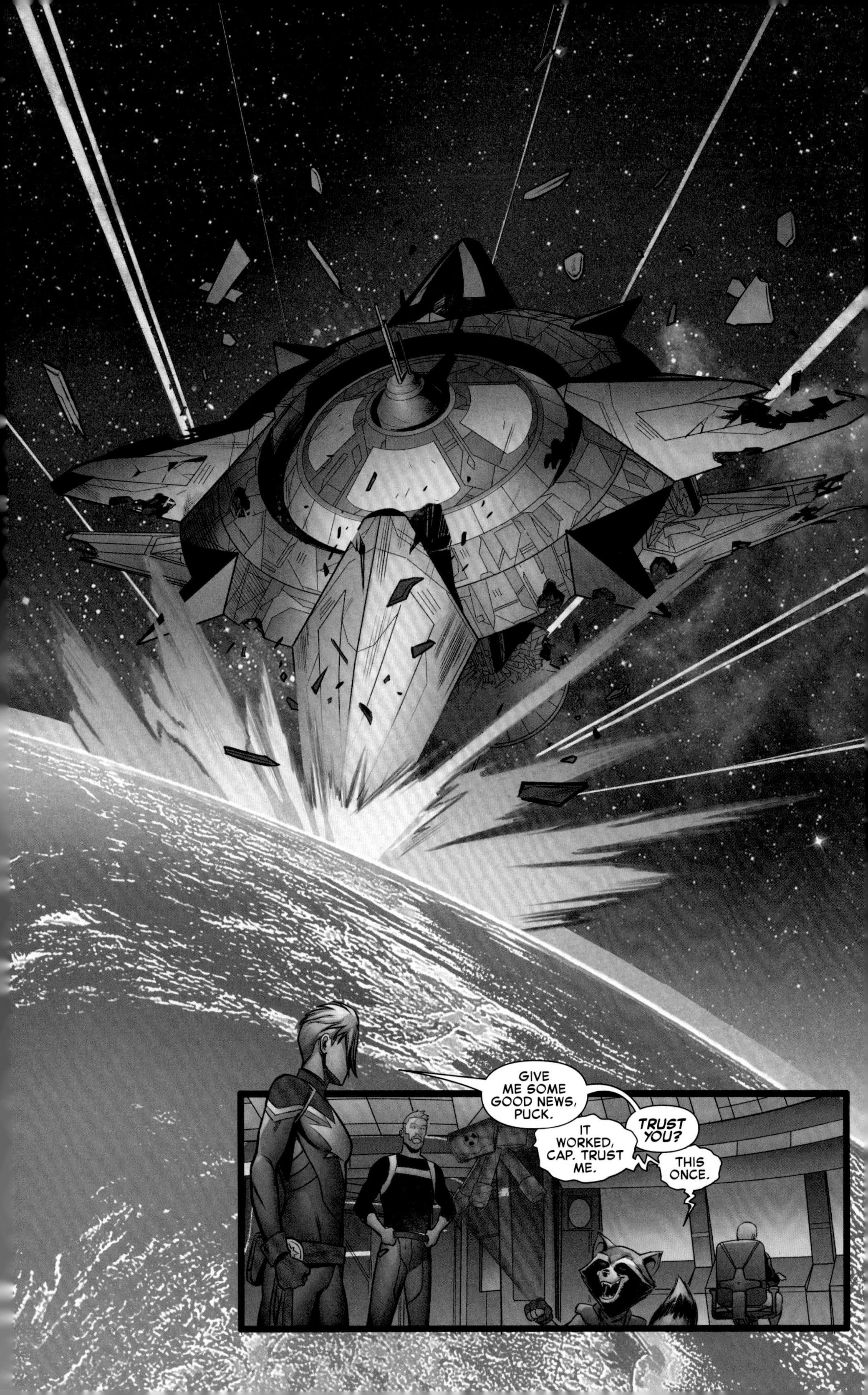
GIVE ME SOME GOOD NEWS, PUCK.
IT WORKED, CAP. TRUST ME.
TRUST YOU?
THIS ONCE.

I MEAN, THOSE CHARGES HAD ENOUGH JUICE TO DESTROY HALF A PLANET.

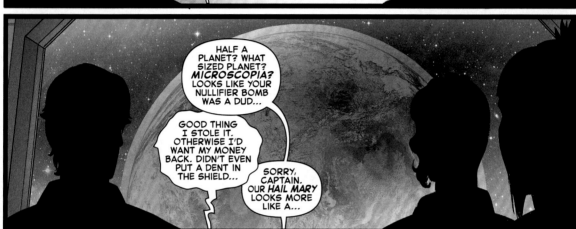

HALF A PLANET? WHAT SIZED PLANET? *MICROSCOPIA?* LOOKS LIKE YOUR NULLIFIER BOMB WAS A DUD...

GOOD THING I STOLE IT. OTHERWISE I'D WANT MY MONEY BACK. DIDN'T EVEN PUT A DENT IN THE SHIELD...

SORRY, CAPTAIN. OUR *HAIL MARY* LOOKS MORE LIKE A...

...A HELL NARY?

A HELLO LARRY?

A HELL NO?

A *HARD PASS?*

YOU WAITED UNTIL *NOW* TO TRY TO MAKE A JOKE, LIEUTENANT?

DESPAIR MAKES ME FUNNY.

THAT WAS FUNNY?

IT'S DESPAIR.

AWAITING FURTHER ORDERS, CAPTAIN.

ORDERS? THAT WAS OUR LAST HOPE. THERE'S ONLY ONE THING LEFT TO DO...

I'M SORRY, WENDY...

AMERICA--THOSE OTHER DIMENSIONS YOU WERE TALKING ABOUT. WE SHOULD TALK EVACUATION...

EXCUSE ME, MA'AM? BEFORE YOU DO THAT...

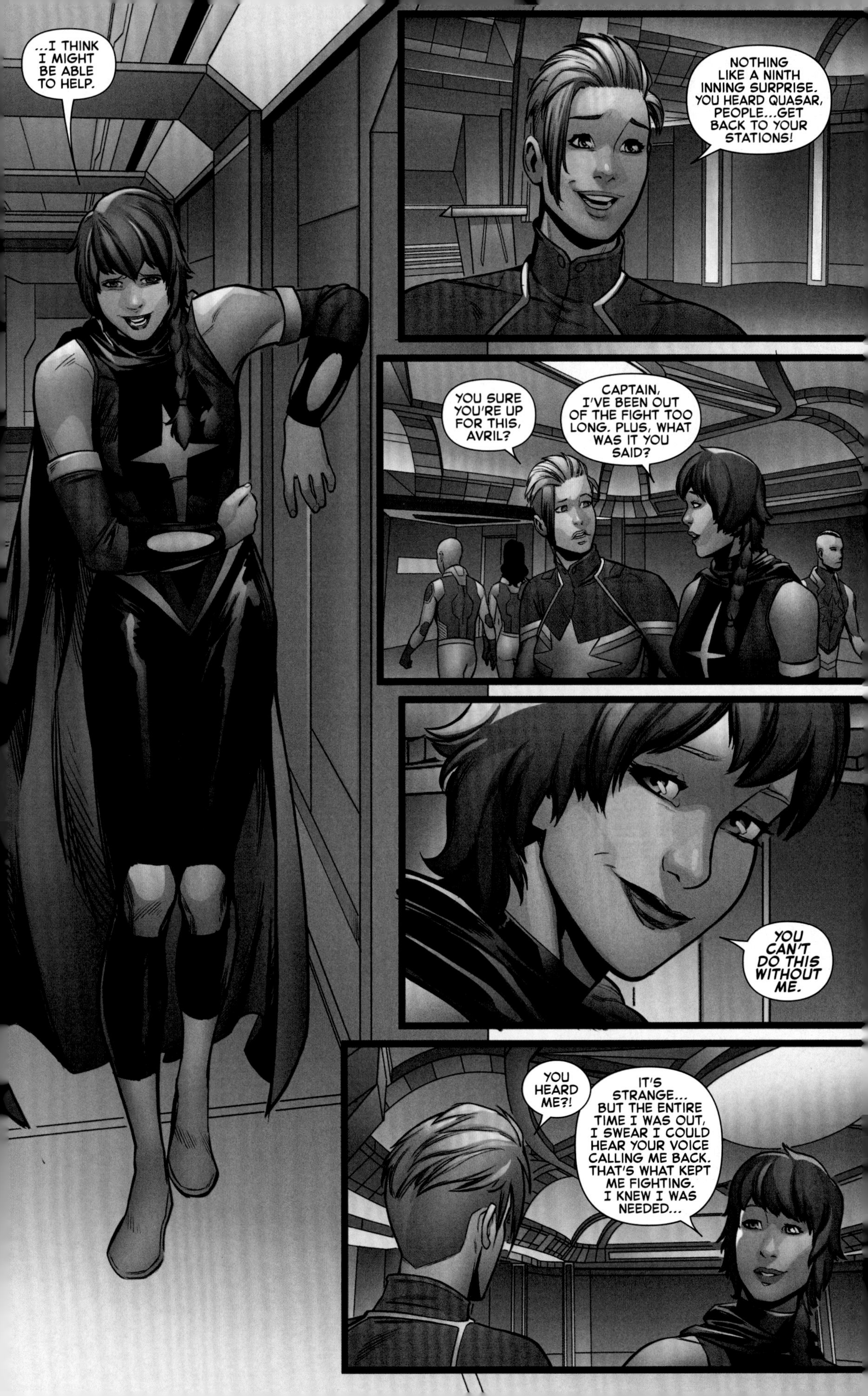
...I THINK I MIGHT BE ABLE TO HELP.
NOTHING LIKE A NINTH INNING SURPRISE. YOU HEARD QUASAR, PEOPLE...GET BACK TO YOUR STATIONS!
YOU SURE YOU'RE UP FOR THIS, AVRIL?
CAPTAIN, I'VE BEEN OUT OF THE FIGHT TOO LONG. PLUS, WHAT WAS IT YOU SAID?
YOU CAN'T DO THIS WITHOUT ME.
IT'S STRANGE... BUT THE ENTIRE TIME I WAS OUT, I SWEAR I COULD HEAR YOUR VOICE CALLING ME BACK. THAT'S WHAT KEPT ME FIGHTING. I KNEW I WAS NEEDED...
YOU HEARD ME?!

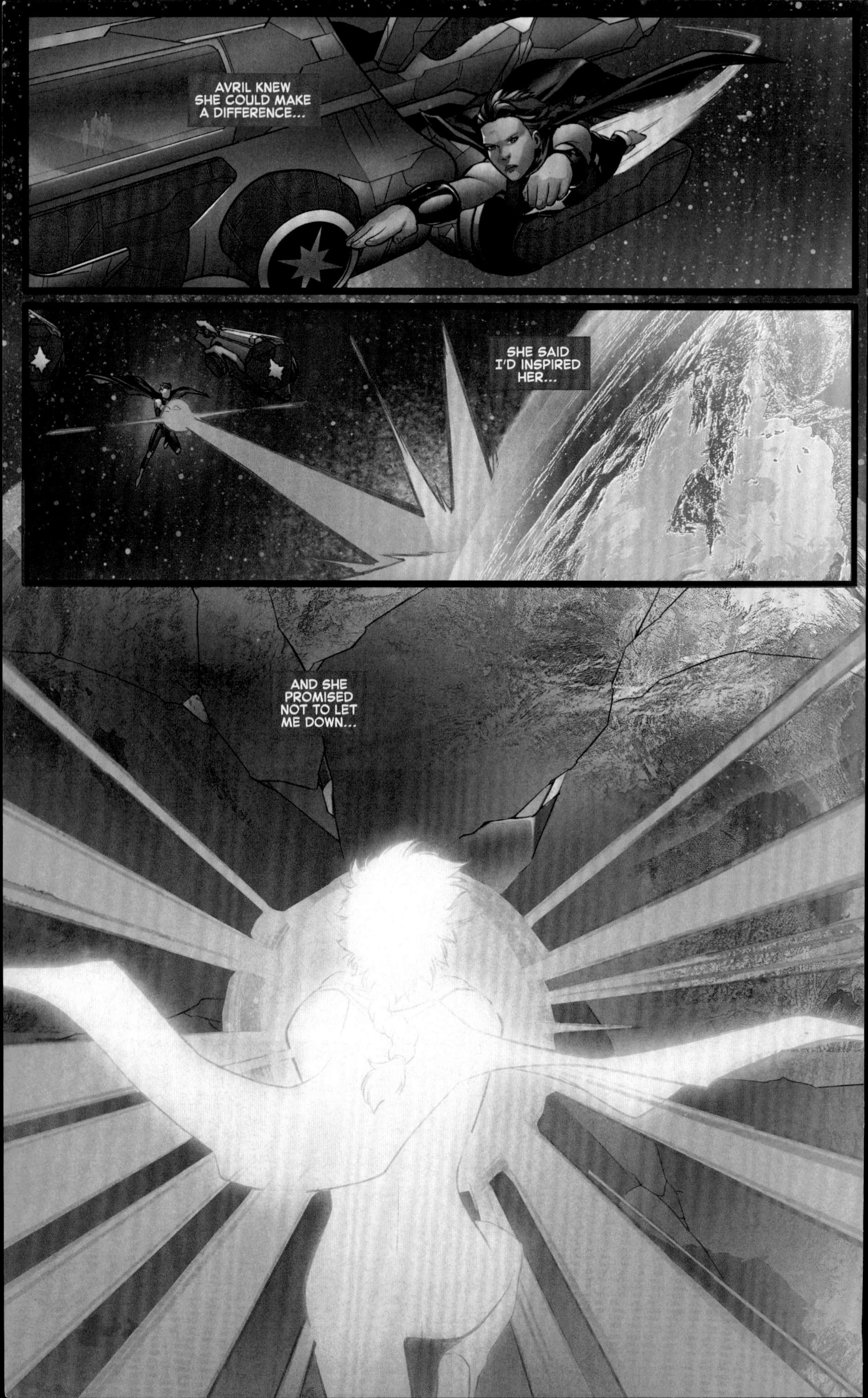
AVRIL KNEW SHE COULD MAKE A DIFFERENCE...
SHE SAID I'D INSPIRED HER...
AND SHE PROMISED NOT TO LET ME DOWN...

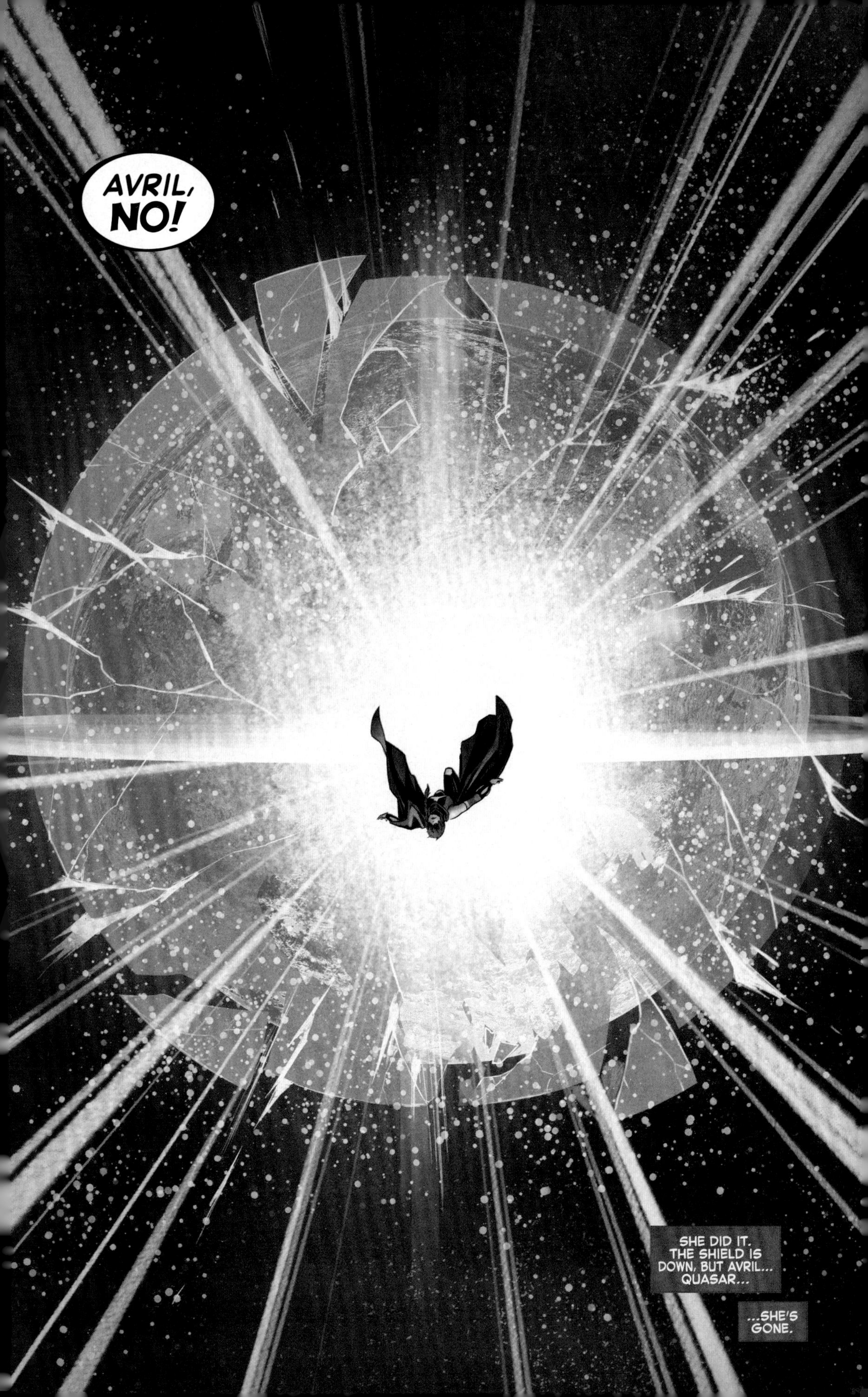
AVRIL, NO!
SHE DID IT. THE SHIELD IS DOWN, BUT AVRIL... QUASAR...
...SHE'S GONE.

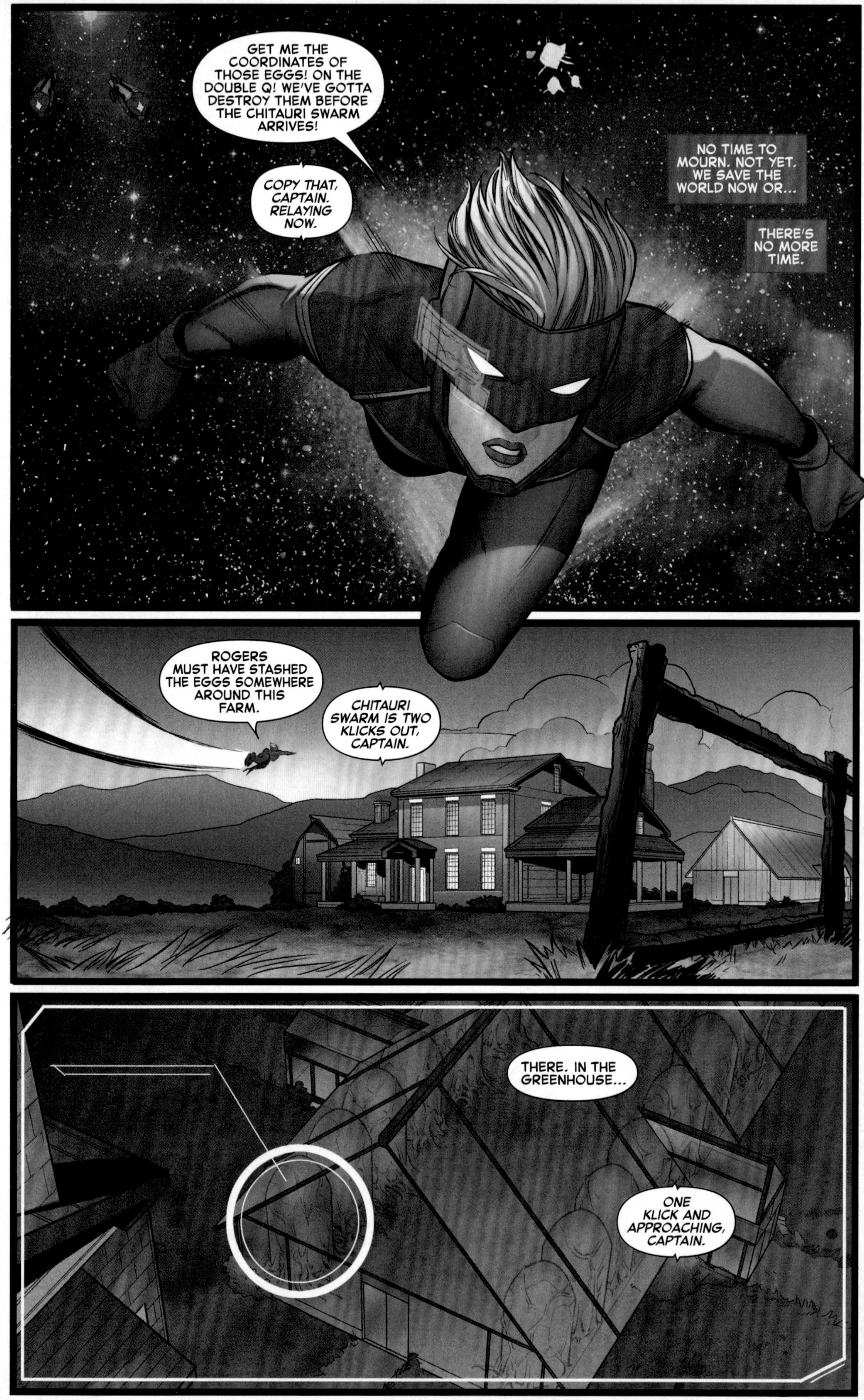
GET ME THE COORDINATES OF THOSE EGGS! ON THE DOUBLE Q! WE'VE GOTTA DESTROY THEM BEFORE THE CHITAURI SWARM ARRIVES!
COPY THAT, CAPTAIN. RELAYING NOW.
NO TIME TO MOURN. NOT YET. WE SAVE THE WORLD NOW OR...
THERE'S NO MORE TIME.
ROGERS MUST HAVE STASHED THE EGGS SOMEWHERE AROUND THIS FARM.
CHITAURI SWARM IS TWO KLICKS OUT, CAPTAIN.
THERE. IN THE GREENHOUSE...
ONE KLICK AND APPROACHING, CAPTAIN.

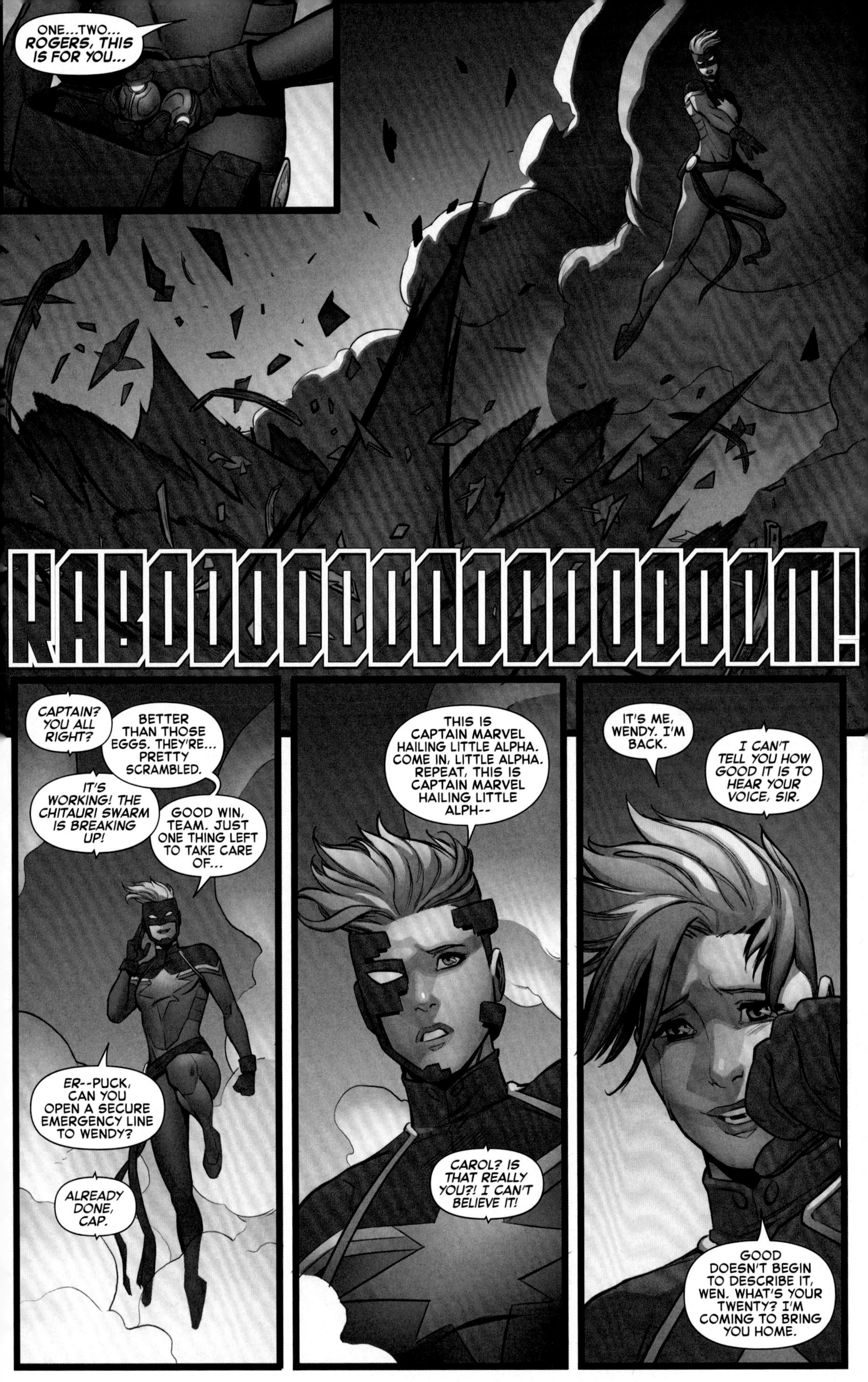
ONE...TWO... ROGERS, THIS IS FOR YOU...
KABOOOOOOOOOOOOOOOM!
CAPTAIN? YOU ALL RIGHT?
BETTER THAN THOSE EGGS. THEY'RE... PRETTY SCRAMBLED.
IT'S WORKING! THE CHITAURI SWARM IS BREAKING UP!
GOOD WIN, TEAM. JUST ONE THING LEFT TO TAKE CARE OF...
ER--PUCK, CAN YOU OPEN A SECURE EMERGENCY LINE TO WENDY?
ALREADY DONE, CAP.
THIS IS CAPTAIN MARVEL HAILING LITTLE ALPHA. COME IN, LITTLE ALPHA. REPEAT, THIS IS CAPTAIN MARVEL HAILING LITTLE ALPH--
CAROL? IS THAT REALLY YOU?! I CAN'T BELIEVE IT!
IT'S ME, WENDY. I'M BACK.
I CAN'T TELL YOU HOW GOOD IT IS TO HEAR YOUR VOICE, SIR.
GOOD DOESN'T BEGIN TO DESCRIBE IT, WEN. WHAT'S YOUR TWENTY? I'M COMING TO BRING YOU HOME.

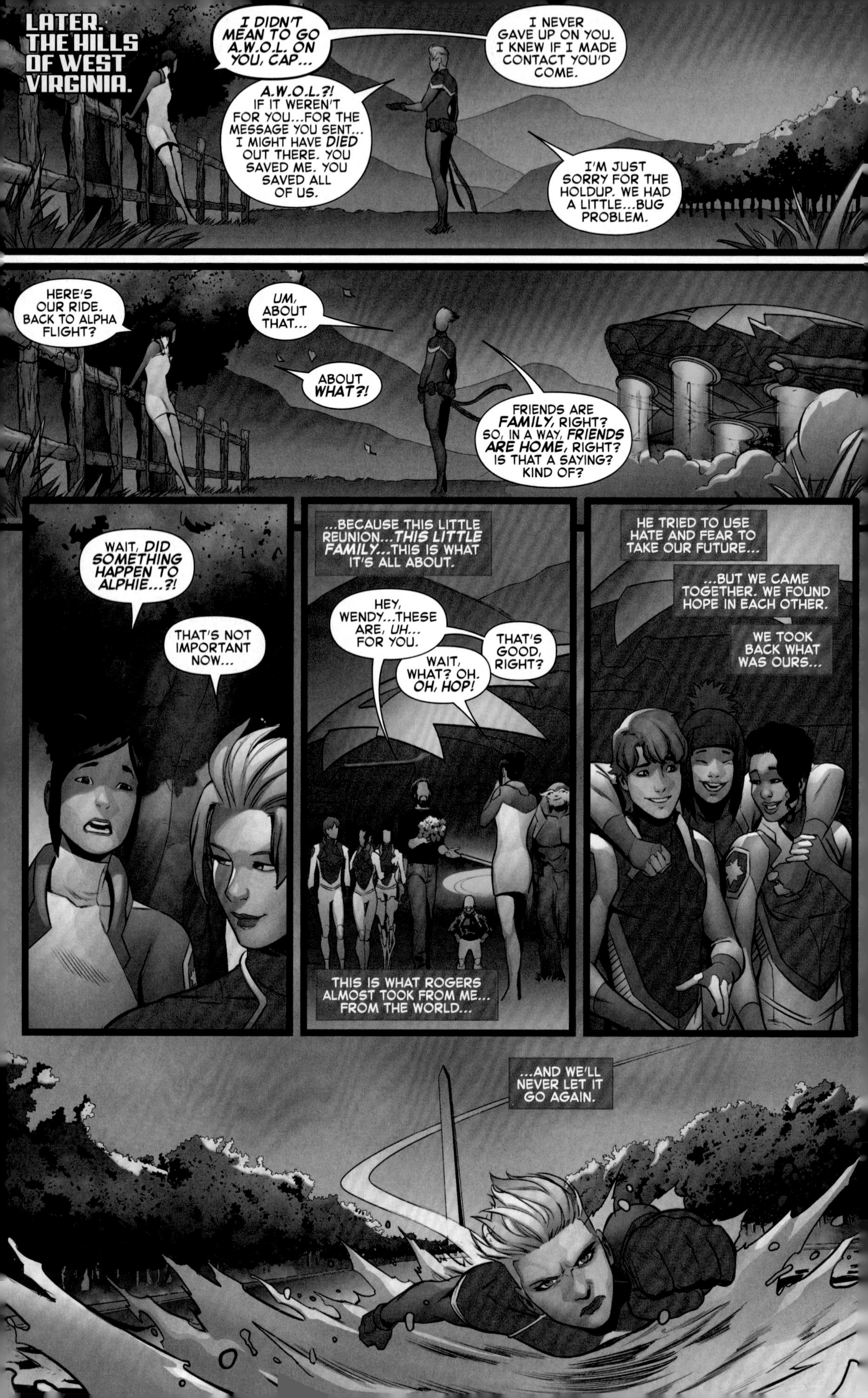
LATER. THE HILLS OF WEST VIRGINIA.
I DIDN'T MEAN TO GO A.W.O.L. ON YOU, CAP...
A.W.O.L.?! IF IT WEREN'T FOR YOU...FOR THE MESSAGE YOU SENT... I MIGHT HAVE DIED OUT THERE. YOU SAVED ME. YOU SAVED ALL OF US.
I NEVER GAVE UP ON YOU. I KNEW IF I MADE CONTACT YOU'D COME.
I'M JUST SORRY FOR THE HOLDUP. WE HAD A LITTLE...BUG PROBLEM.
HERE'S OUR RIDE. BACK TO ALPHA FLIGHT?
UM, ABOUT THAT...
ABOUT WHAT?!
FRIENDS ARE FAMILY, RIGHT? SO, IN A WAY, FRIENDS ARE HOME, RIGHT? IS THAT A SAYING? KIND OF?
WAIT, DID SOMETHING HAPPEN TO ALPHIE...?!
THAT'S NOT IMPORTANT NOW...
...BECAUSE THIS LITTLE REUNION...THIS LITTLE FAMILY...THIS IS WHAT IT'S ALL ABOUT.
HEY, WENDY...THESE ARE, UH... FOR YOU.
THAT'S GOOD, RIGHT?
WAIT, WHAT? OH. OH, HOP!
THIS IS WHAT ROGERS ALMOST TOOK FROM ME... FROM THE WORLD...
HE TRIED TO USE HATE AND FEAR TO TAKE OUR FUTURE...
...BUT WE CAME TOGETHER. WE FOUND HOPE IN EACH OTHER.
WE TOOK BACK WHAT WAS OURS...
...AND WE'LL NEVER LET IT GO AGAIN.

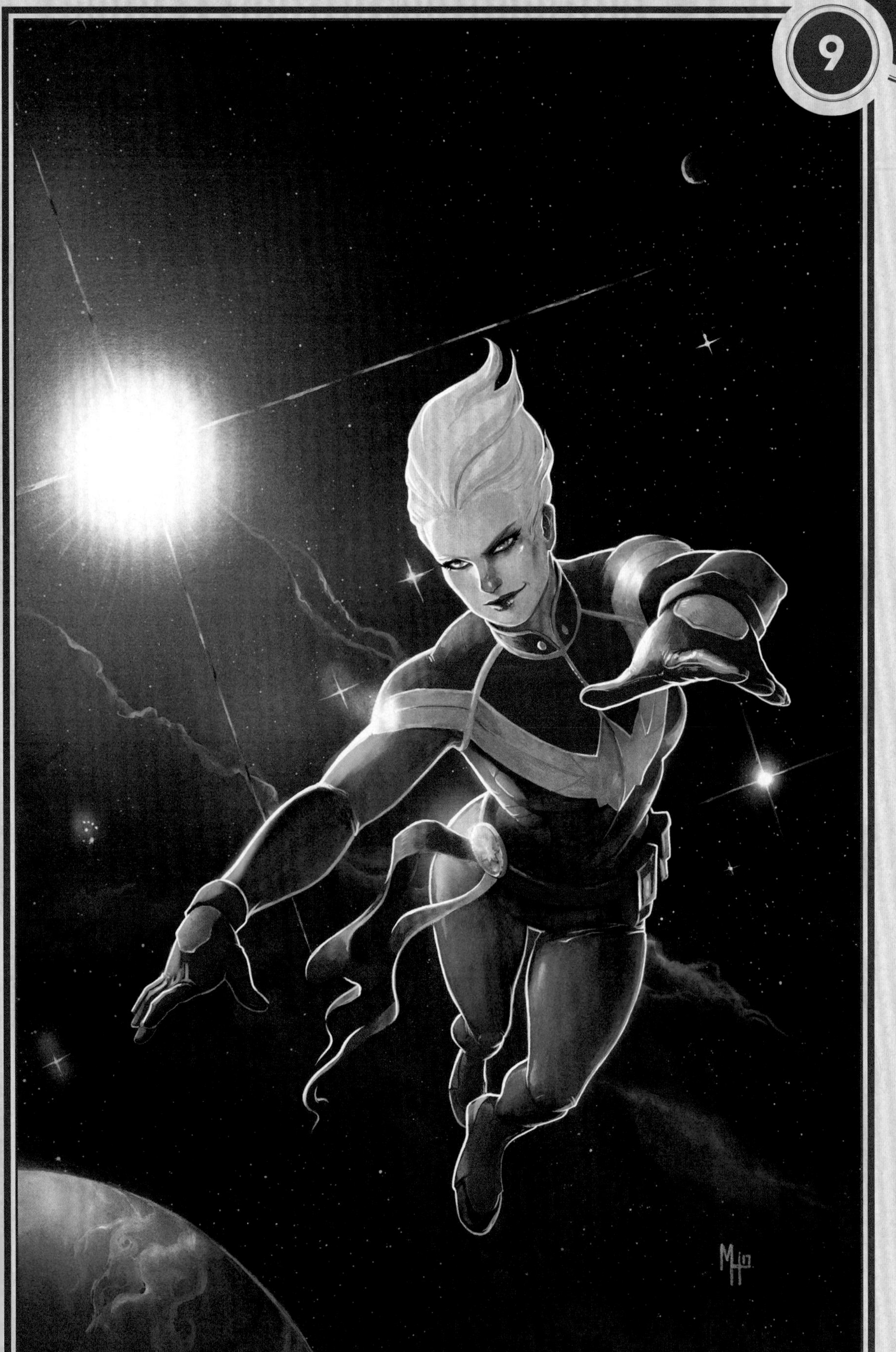
9

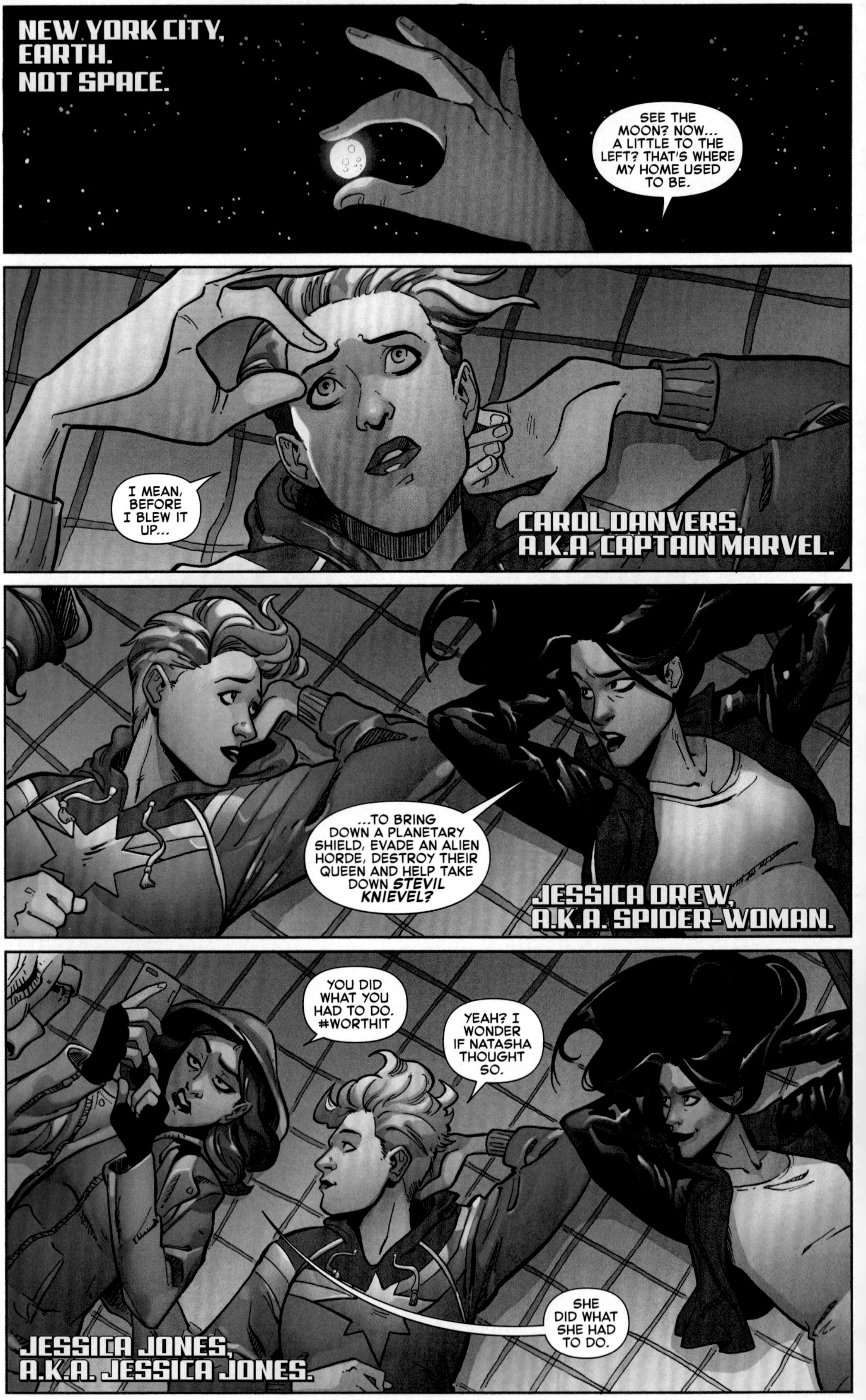
NEW YORK CITY, EARTH. NOT SPACE.
SEE THE MOON? NOW... A LITTLE TO THE LEFT? THAT'S WHERE MY HOME USED TO BE.
I MEAN, BEFORE I BLEW IT UP...
CAROL DANVERS, A.K.A. CAPTAIN MARVEL.
...TO BRING DOWN A PLANETARY SHIELD, EVADE AN ALIEN HORDE, DESTROY THEIR QUEEN AND HELP TAKE DOWN STEVIL KNIEVEL?
JESSICA DREW, A.K.A. SPIDER-WOMAN.
YOU DID WHAT YOU HAD TO DO. #WORTHIT
YEAH? I WONDER IF NATASHA THOUGHT SO.
SHE DID WHAT SHE HAD TO DO.
JESSICA JONES, A.K.A. JESSICA JONES.

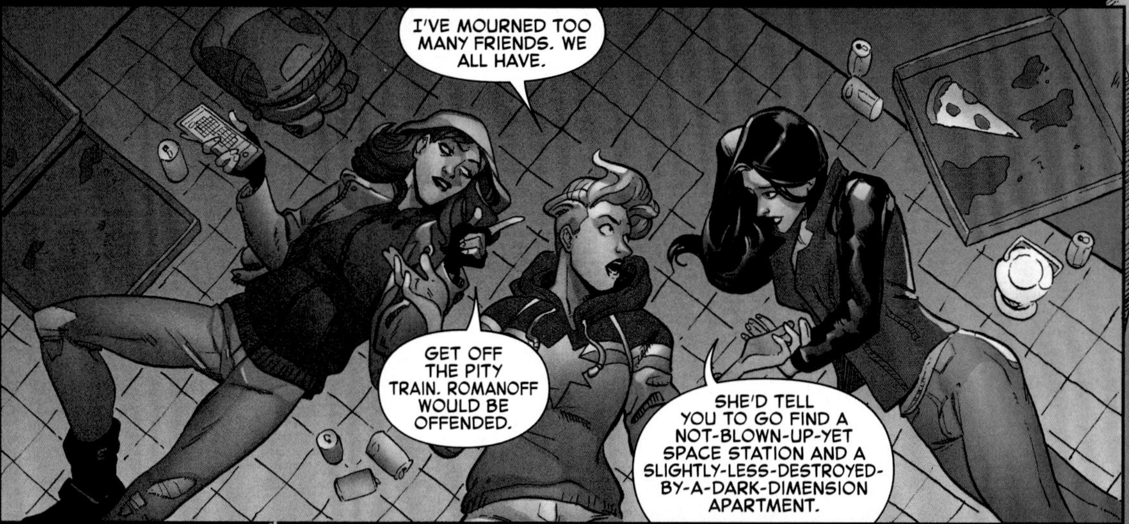
I'VE MOURNED TOO MANY FRIENDS. WE ALL HAVE.
GET OFF THE PITY TRAIN. ROMANOFF WOULD BE OFFENDED.
SHE'D TELL YOU TO GO FIND A NOT-BLOWN-UP-YET SPACE STATION AND A SLIGHTLY-LESS-DESTROYED-BY-A-DARK-DIMENSION APARTMENT.
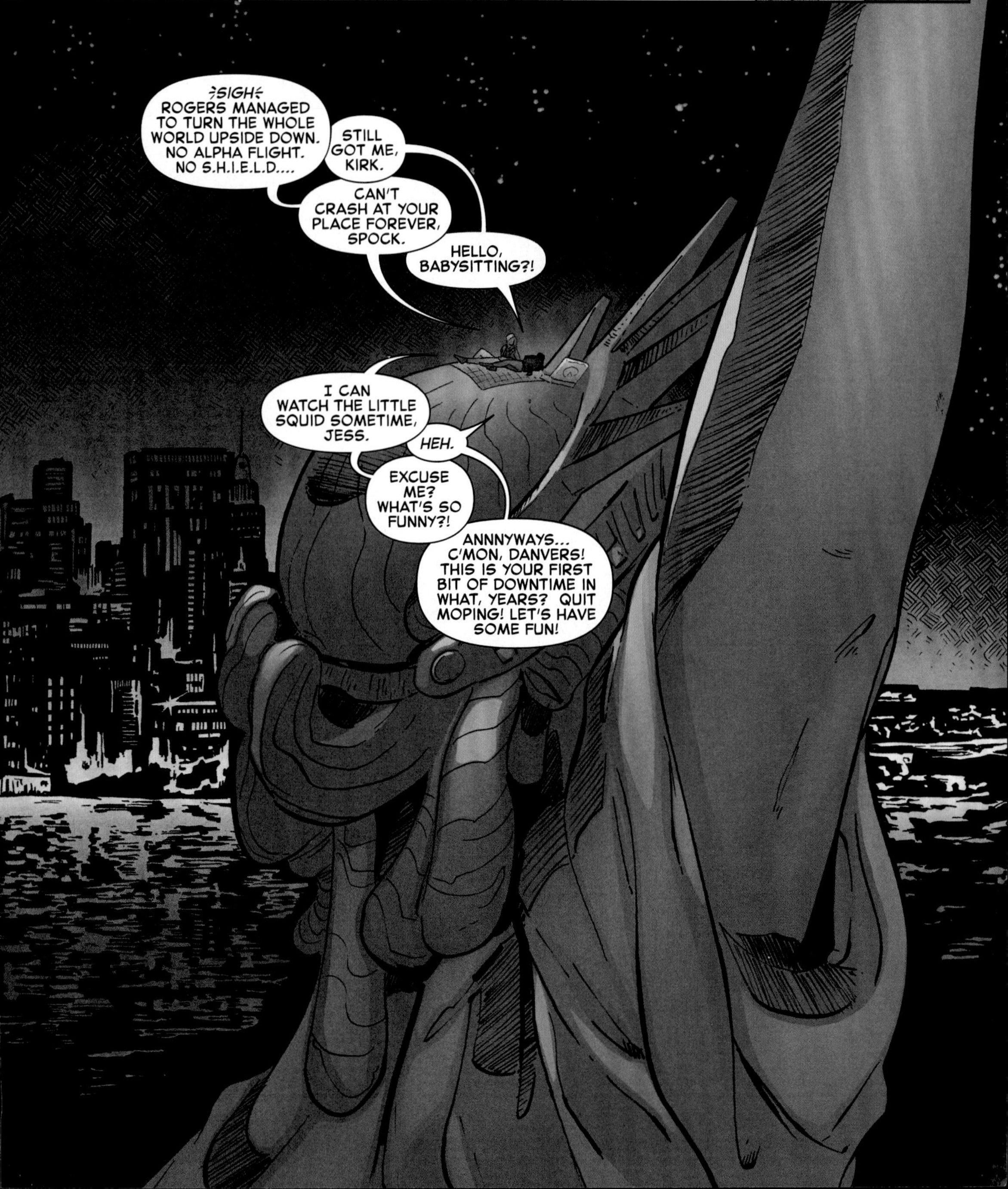
SIGH ROGERS MANAGED TO TURN THE WHOLE WORLD UPSIDE DOWN. NO ALPHA FLIGHT. NO S.H.I.E.L.D....
STILL GOT ME, KIRK.
CAN'T CRASH AT YOUR PLACE FOREVER, SPOCK.
HELLO, BABYSITTING?!
I CAN WATCH THE LITTLE SQUID SOMETIME, JESS.
HEH.
EXCUSE ME? WHAT'S SO FUNNY?!
ANNNYWAYS... C'MON, DANVERS! THIS IS YOUR FIRST BIT OF DOWNTIME IN WHAT, YEARS? QUIT MOPING! LET'S HAVE SOME FUN!

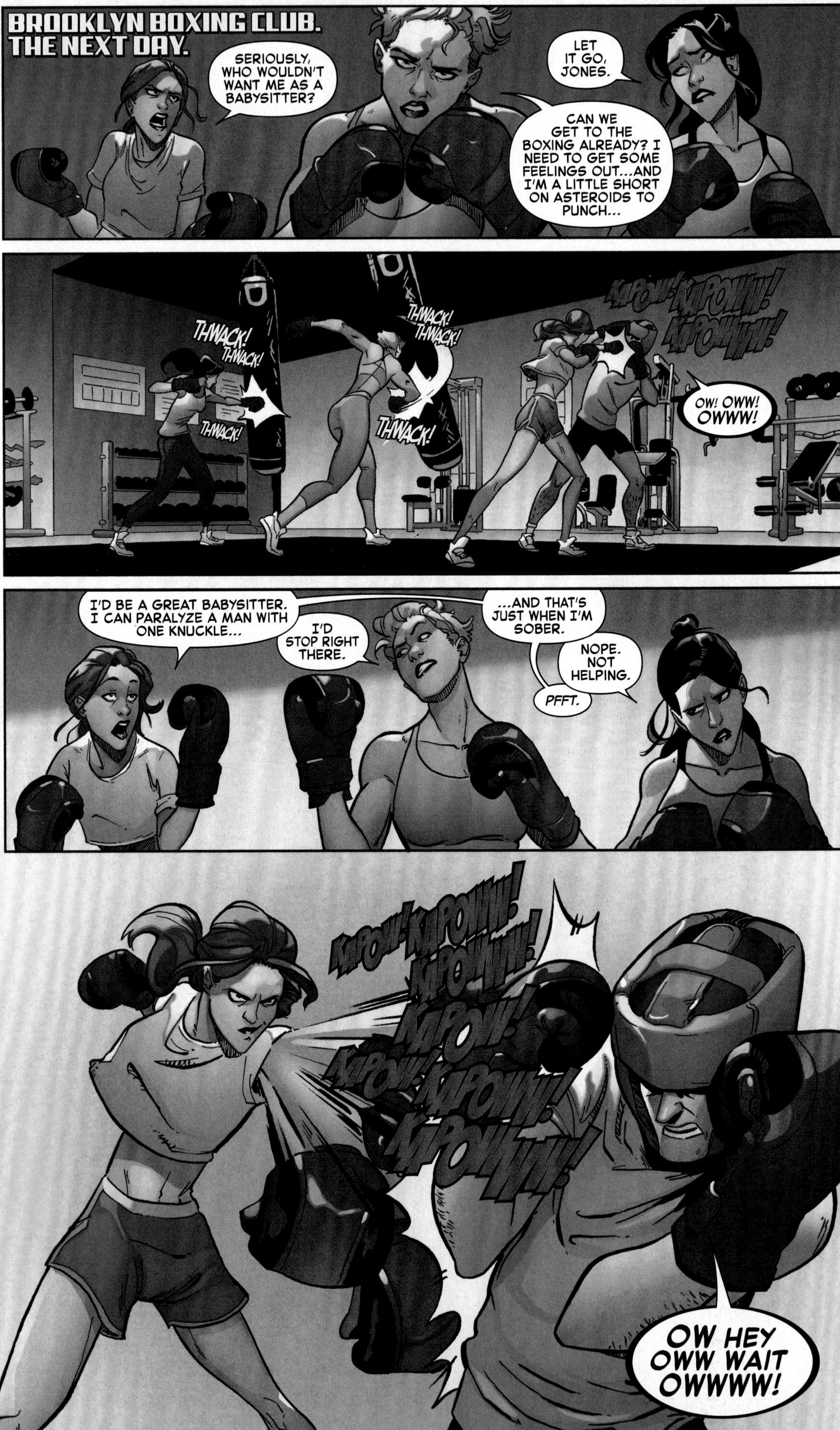
BROOKLYN BOXING CLUB. THE NEXT DAY.
SERIOUSLY, WHO WOULDN'T WANT ME AS A BABYSITTER?
LET IT GO, JONES.
CAN WE GET TO THE BOXING ALREADY? I NEED TO GET SOME FEELINGS OUT...AND I'M A LITTLE SHORT ON ASTEROIDS TO PUNCH...
THWACK! THWACK!
THWACK!
THWACK! THWACK!
THWACK!
KAPOW! KAPOWW! KAPOWWW!
OW! OWW! OWWW!
I'D BE A GREAT BABYSITTER. I CAN PARALYZE A MAN WITH ONE KNUCKLE...
I'D STOP RIGHT THERE.
...AND THAT'S JUST WHEN I'M SOBER.
NOPE. NOT HELPING.
PFFT.
KAPOW! KAPOWW! KAPOWWW!
KAPOW!
KAPOW! KAPOWW!
KAPOWWW!
OW HEY OWW WAIT OWWWW!

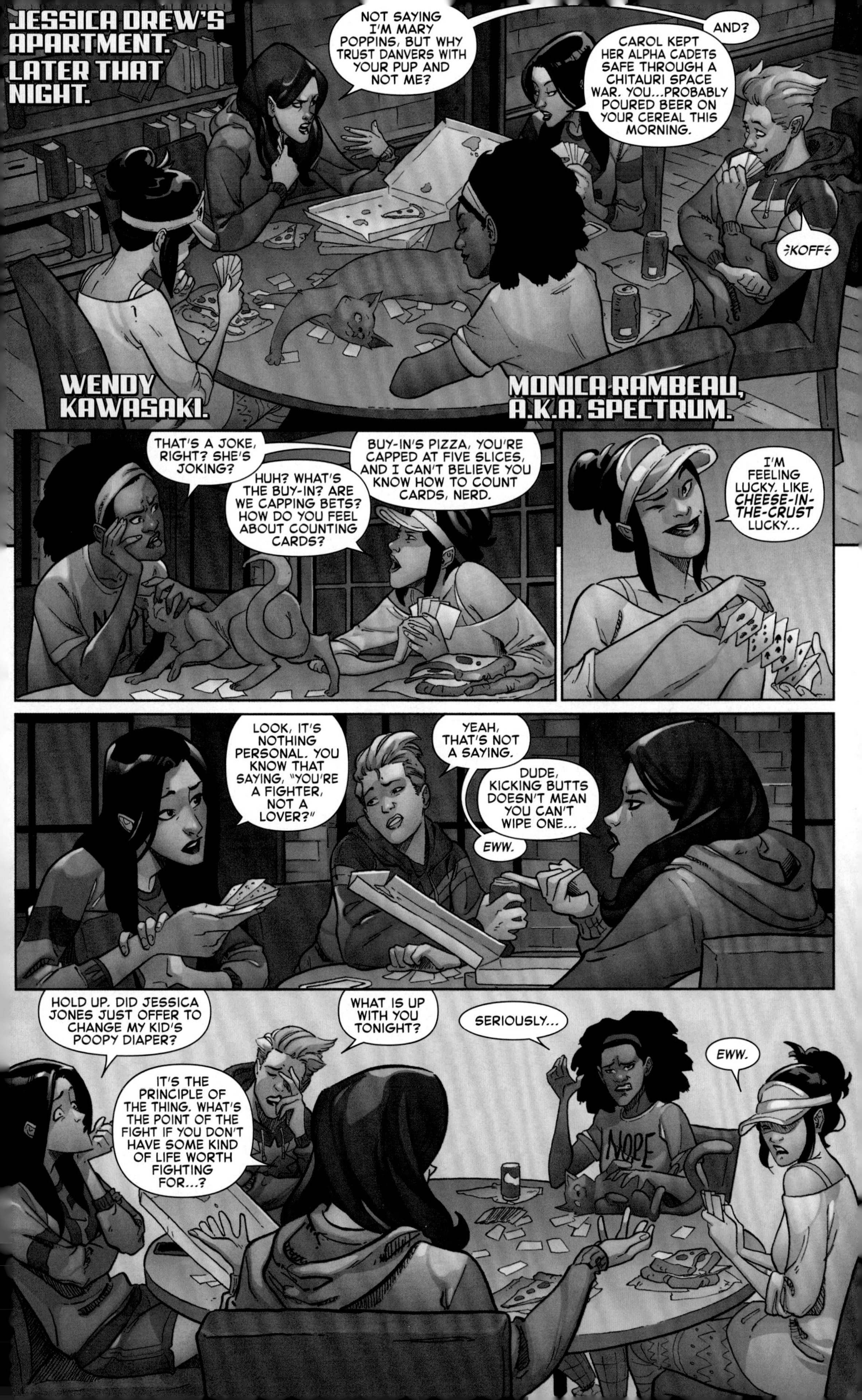
JESSICA DREW'S APARTMENT. LATER THAT NIGHT.
NOT SAYING I'M MARY POPPINS, BUT WHY TRUST DANVERS WITH YOUR PUP AND NOT ME?
AND?
CAROL KEPT HER ALPHA CADETS SAFE THROUGH A CHITAURI SPACE WAR. YOU...PROBABLY POURED BEER ON YOUR CEREAL THIS MORNING.
KOFF
WENDY KAWASAKI.
MONICA RAMBEAU, A.K.A. SPECTRUM.
THAT'S A JOKE, RIGHT? SHE'S JOKING?
HUH? WHAT'S THE BUY-IN? ARE WE CAPPING BETS? HOW DO YOU FEEL ABOUT COUNTING CARDS?
BUY-IN'S PIZZA, YOU'RE CAPPED AT FIVE SLICES, AND I CAN'T BELIEVE YOU KNOW HOW TO COUNT CARDS, NERD.
I'M FEELING LUCKY. LIKE, CHEESE-IN-THE-CRUST LUCKY...
LOOK, IT'S NOTHING PERSONAL. YOU KNOW THAT SAYING, "YOU'RE A FIGHTER, NOT A LOVER?"
YEAH, THAT'S NOT A SAYING.
DUDE, KICKING BUTTS DOESN'T MEAN YOU CAN'T WIPE ONE...
EWW.
HOLD UP. DID JESSICA JONES JUST OFFER TO CHANGE MY KID'S POOPY DIAPER?
IT'S THE PRINCIPLE OF THE THING. WHAT'S THE POINT OF THE FIGHT IF YOU DON'T HAVE SOME KIND OF LIFE WORTH FIGHTING FOR...?
WHAT IS UP WITH YOU TONIGHT?
SERIOUSLY...
EWW.
NOPE

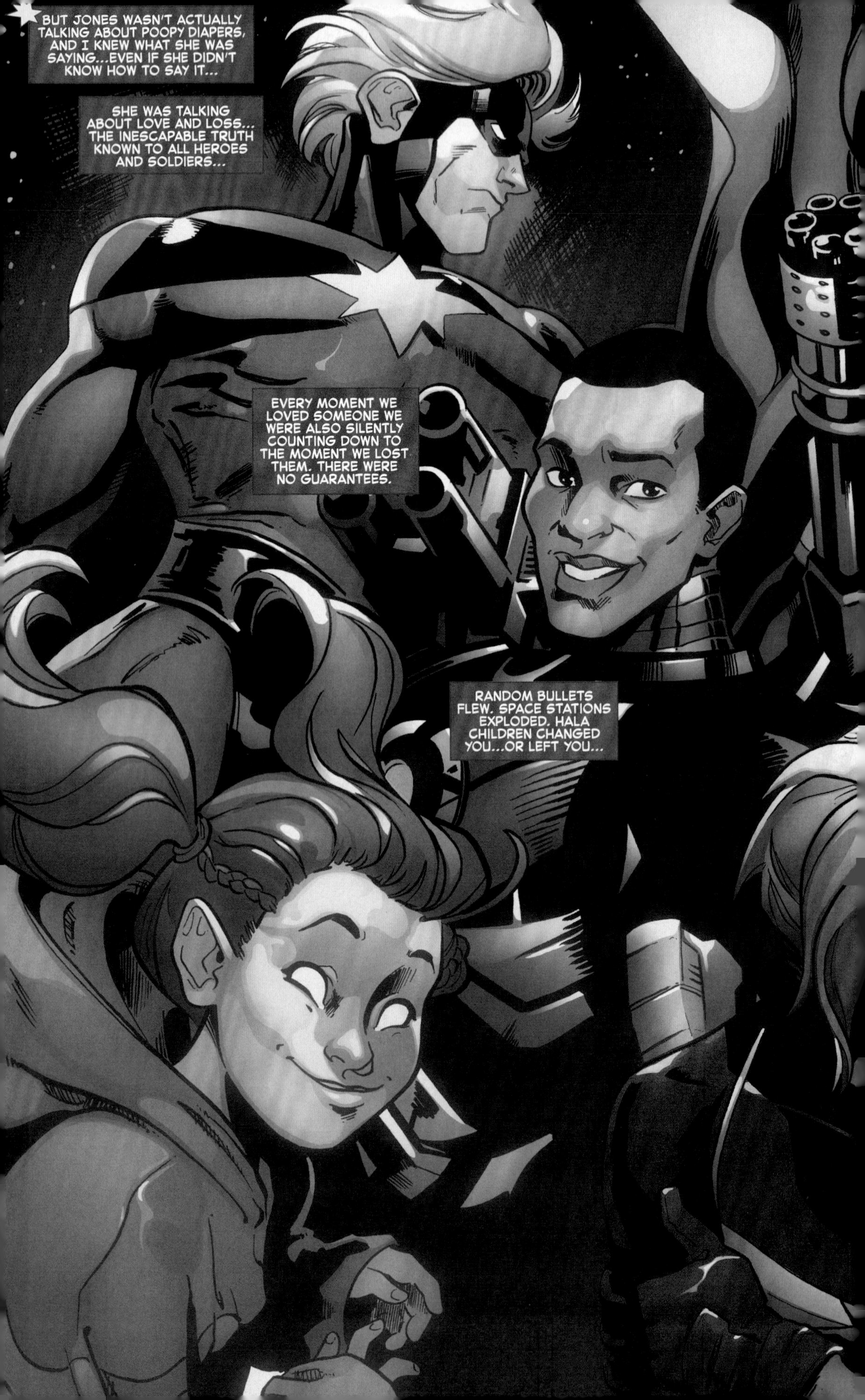
BUT JONES WASN'T ACTUALLY TALKING ABOUT POOPY DIAPERS, AND I KNEW WHAT SHE WAS SAYING...EVEN IF SHE DIDN'T KNOW HOW TO SAY IT...
SHE WAS TALKING ABOUT LOVE AND LOSS... THE INESCAPABLE TRUTH KNOWN TO ALL HEROES AND SOLDIERS...
EVERY MOMENT WE LOVED SOMEONE WE WERE ALSO SILENTLY COUNTING DOWN TO THE MOMENT WE LOST THEM. THERE WERE NO GUARANTEES.
RANDOM BULLETS FLEW. SPACE STATIONS EXPLODED. HALA CHILDREN CHANGED YOU...OR LEFT YOU...

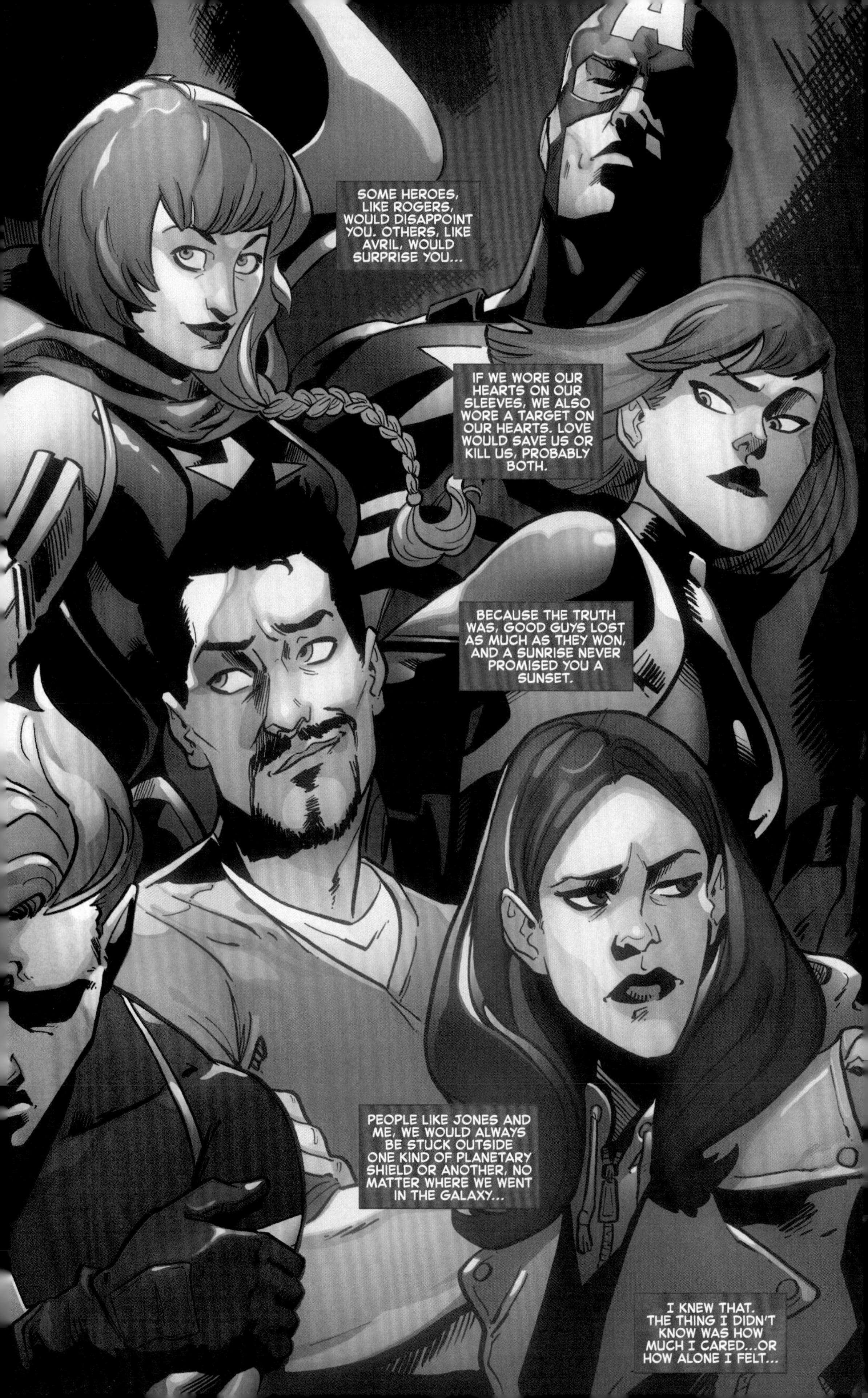
SOME HEROES, LIKE ROGERS, WOULD DISAPPOINT YOU. OTHERS, LIKE AVRIL, WOULD SURPRISE YOU...
IF WE WORE OUR HEARTS ON OUR SLEEVES, WE ALSO WORE A TARGET ON OUR HEARTS. LOVE WOULD SAVE US OR KILL US, PROBABLY BOTH.
BECAUSE THE TRUTH WAS, GOOD GUYS LOST AS MUCH AS THEY WON, AND A SUNRISE NEVER PROMISED YOU A SUNSET.
PEOPLE LIKE JONES AND ME, WE WOULD ALWAYS BE STUCK OUTSIDE ONE KIND OF PLANETARY SHIELD OR ANOTHER, NO MATTER WHERE WE WENT IN THE GALAXY...
I KNEW THAT. THE THING I DIDN'T KNOW WAS HOW MUCH I CARED...OR HOW ALONE I FELT...

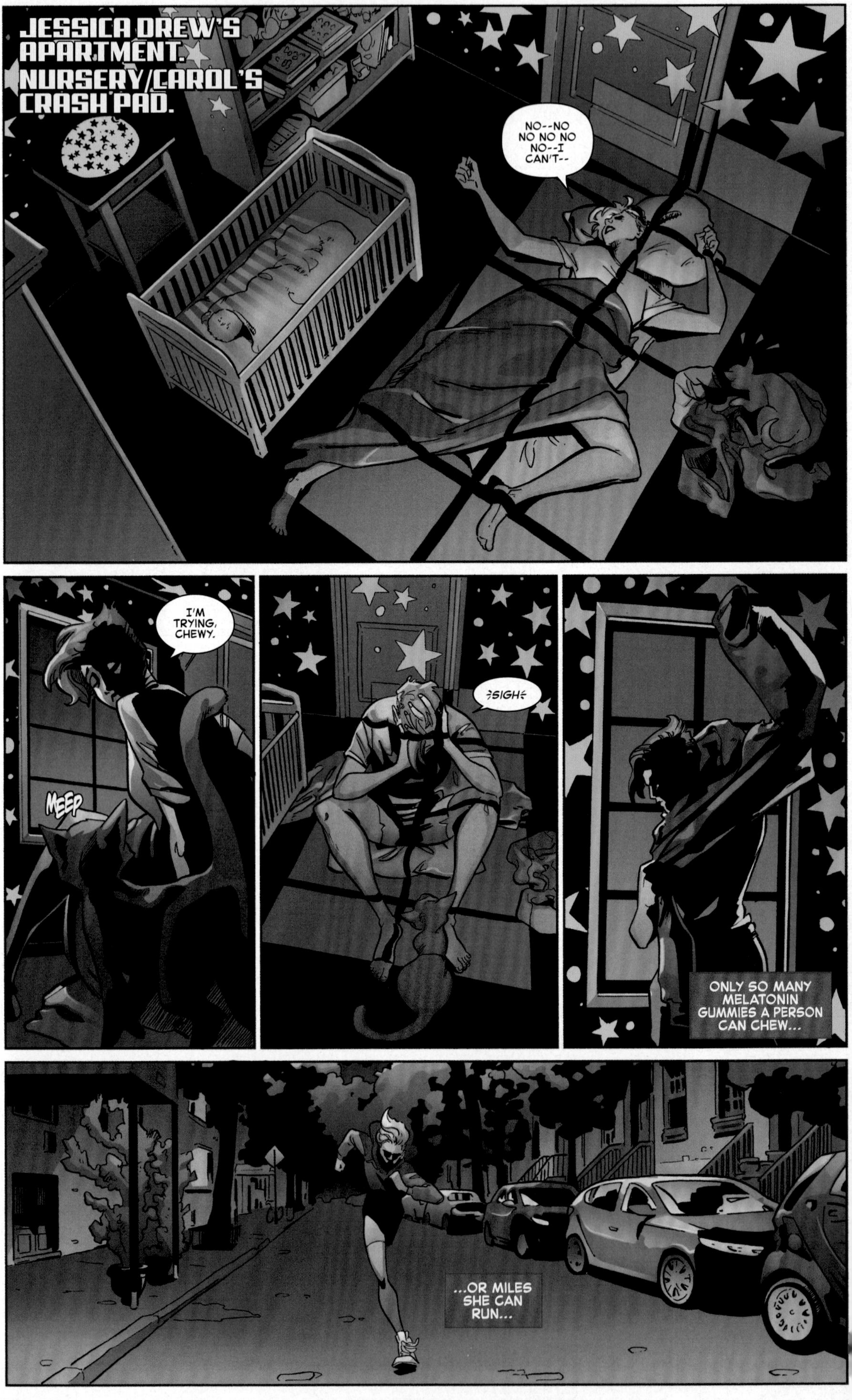
JESSICA DREW'S APARTMENT. NURSERY/CAROL'S CRASH PAD.
NO--NO NO NO NO NO--I CAN'T--
I'M TRYING, CHEWY.
MEEP
⇢SIGH⇠
ONLY SO MANY MELATONIN GUMMIES A PERSON CAN CHEW...
...OR MILES SHE CAN RUN...

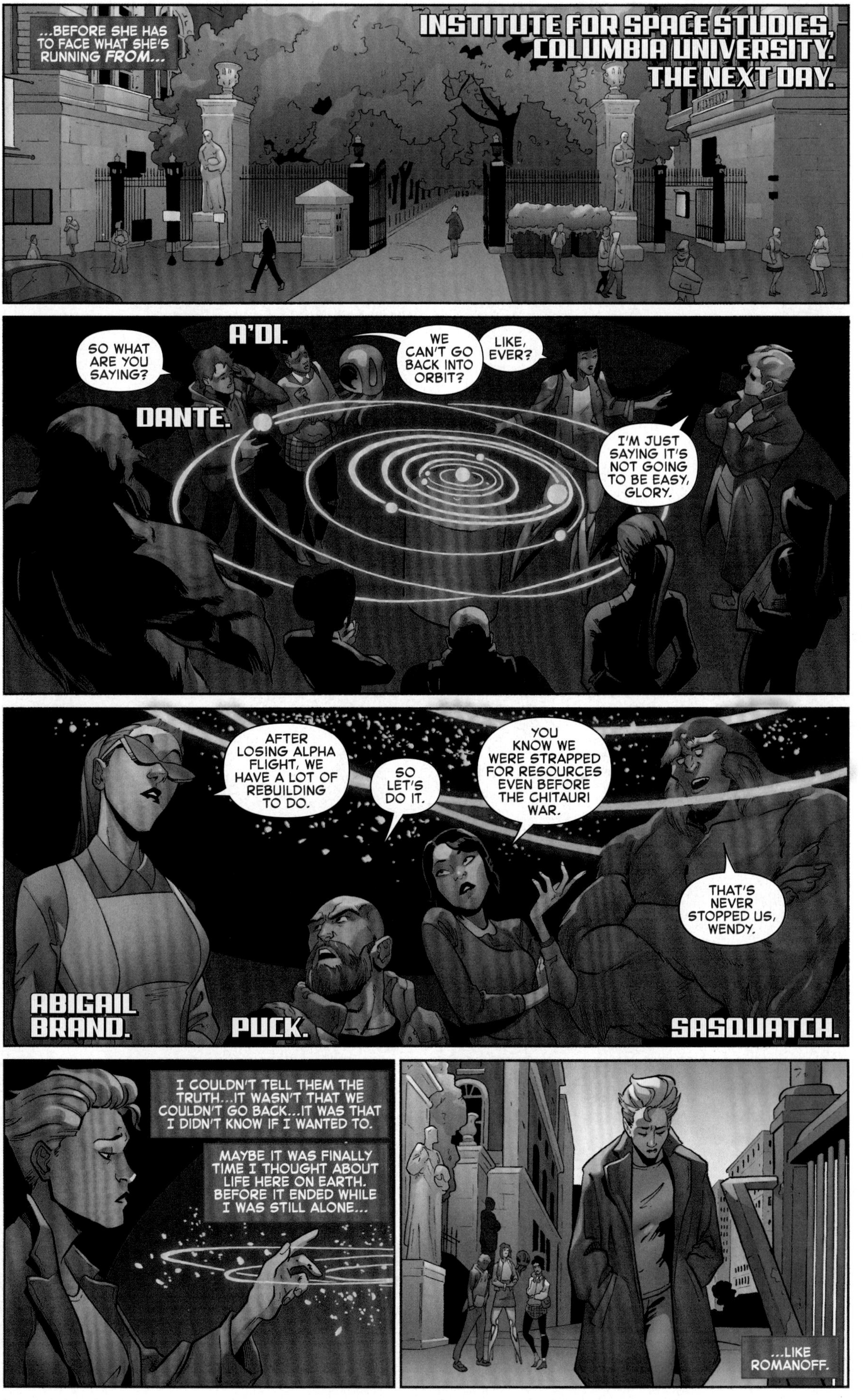
...BEFORE SHE HAS TO FACE WHAT SHE'S RUNNING FROM...
INSTITUTE FOR SPACE STUDIES, COLUMBIA UNIVERSITY. THE NEXT DAY.
A'DI.
DANTE.
SO WHAT ARE YOU SAYING?
WE CAN'T GO BACK INTO ORBIT?
LIKE, EVER?
I'M JUST SAYING IT'S NOT GOING TO BE EASY, GLORY.
ABIGAIL BRAND.
PUCK.
SASQUATCH.
AFTER LOSING ALPHA FLIGHT, WE HAVE A LOT OF REBUILDING TO DO.
SO LET'S DO IT.
YOU KNOW WE WERE STRAPPED FOR RESOURCES EVEN BEFORE THE CHITAURI WAR.
THAT'S NEVER STOPPED US, WENDY.
I COULDN'T TELL THEM THE TRUTH...IT WASN'T THAT WE COULDN'T GO BACK...IT WAS THAT I DIDN'T KNOW IF I WANTED TO.
MAYBE IT WAS FINALLY TIME I THOUGHT ABOUT LIFE HERE ON EARTH. BEFORE IT ENDED WHILE I WAS STILL ALONE...
...LIKE ROMANOFF.

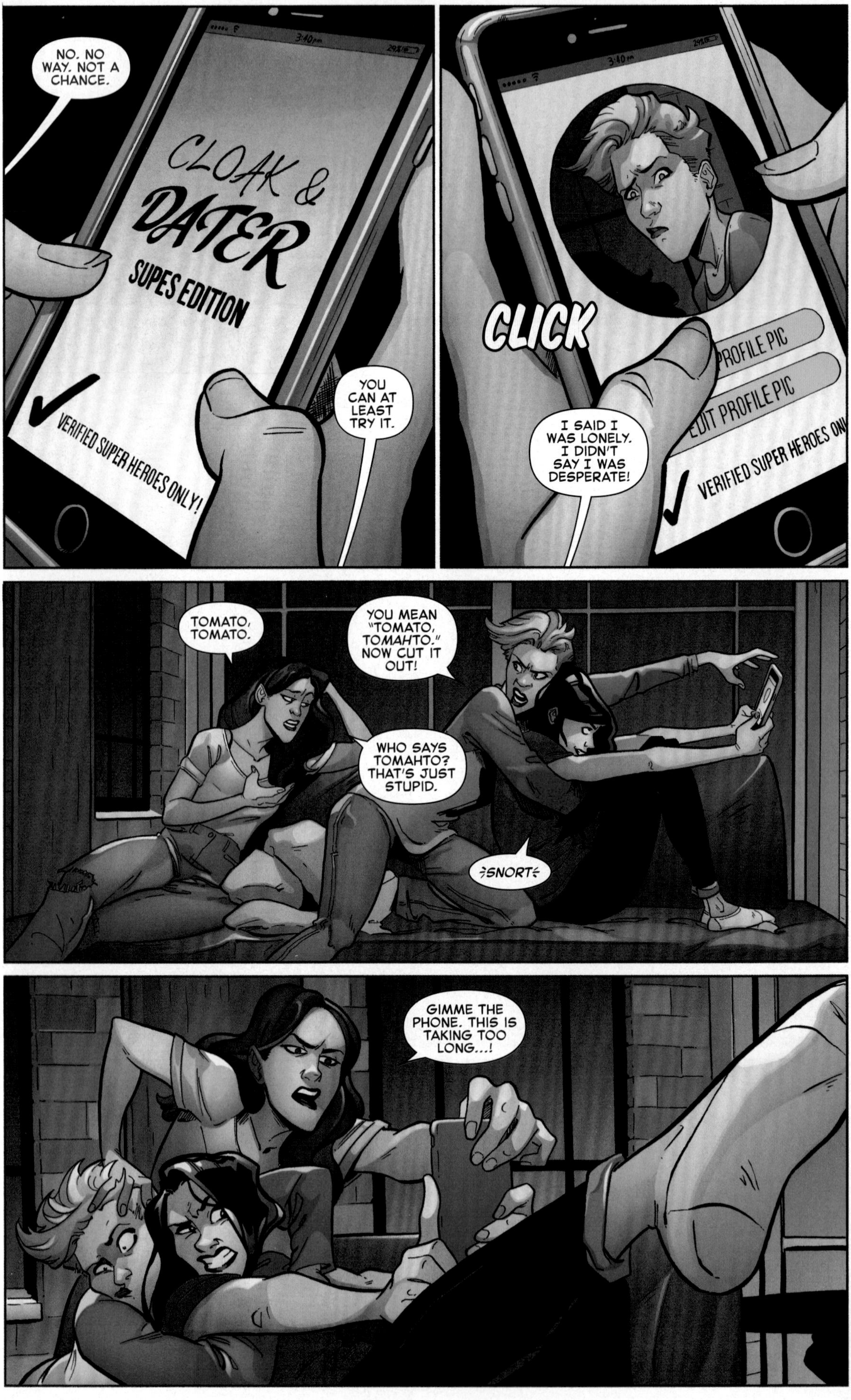
NO. NO WAY. NOT A CHANCE.
CLOAK & DATER
SUPES EDITION
VERIFIED SUPER HEROES ONLY!
YOU CAN AT LEAST TRY IT.
CLICK
PROFILE PIC
EDIT PROFILE PIC
I SAID I WAS LONELY. I DIDN'T SAY I WAS DESPERATE!
VERIFIED SUPER HEROES ON
TOMATO, TOMATO.
YOU MEAN "TOMATO, TOMAHTO." NOW CUT IT OUT!
WHO SAYS TOMAHTO? THAT'S JUST STUPID.
SNORT
GIMME THE PHONE. THIS IS TAKING TOO LONG...!

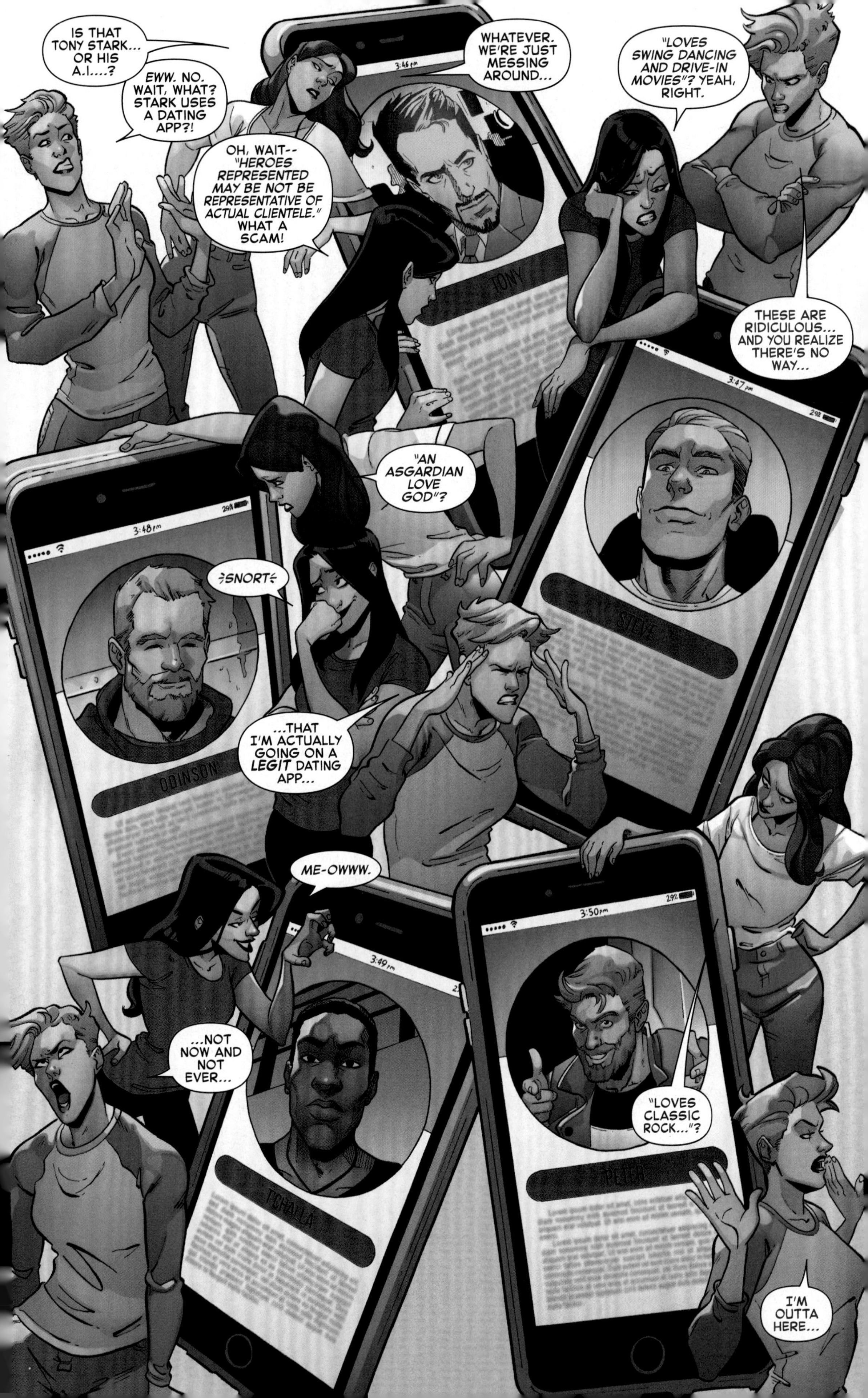
IS THAT TONY STARK... OR HIS A.I....?
EWW. NO. WAIT, WHAT? STARK USES A DATING APP?!
WHATEVER. WE'RE JUST MESSING AROUND...
OH, WAIT-- "HEROES REPRESENTED MAY BE NOT BE REPRESENTATIVE OF ACTUAL CLIENTELE." WHAT A SCAM!
"LOVES SWING DANCING AND DRIVE-IN MOVIES"? YEAH, RIGHT.
3:46 pm
TONY
THESE ARE RIDICULOUS... AND YOU REALIZE THERE'S NO WAY...
3:47 pm
STEVE
"AN ASGARDIAN LOVE GOD"?
3:48 pm
SNORT
ODINSON
...THAT I'M ACTUALLY GOING ON A LEGIT DATING APP...
ME-OWWW.
3:49 pm
3:50 pm
...NOT NOW AND NOT EVER...
"LOVES CLASSIC ROCK..."?
T'CHALLA
PETER
I'M OUTTA HERE...

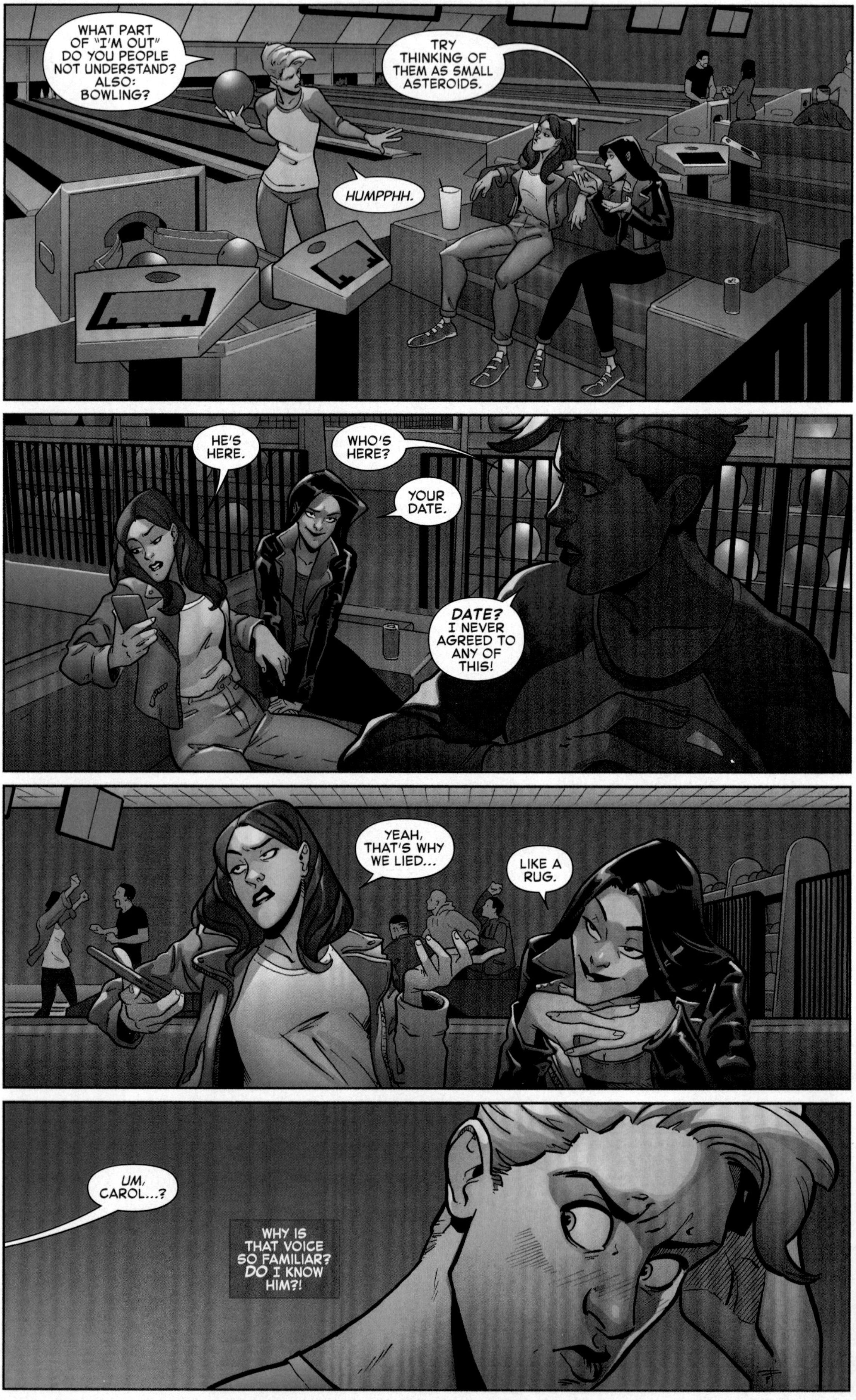
WHAT PART OF "I'M OUT" DO YOU PEOPLE NOT UNDERSTAND? ALSO: BOWLING?
TRY THINKING OF THEM AS SMALL ASTEROIDS.
HUMPPHH.
HE'S HERE.
WHO'S HERE?
YOUR DATE.
DATE? I NEVER AGREED TO ANY OF THIS!
YEAH, THAT'S WHY WE LIED...
LIKE A RUG.
UM, CAROL...?
WHY IS THAT VOICE SO FAMILIAR? DO I KNOW HIM?!

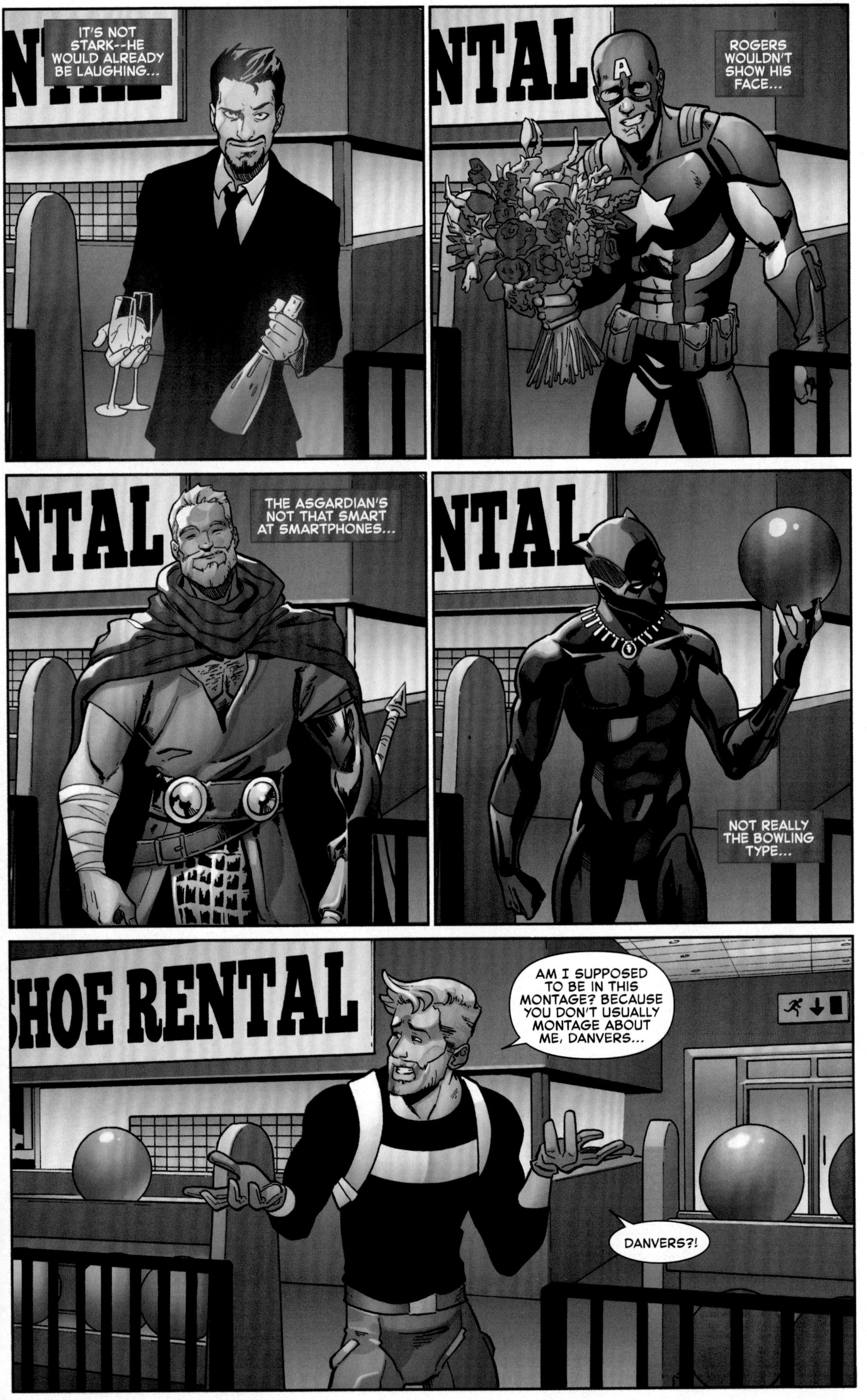

IT'S NOT STARK--HE WOULD ALREADY BE LAUGHING...
NTAL
ROGERS WOULDN'T SHOW HIS FACE...
NTAL
THE ASGARDIAN'S NOT THAT SMART AT SMARTPHONES...
NTAL
NOT REALLY THE BOWLING TYPE...
SHOE RENTAL
AM I SUPPOSED TO BE IN THIS MONTAGE? BECAUSE YOU DON'T USUALLY MONTAGE ABOUT ME, DANVERS...
DANVERS?!

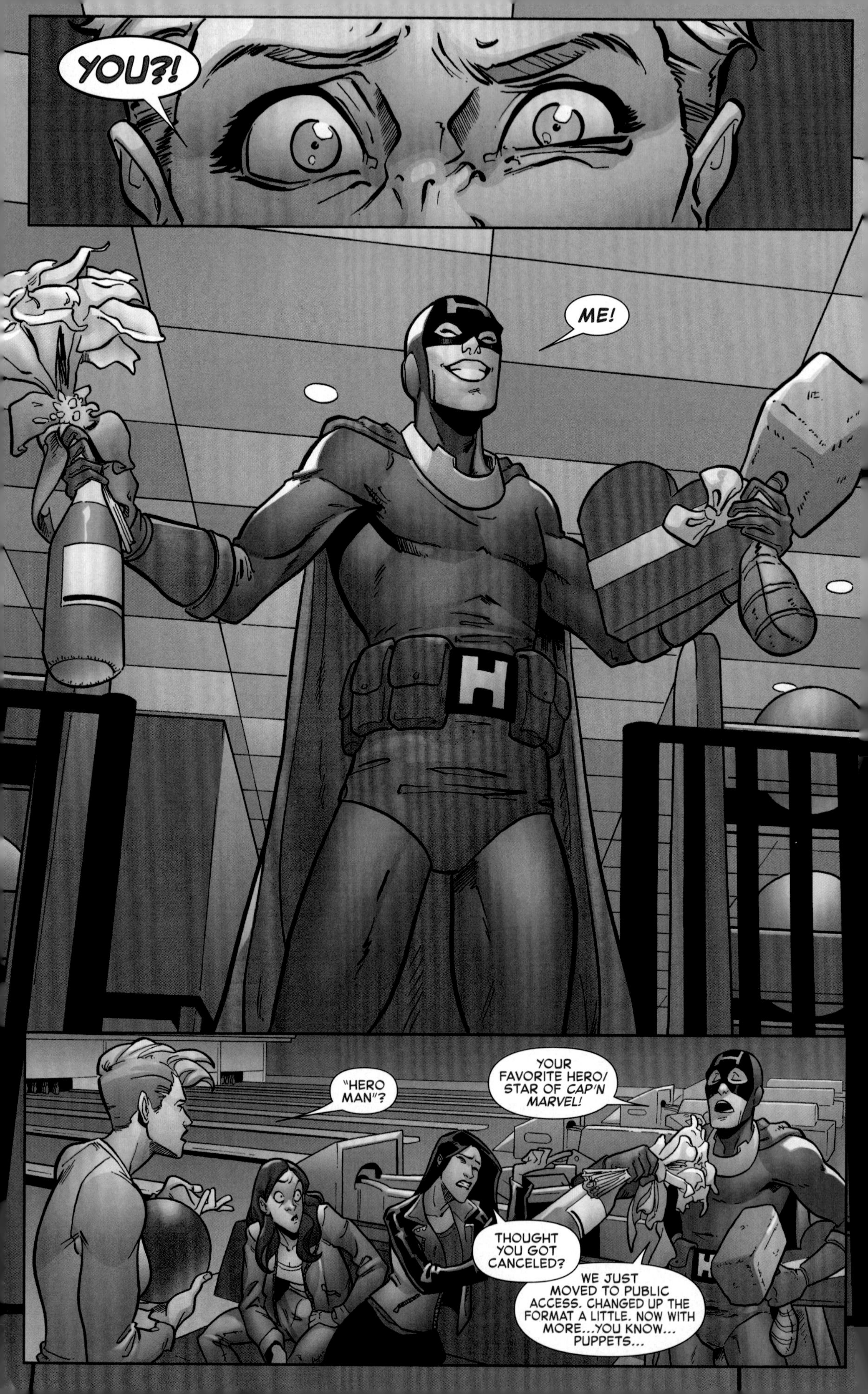
YOU?!
ME!
"HERO MAN"?
YOUR FAVORITE HERO/ STAR OF CAP'N MARVEL!
THOUGHT YOU GOT CANCELED?
WE JUST MOVED TO PUBLIC ACCESS. CHANGED UP THE FORMAT A LITTLE. NOW WITH MORE...YOU KNOW... PUPPETS...

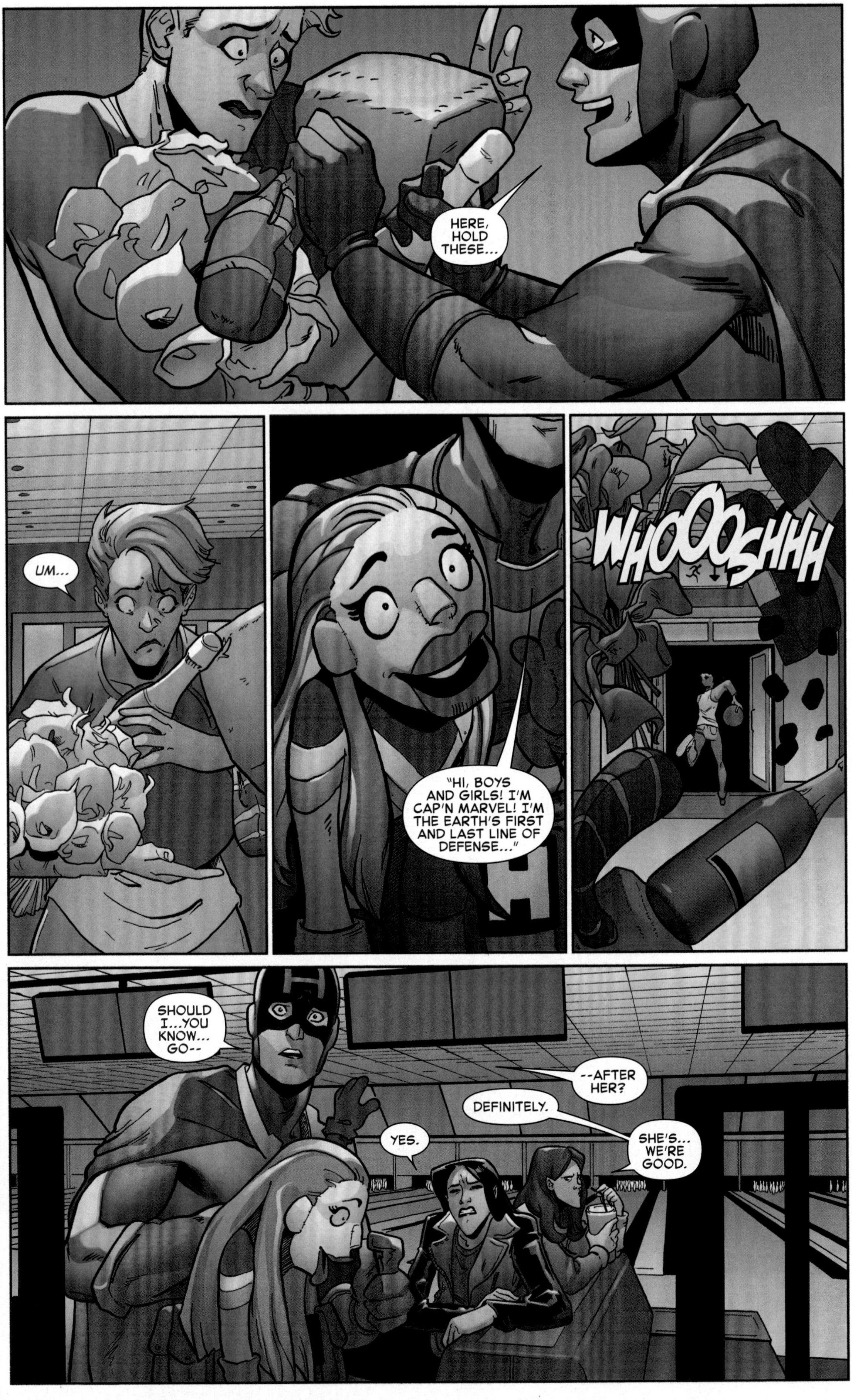
HERE, HOLD THESE...
UM...
"HI, BOYS AND GIRLS! I'M CAP'N MARVEL! I'M THE EARTH'S FIRST AND LAST LINE OF DEFENSE..."
WHOOOSHHH
SHOULD I...YOU KNOW... GO--
--AFTER HER?
DEFINITELY.
YES.
SHE'S... WE'RE GOOD.

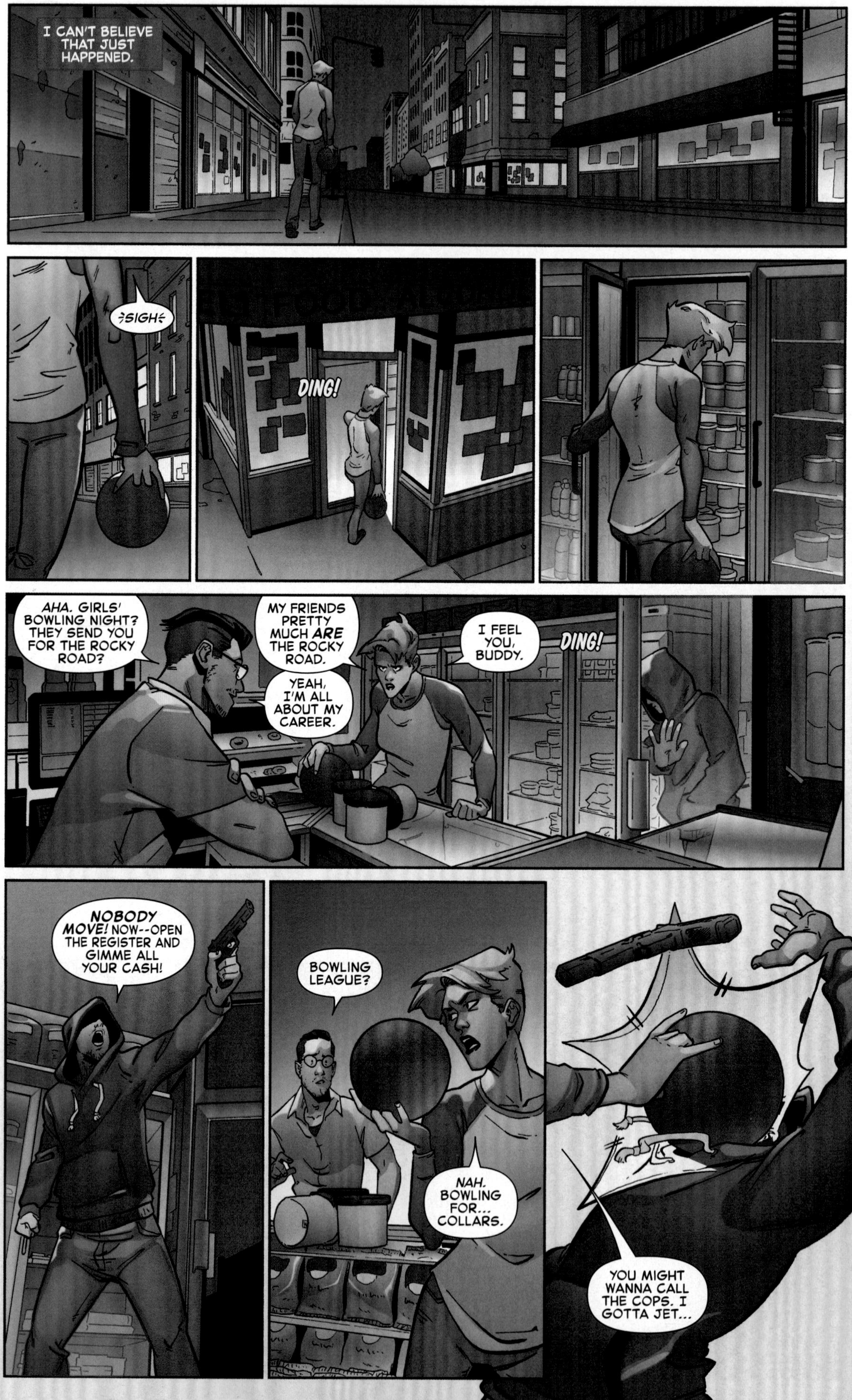
I CAN'T BELIEVE THAT JUST HAPPENED.
SIGH
DING!
AHA. GIRLS' BOWLING NIGHT? THEY SEND YOU FOR THE ROCKY ROAD?
MY FRIENDS PRETTY MUCH ARE THE ROCKY ROAD.
YEAH, I'M ALL ABOUT MY CAREER.
I FEEL YOU, BUDDY.
DING!
NOBODY MOVE! NOW--OPEN THE REGISTER AND GIMME ALL YOUR CASH!
BOWLING LEAGUE?
NAH. BOWLING FOR... COLLARS.
YOU MIGHT WANNA CALL THE COPS. I GOTTA JET...

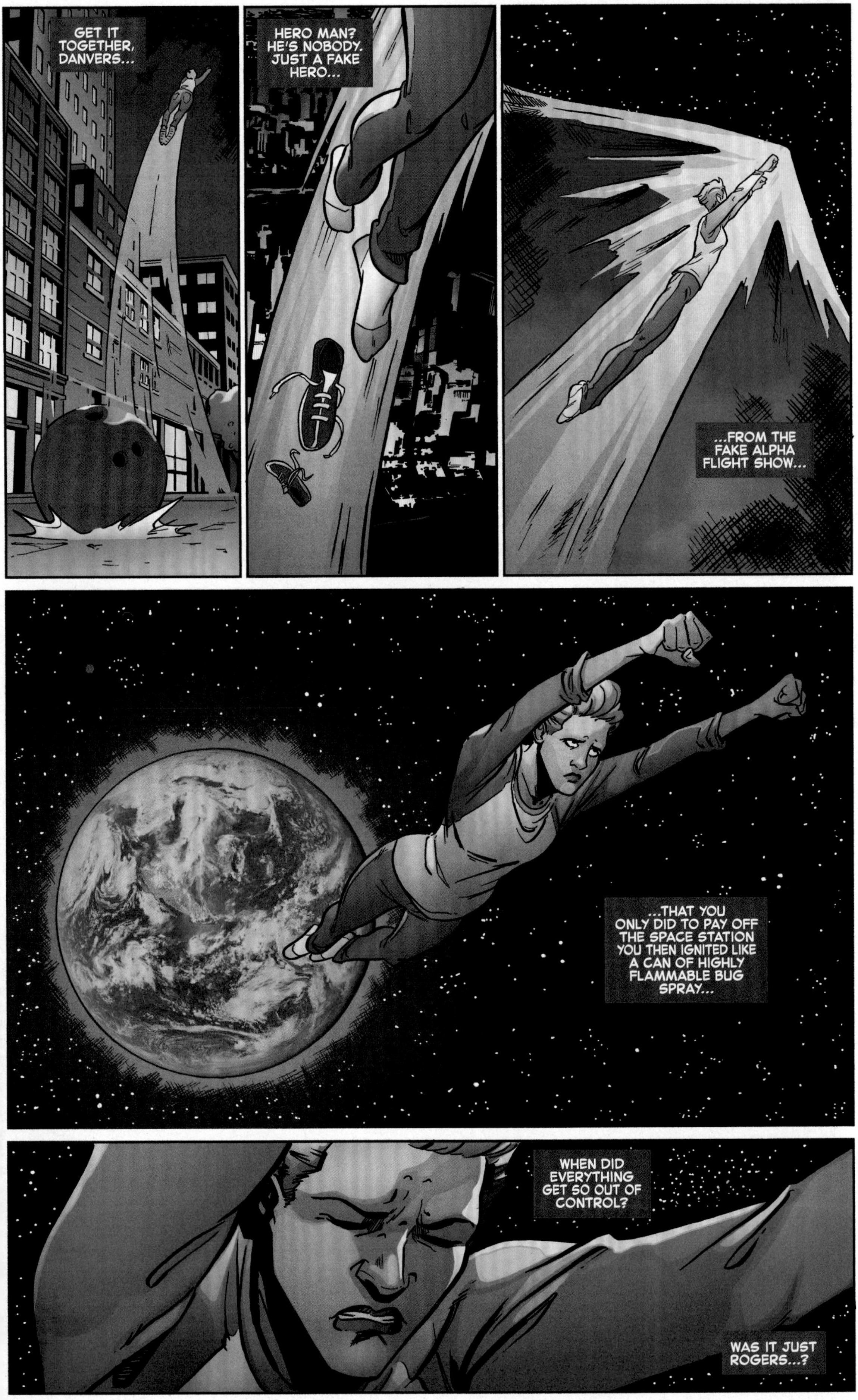
GET IT TOGETHER, DANVERS...
HERO MAN? HE'S NOBODY. JUST A FAKE HERO...
...FROM THE FAKE ALPHA FLIGHT SHOW...
...THAT YOU ONLY DID TO PAY OFF THE SPACE STATION YOU THEN IGNITED LIKE A CAN OF HIGHLY FLAMMABLE BUG SPRAY...
WHEN DID EVERYTHING GET SO OUT OF CONTROL?
WAS IT JUST ROGERS...?

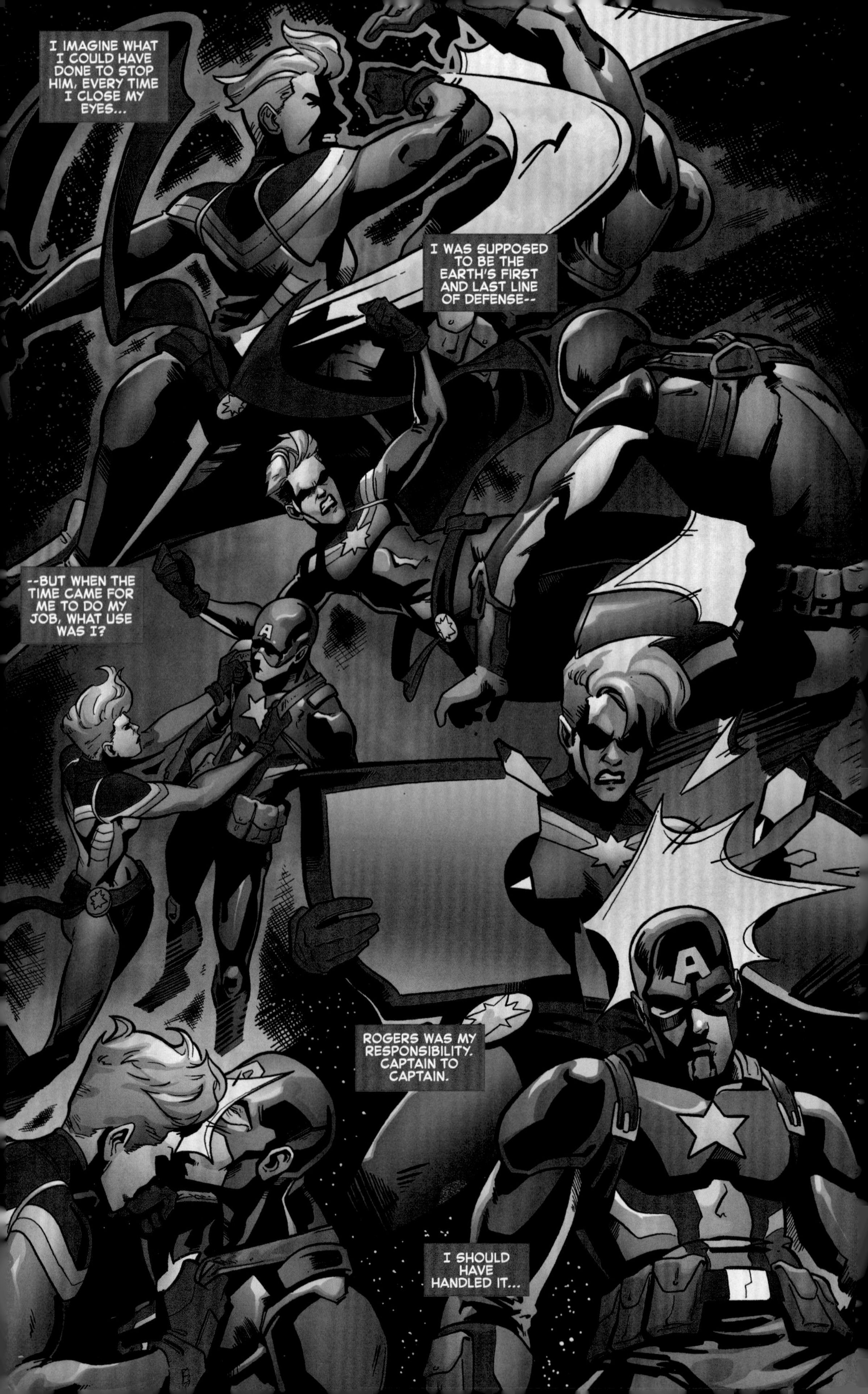
I IMAGINE WHAT I COULD HAVE DONE TO STOP HIM, EVERY TIME I CLOSE MY EYES...
I WAS SUPPOSED TO BE THE EARTH'S FIRST AND LAST LINE OF DEFENSE--
--BUT WHEN THE TIME CAME FOR ME TO DO MY JOB, WHAT USE WAS I?
ROGERS WAS MY RESPONSIBILITY. CAPTAIN TO CAPTAIN.
I SHOULD HAVE HANDLED IT...

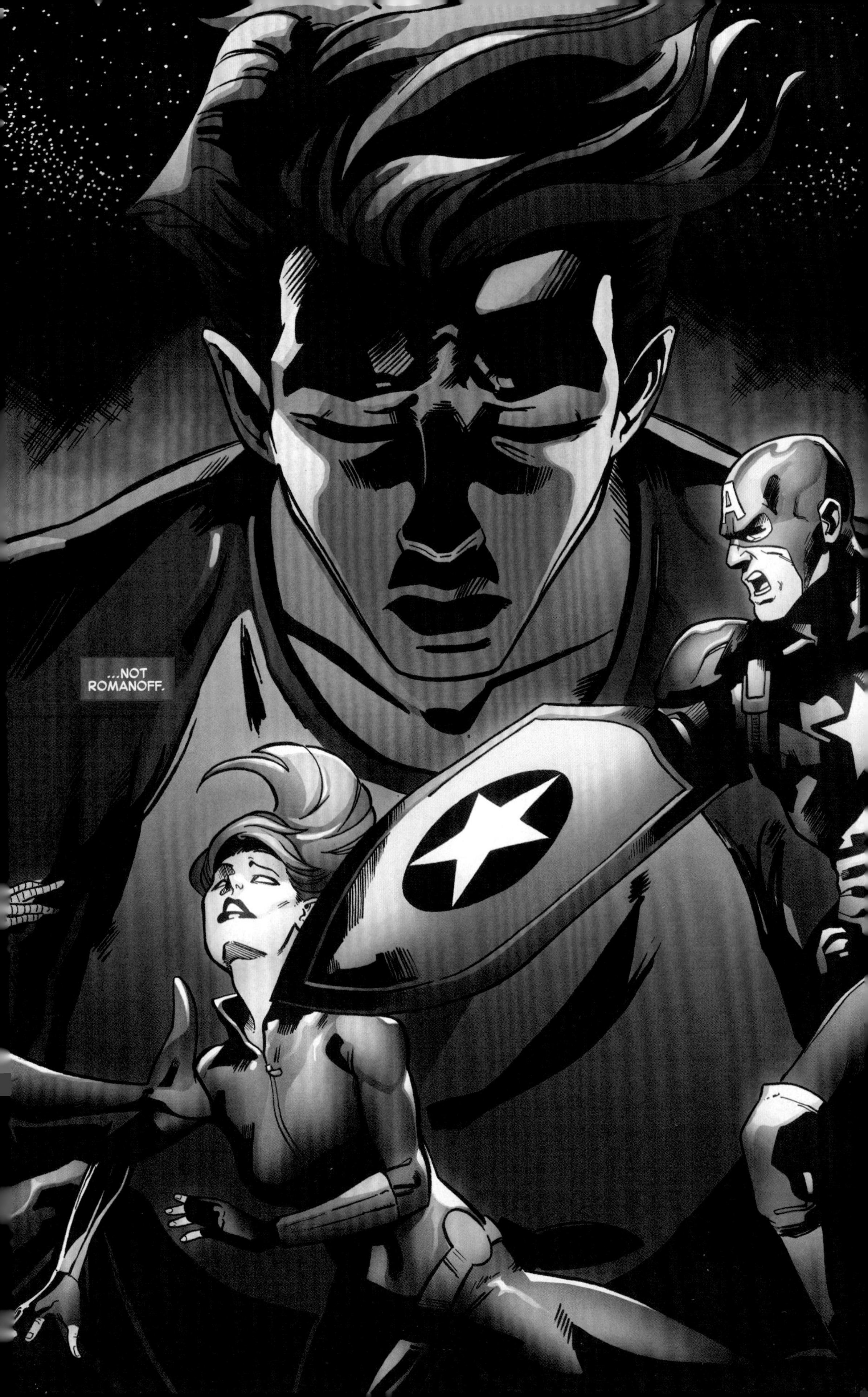
...NOT ROMANOFF.

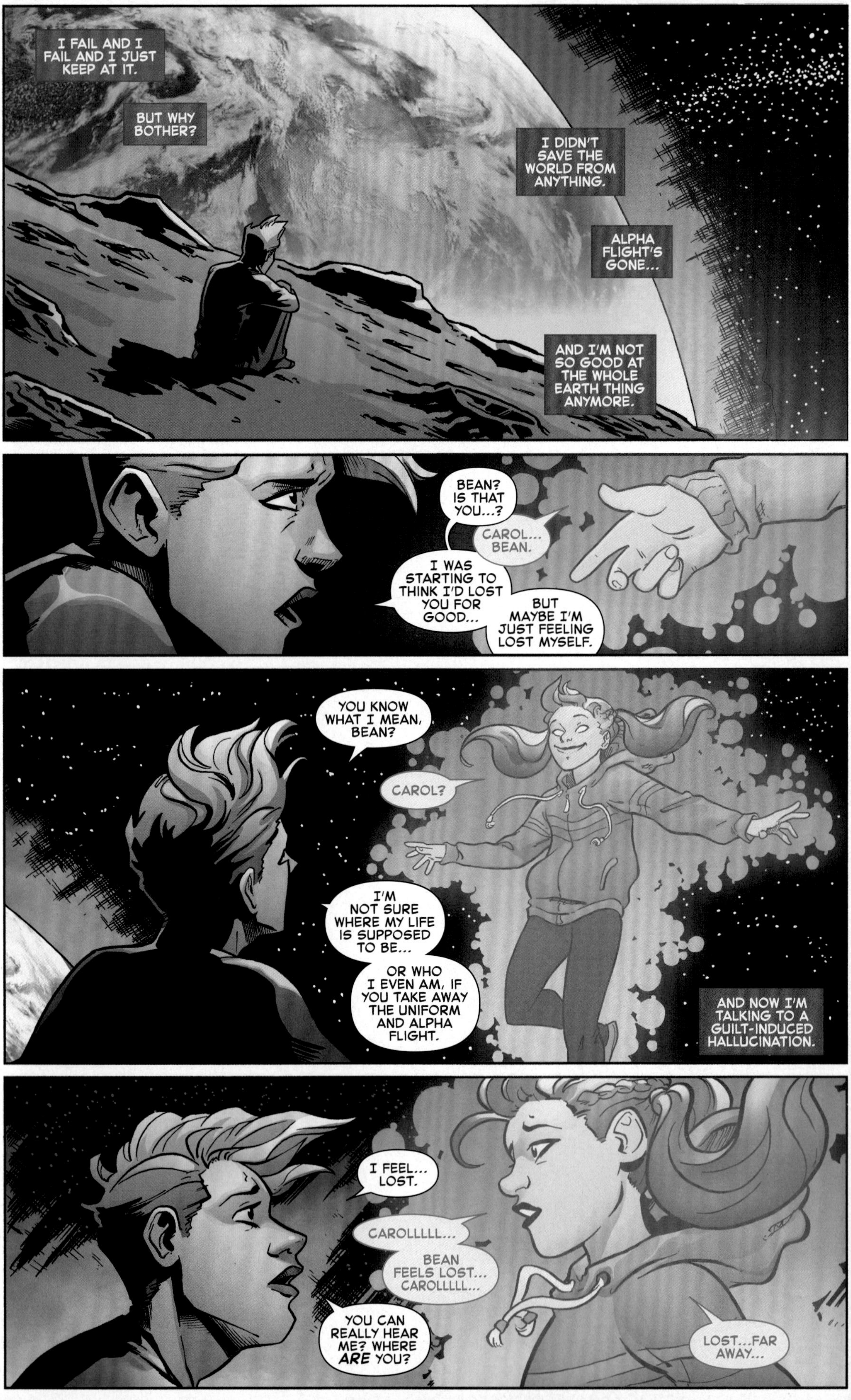
I FAIL AND I FAIL AND I JUST KEEP AT IT.
BUT WHY BOTHER?
I DIDN'T SAVE THE WORLD FROM ANYTHING.
ALPHA FLIGHT'S GONE...
AND I'M NOT SO GOOD AT THE WHOLE EARTH THING ANYMORE.
BEAN? IS THAT YOU...?
CAROL... BEAN.
I WAS STARTING TO THINK I'D LOST YOU FOR GOOD...
BUT MAYBE I'M JUST FEELING LOST MYSELF.
YOU KNOW WHAT I MEAN, BEAN?
CAROL?
I'M NOT SURE WHERE MY LIFE IS SUPPOSED TO BE...
OR WHO I EVEN AM, IF YOU TAKE AWAY THE UNIFORM AND ALPHA FLIGHT.
AND NOW I'M TALKING TO A GUILT-INDUCED HALLUCINATION.
I FEEL... LOST.
CAROLLLLL...
BEAN FEELS LOST... CAROLLLLL...
YOU CAN REALLY HEAR ME? WHERE ***ARE*** YOU?
LOST...FAR AWAY...

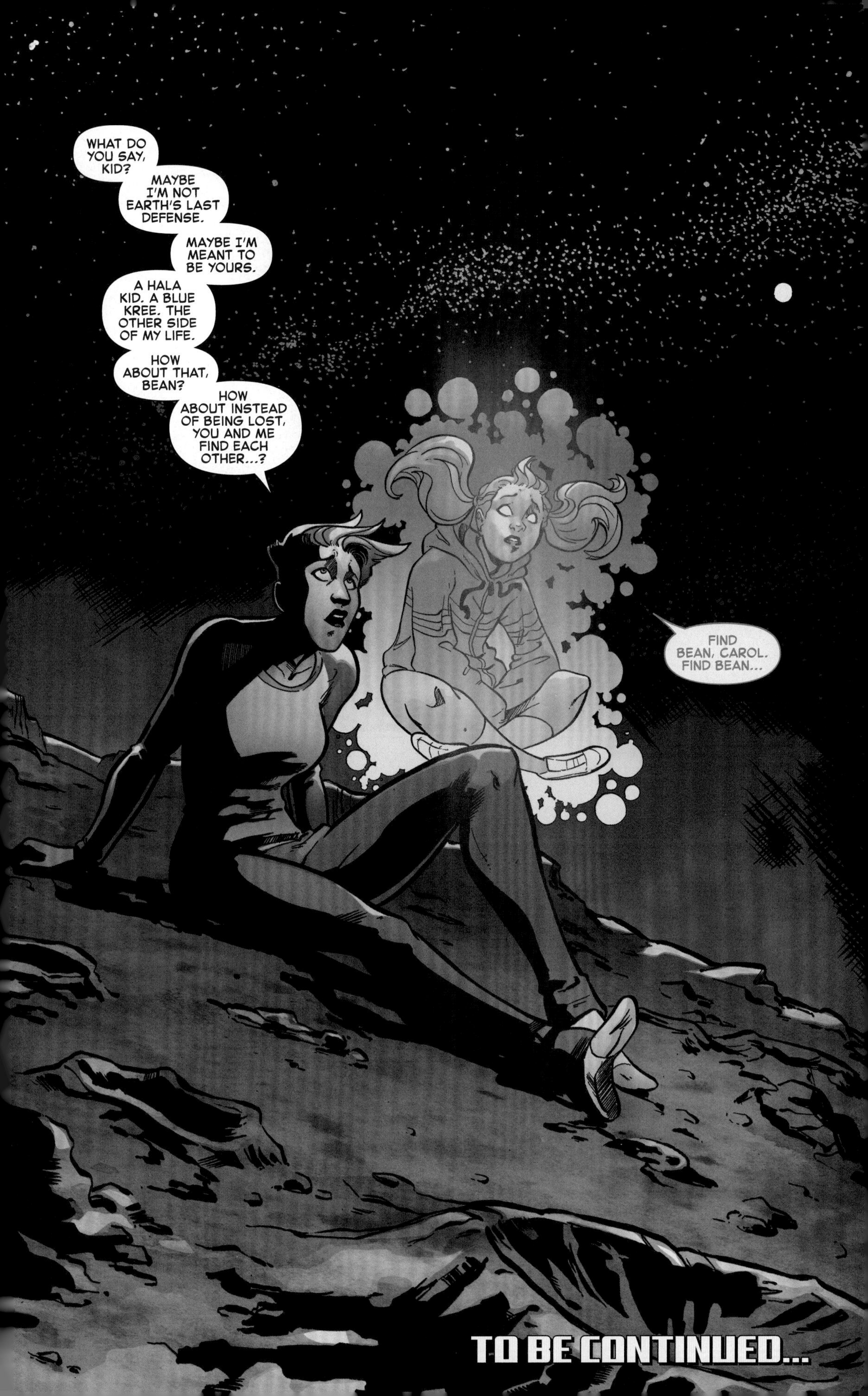
WHAT DO YOU SAY, KID?
MAYBE I'M NOT EARTH'S LAST DEFENSE.
MAYBE I'M MEANT TO BE YOURS.
A HALA KID. A BLUE KREE. THE OTHER SIDE OF MY LIFE.
HOW ABOUT THAT, BEAN?
HOW ABOUT INSTEAD OF BEING LOST, YOU AND ME FIND EACH OTHER...?
FIND BEAN, CAROL. FIND BEAN...
TO BE CONTINUED...

#5, PAGES 14-15 ART PROCESS BY
MICHELE BANDINI

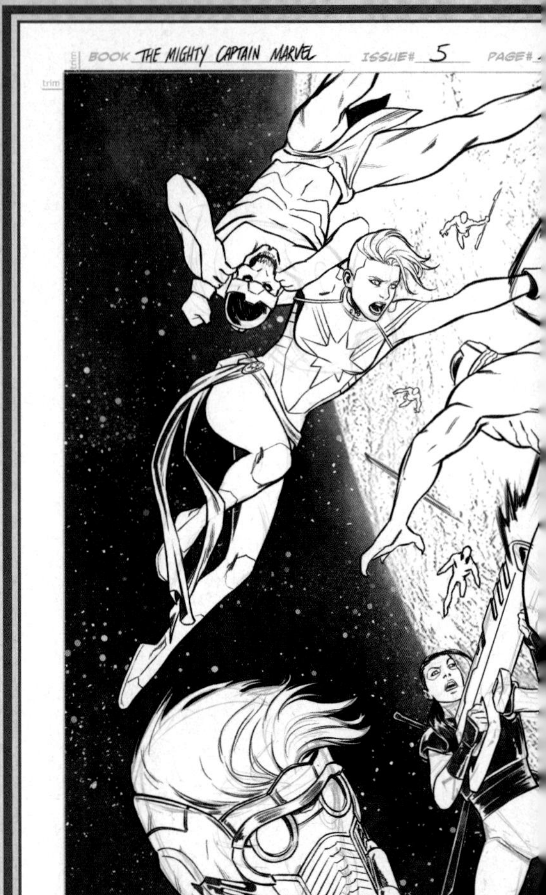
BOOK THE MIGHTY CAPTAIN MARVEL ISSUE# 5

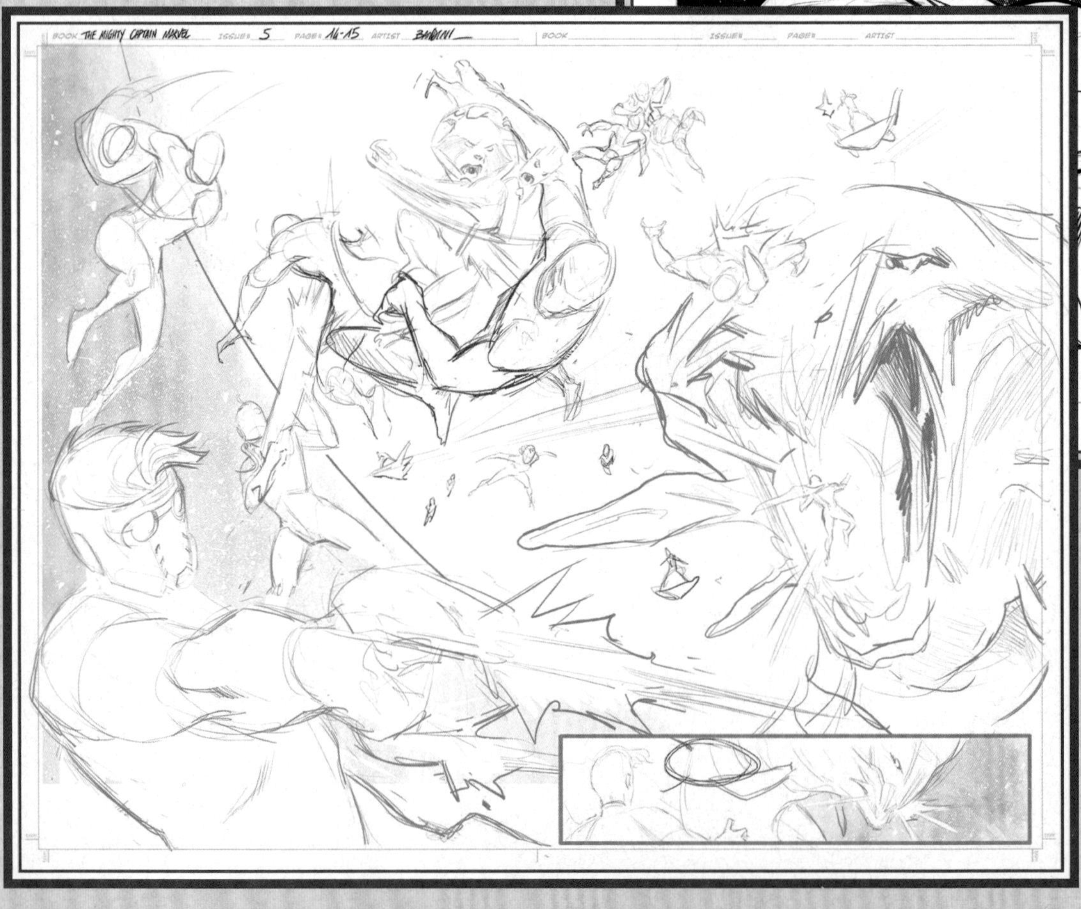
BOOK THE MIGHTY CAPTAIN MARVEL ISSUE# 5 PAGE# 14-15 ARTIST BANDINI

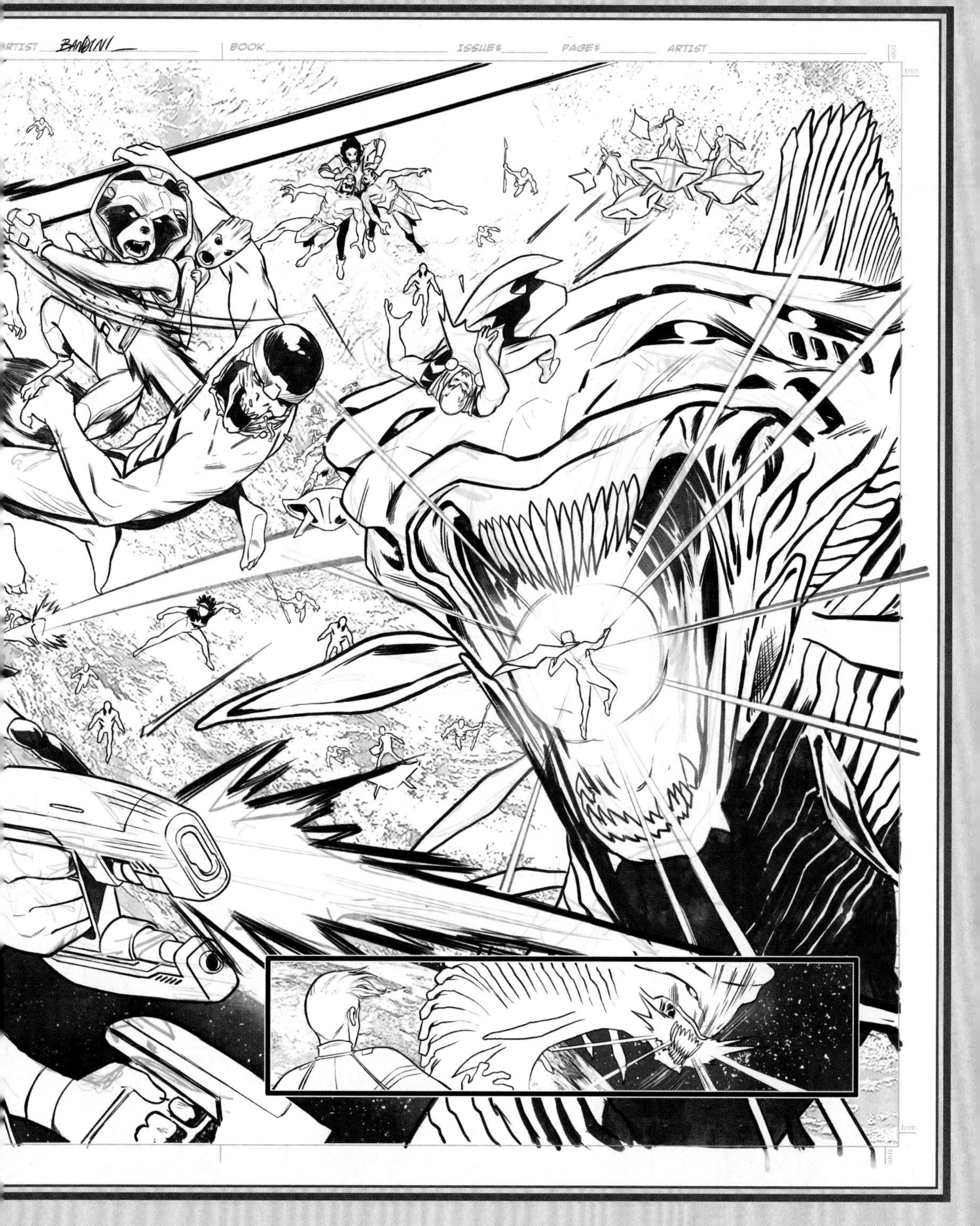

ARTIST BANDINI
BOOK
ISSUE#
PAGE#
ARTIST
trim

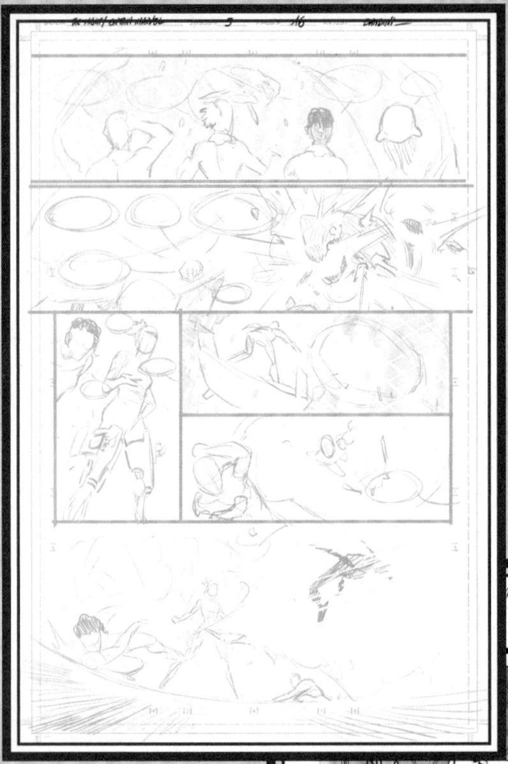

#5, PAGE 16 ART PROCESS BY
MICHELE BANDINI

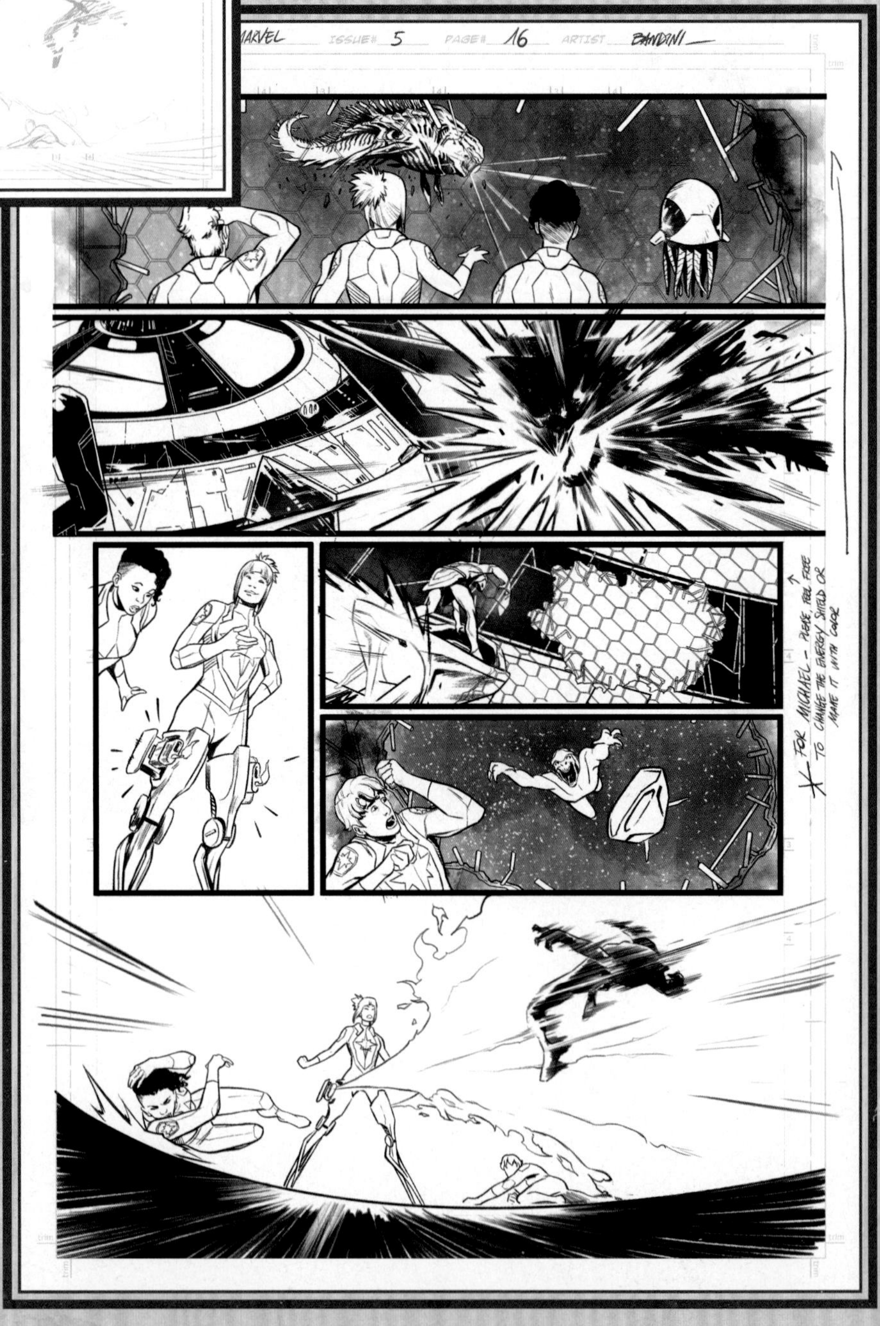
MARVEL ISSUE# 5 PAGE# 16 ARTIST BANDINI
FOR MICHAEL - PLEASE, FEEL FREE TO CHANGE THE ENERGY SHIELD OR MAKE IT WITH COLOR

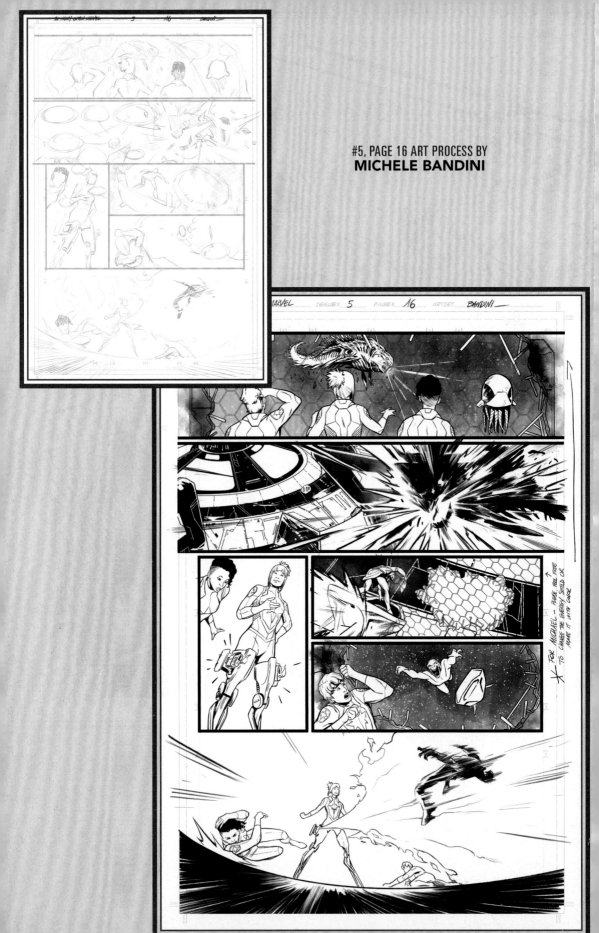